Organisation and Development of Educational System

Organisation and Development of Educational System

Pankaj Kumar Desai

ALTAR

ALTAR PUBLISHING HOUSE
NEW DELHI (INDIA)

Published by

ALTAR PUBLISHING HOUSE
L- 9 A, IInd FLOOR, STREET NO.42
SADATPUR EXTENSION
DELHI-110094 (INDIA)
CELL- 0-9899346553, 0-9868990429

Organisation and Development of Educational System

Edition 2010
ISBN 978-81-910524-2-8

Printed in India
at Asian Offset Printers, Delhi

Preface

The Indian education system comprises pre-school, primary school, secondary school, higher secondary school, and higher education (graduation and post-graduation). Although primary school is compulsory, this has been difficult to achieve in practice and India is still struggling to raise its literacy rates. Through school, students are taught a uniform set of subjects including languages, mathematics, sciences, and social sciences. Higher education in India provides an opportunity to specialize in a field and includes technical schools, colleges, and universities.

Higher education in India has evolved in distinct and divergent streams with each stream monitored by an apex body, indirectly controlled by the Ministry of Human Resource Development and funded by the state governments. The important universities are called Central Universities and these are maintained by the Union Government. The private sector also has a strong presence in Indian higher education. The Indian Institutes of Technology (IIT), National Law School, Bangalore; All India Institute of Medical Sciences; Indian School of Business, Hyderabad; and the Indian Institutes of Management (IIMs) are renowned for their superior standards of education and compete with the best in the world.

This book provides an analytical overview of the organisation and development Indian education system, that is both qualitative and quantitative, and a discussion of current policies, programmes, and issues concerning different aspects of education in India. This book has been prepared strictly according to the B.Ed. syllabus, prescribed by universities. It would serve as perfect reference material for all teachers, teacher-students and other readers also.

Author

Contents

Contents

1

Indian Educational System: Structure and Organisation

Education has always been a very important concern for any society. Looking back in to the rich past of the India, one can easily observe that our educational heritage is only one among various other elements that have captured the attention of the world. While the United Nations is worried about the presence of a large number of illiterates, various other countries are amazed by the quality of some of the human resources that the Indian education system has produced. The growth of the Indian economy in the recent past and the compulsion to sustain it is also forcing the Indian government to accelerate the process of developing all the branches of the Indian education system. Therefore, it would be very interesting to understand and analyse the various structures of education in India, its present condition and future developments.

The *Vedas*, *Puranas*, *Ayurveda*,*Yoga*, Kautilya's *Arthasahtra* are only some of the milestones that the traditional Indian knowledge system boasts of. There are evidences of imparting formal education in ancient India under the Gurukul system. Under the Gurukul system, young boys who were passing through the Brahmacharya stage of life had to stay at the Guru or the teacher's home and complete their education. Although the ancient system of education has produced many geniuses and still a major area of research, it was hardly egalitarian. Women and people of lower castes gradually lost their right to educate themselves. The spread of Jainism, Buddhism, Bhakti and Sufi movements did have some liberating effects on the condition of the women, sudras and atisudras. But it is the English language and the reformation movements of the 19th century that had the most liberating effect in pre-independent India. Thus, the Britishers, although rightly criticised for devastating the Indian economy, can also be credited for bringing a revolution in the Indian education system.

Soon after gaining independence in 1947, making education available to all had become a priority for the government. As discrimination on the basis of caste and gender has been a major impediment in the healthy development of the Indian society, they have been made unlawful by the Indian constitution. The 86th constitutional amendment has also made elementary education a fundamental right for the children between the age group- 6 to 14. According to the 2001 census, the total literacy rate in India is 65.38%. The female literacy rate is only 54.16%. The gap between rural and urban literacy rate is also very significant in India. This is evident from the fact that only 59.4% of rural population are literate as against 80. 3% urban population according to the 2001 census.

In order to develop the higher education system, the government had established the University Grants Commission in 1953. The primary role of UGC has been to regulate the standard and spread of higher education in India. There has been a marked progress in the expansion of higher education if we look at the increase of higher educational institutes in India. The higher education system in India comprise of more than 17000 colleges, 20 central universities, 217 State Universities, 106 Deemed to Universities and 13 institutes of National importance. This number will soon inflate as the setting up of 30 more central universities, 8 new IITs, 7 IIMs and 5 new Indian Institutes of Science are now proposed.

The present education system in India mainly comprises of primary education, secondary education, senior secondary education and higher education. Elementary education consists of eight years of education. Each of secondary and senior secondary education consists of two years of education. Higher education in India starts after passing the higher secondary education or the 12th standard. Depending on the stream, doing graduation in India can take three to five years. Post graduate courses are generally of two to three years of duration. After completing post graduation, scope for doing research in various educational institutes also remains open.

There are quite a good number of educational institutes in India that can compete with the best educational institutes of the world. The Indian Institutes of Technology (IITs), Indian Institutes of Management (IIMs), Indian Institutes of Science, National Law Schools, Jawaharlal Nehru University are some such institutes.

As education is the means for bringing socioeconomic transformation in a society, various measures are being taken to enhance the access of education to the marginalised sections of the society. One such measure is the introduction of the reservation system in the institutes of higher education. Under the present law, 7.5% seats in the higher educational institutes are reserved for the scheduled tribes, 15% for scheduled castes and 27% for the non creamy layers of the Other Backward Classes (OBCs). Under the Indian constitution, various minority groups can also set up their own educational institutes. Efforts are also being taken to improve the access to higher education among the women of India by setting up various educational institutes exclusively for them or reserving seats in the already existing institutes. The growing acceptance of distance learning courses and expansion of the open university system is also contributing a lot in the democratisation of higher education in India.

Educational Structure

Educational structure has become comprehensive and differential. The educational system is being reorganised to the changing needs and realities. Educational system has undergone several assessments in order to improve and to become responsive to the challenges of modernisation and goals of national developments. Demographical changes have been made. Alternate strategies of education have resulted in restructuring of education and emergence of alternate structures. Alternate non-formal structures as complementary to formal structures have been developed parallel as complement or supplement to formal education structure.

Educational content/curricula/teaching-learning materials are becoming more functional and less academic, more diversified and less omnibus, and more operational and less disciplinary. The approach for developing the learning materials has become an integrated approach to knowledge with focus on reallife problems. Divergent learning materials are being developed. Local specific learning sequences are being experimented. Content is being based on relevance, flexibility, needs, and local specifics. Curricula are being revised to contain new areas of population education, health and nutrition education, community education, and value-oriented education.

The National Council of Educational Research and Training (NCERT) is the apex body for school education in India. The NCERT provides support and technical assistance to a number of schools in India and oversees many aspects of enforcement of education policies. In India, the various bodies governing school education system are:

— The state government boards, in which the majority of Indian children are enrolled.
— The Central Board of Secondary Education (CBSE) board.
— The Council for the Indian School Certificate Examinations (CISCE) board.
— The National Institute of Open Schooling.
— International schools affiliated to the International Baccalaureate Programme and/or the Cambridge International Examinations.
— Islamic Madrasah schools, whose boards are controlled by local state governments, or autonomous, or affiliated with Darul Uloom Deoband.
— Autonomous schools like Woodstock School, Auroville, Patha Bhavan and Ananda Marga Gurukula.

Primary Education

The Indian government lays emphasis to primary education upto the age of fourteen years. The Indian government has also banned child labor in order to ensure that the children do not enter unsafe working conditions. However, both free education and the ban on child labor are difficult to enforce due to economic disparity and social conditions. The District Primary Education Programme (DPEP) was launched in 1994 with an aim to universalise primary education in India by reforming and vitalising the existing primary education system. 85%

of the DPEP is funded by the central government and the remaining 15 percent is funded by the state. The DPEP, which has opened 160000 new schools including 84000 alternative education schools delivering alternative education to approximately 3.5 million children, is also supported by UNICEF and other international programmes. This primary education scheme has also shown a high Gross Enrollment Ratio of 93-95% for the last three years in some states. Significant improvement in staffing and enrollment of girls has also been made as a part of this scheme. The overall primary school conditions in India as a whole continued to remain lag behind internationally due to understaffing coupled with lack of developed infrastructure and sufficient financing.

Secondary Education

The National Policy on Education (NPE), 1986, has provided for environment awareness, science and technology education, and introduction of traditional elements such as Yoga into the Indian secondary school system. A significant feature of India's secondary school system is the emphasis on inclusion of the disadvantaged sections of the society Professionals from established institutes are often called to support in vocational training. Another feature of India's secondary school system is its emphasis on profession based vocational training to help students attain skills for finding a vocation of his/her choosing.

A special Integrated Education for Disabled Children (IEDC) programme was started in 1974. Another notable special programme, the Kendriya Vidyalaya project, was started for the employees of the central government of India, who are distributed throughout the country. The government started the Kendriya Vidyalaya project in 1965 to provide uniform education in institutions following the same syllabus at the same pace regardless of the location to which the employee's family has been transferred.

Tertiary Education

India's higher education system is the third largest in the world, after China and the United States. The main governing body at the tertiary level is the University Grants Commission (India), which enforces its standards, advises the government, and helps coordinate between the centre and the state. Accreditation for higher learning is overseen by 12 autonomous institutions established by the University Grants Commission.

As of 2009, India has 20 central universities, 215 state universities, 100 deemed universities, 5 institutions established and functioning under the State Act, and 13 institutes which are of national importance. Other institutions include 16000 colleges, including 1800 exclusive women's colleges, functioning under these universities and institutions. The emphasis in the tertiary level of education lies on science and technology. Indian educational institutions by 2004 consisted of a large number of technology institutes. As of 2006 some 1200 engineering colleges awarded degrees in India and approximately 380000 students were admitted in them. Distance learning is also a feature of the Indian higher education system.

Some institutions of India, such as the Indian Institutes of Technology (IITs), have been globally acclaimed for their standard of education. The IITs enrol about 4000 students annually and the alumni have contributed to both the growth of the private sector and the public sectors of India. IIT graduates of India have also contributed significantly to the global software industry, with an estimated 30000 graduates employed in the United States as of 2006.

Technical Education

From the first Five Year Plan onwards India's emphasis was to develop a pool of scientifically inclined manpower. India's National Policy on Education (NPE) provisioned for an apex body for regulation and development of higher technical education, which came into being as the All India Council for Technical Education (AICTE) in 1987 through an act of the Indian parliament. At the level of the centre the Indian Institutes of Technology are deemed of national importance. The Indian Institutes of Management are also among the nation's premier education facilities. Several Regional Engineering Colleges (REC) have been converted into National Institutes of Technology. The UGC has inter-university centres at a number of locations throughout India to promote common research, eg. the Nuclear Science Centre at the Jawaharlal Nehru University, New Delhi.

Literacy

2001 government statistics hold the national literacy to be around 64.84%. Government statistics of 2001 also hold that the rate of increase of literacy is more in rural areas than in urban areas. Female literacy is was at a national average of 53.63% whereas the male literacy was 75.26%. Within the Indian states, Kerala has shown the highest literacy rates of 90.02% whereas Bihar averaged lower than 50% literacy, the lowest in India. The 2001 statistics also indicated that the total number of 'absolute non literates' in the country was 304 million.

World Bank statistics found that fewer than 40 percent of adolescents in India attend secondary schools. The Economist reports that half of 10-year-old rural children could not read at a basic level, over 60% were unable to do division, and half dropped out by the age 14. Only one in ten young people have access to tertiary education. Out of those who receive higher education, Mercer Consulting estimates that only a quarter of graduates are "employable". An optimistic estimate is that only one in five job-seekers in India has ever had any sort of vocational training.

Private Education

Because of poor quality of public education, 27% of Indian children are privately educated. Private schools provide often superior results at a fraction of the unit cost of government schools. Private schools cover the entire curriculum and offer extra-curricular activities such as science fairs, general knowledge, sports, music and drama.

Most teachers in private schools are female, graduates and reasonably experienced. The competition in the school market is intense, yet most schools make profit. Even the poorest often go to private schools despite the fact that government schools are free. A study found that 65% of schoolchildren in Hyderabad's slums attend private schools.

Private schools are often operating illegally. A 2001 study found that it takes 14 different licenses from four different authorities to open a private school in New Delhi and could take years if done legally.

Women's Education

Women have much lower literacy rate. Compared to boys, far fewer girls are enrolled in the schools, and many of them drop out. According to a 1998 report by U.S. Department of Commerce, the chief barrier to female education in India are inadequate school facilities (such as sanitary facilities), shortage of female teachers and gender bias in curriculum (majority of the female characters being depicted as weak and helpless).

The number of literate women among the female population of India was between 2-6% from the British Raj onwards to the formation of the Republic of India in 1947. Concerted efforts led to improvement from 15.3% in 1961 to 28.5% in 1981. By 2001 the literacy for women had exceeded 50% of the overall female population, though these statistics were still very low compared to world standards and even male literacy within India.

Since 1947 the Indian government has tried to provide incentives for girls' school attendance through programs for midday meals, free books, and uniforms. This welfare thrust raised primary enrollment between 1951 and 1981. In 1986 the National Policy on Education decided to restructure education in tune with the social framework of each state, and with larger national goals. It emphasised that education was necessary for democracy, and central to the improvement of women's condition.

The new policy aimed at social change through revised texts, curricula, increased funding for schools, expansion in the numbers of schools, and policy improvements. Emphasis was placed on expanding girls' occupational centres and primary education; secondary and higher education; and rural and urban institutions. The report tried to connect problems like low school attendance with poverty, and the dependence on girls for housework and sibling day care. The National Literacy Mission also worked through female tutors in villages. Although the minimum marriage age is now eighteen for girls, many continue to be married much earlier. Therefore, at the secondary level, female dropout rates are high.

Rural Education

Following independence, the Republic of India viewed education as an effective tool for bringing social change through community development. The administrative control was effectively initiated in the 1950s, when, in 1952, the government grouped villages under a Community Development Block-an authority under national programme which could control education in up to 100 villages. A Block Development Officer oversaw a geographical area of 150 square miles which could contain a population of as many as 70000 people.

The community development programmes comprise agriculture, animal husbandry, cooperation, rural industries, rural engineering, health and sanitation including family welfare,. family planning, women welfare, child care and nutrition, education including adult education, social education and literacy, youth welfare and community organisation. In each of these areas of development there are several programmes, schemes and activities which are additive, expanding and tapering off covering the total community, some segments, or specific target populations such as small and marginal farmers, artisans, women and in general people below the poverty line.

Despite some setbacks the rural education programmes continued throughout the 1950s, with support from private institutions. A sizable network of rural education had been established by the time the *Gandhigram Rural Institute* was established and 5, 200 Community Development Blocks were established in India. Nursery schools, elementary schools, secondary school, and schools for adult education for women were set up. The government continued to view rural education as an agenda that could be relatively free from bureaucratic backlog and general stagnation. However, in some cases lack of financing balanced the gains made by rural education institutes of India. Some ideas failed to find acceptability among India's poor and investments made by the government sometimes yielded little results.

Issues in Educational Sector

One study found out that 25% of public sector teachers and 40% of public sector medical workers were absent during the survey. Among teachers who were paid to teach, absence rates ranged from 15% in

Maharashtra to 71% in Bihar. Only 1 in nearly 3000 public school head teachers had ever dismissed a teacher for repeated absence. A study on teachers by Kremer etc. found that 'only about half were teaching, during unannounced visits to a nationally representative sample of government primary schools in India.'

Modern education in India is often criticised for being based on rote learning rather than problem solving. *BusinessWeek* denigrates the Indian curriculum saying it revolves around rote learning and Express India suggests that students are focused on cramming. A study of 188 government-run primary schools found that 59% of the schools had no drinking water and 89% had no toilets. 2003-04 data by National Institute of Educational Planning and Administration revealed that only 3.5% of primary schools in Bihar and Chhattisgarh had toilets for girls. In Madhya Pradesh, Maharashtra, Andhra Pradesh, Gujarat, Rajasthan and Himachal Pradesh, rates were 12-16%.

Fake degrees are a problem. One raid in Bihar found 0.1 million fake certificates. In February 2009, the University Grant Commission found 19 fake institutions operating in India. Only 16% of manufacturers in India offer in-service training to their employees, compared with over 90% in China.

Educational Initiatives

Following India's independence a number of rules were formulated for the backward Scheduled Castes and the Scheduled Tribes of India, and in 1960 a list identifying 405 Scheduled Castes and 225 Scheduled Tribes was published by the central government. An amendment was made to the list in 1975, which identified 841 Scheduled Castes and 510 Scheduled Tribes. The total percentage of Scheduled Castes and Scheduled Tribes combined was found to be 22.5 percent with the Scheduled Castes accounting for 17 percent and the Scheduled Tribes accounting for the remaining 7.5 percent. Following the report many Scheduled Castes and Scheduled Tribes increasingly referred to themselves as Dalit, a Marathi language terminology used by B. R. Ambedkar which literally means "oppressed".

The Scheduled Castes and Scheduled Tribes are provided for in many of India's educational programmes. Special reservations are also provided for the Scheduled Castes and Scheduled Tribes in India, eg. a reservation of 15% in Kendriya Vidhyala for Scheduled Castes and another reservation of 7.5% in Kendriya Vidhyala for Scheduled Tribes. Similar reservations are held by the Scheduled Castes and Scheduled Tribes in many schemes and educational facilities in India. The remote and far-flung regions of North East India are provided for under the Non Lapsable Central pool of Resources (NLCPR) since 1998-1999. The NLCPR aims to provide funds for infrastructure development in these remote areas.

The government objective for the Sarva Shiksha Abhiyan (SSA), started in 2001, is to provide education to children between 6-14 years by 2010. The programme focuses specially on girls and children with challenged social or financial backgrounds. The SSA also aims to provide practical infrastructure and relevant source material in form of free textbooks to children in remote areas. The SSA also aims at widening computer education in rural areas. However, some objectives of the SSA, eg. enrollment of all children under the scheme in schools by 2005 remain unfulfilled. Education Guarantee Scheme and Alternative and Innovative Education are components of the SSA.

Women from remote, underdeveloped areas or from weaker social groups in Andra Pradesh, Assam, Bihar, Jharkhand, Karnataka, Kerala, Gujarat, Uttar Pradesh, and Uttarakhand, fall under the Mahila Samakhya Scheme, initiated in 1989. Apart from provisions for education this programme also aims to raise awareness by holding meetings and seminars at rural levels. The government allowed 340 million rupees during 2007-08 to carry out this scheme over 83 districts including more than 21, 000 villages.

Currently there are 68 Bal Bhavans and 10 Bal Kendra affiliated to the National Bal Bhavan. The scheme involves educational and social activities and recognising children with a marked talent for a particular educational stream. A number of programmes and activities are held under this scheme, which also involves cultural exchanges and participation in several international forums.

India's minorities, especially the ones considered 'educationally backward' by the government, are provided for in the 1992 amendment of the Indian National Policy on Education (NPE). The government initiated the Scheme of Area Intensive Programme for Educationally

Backward Minorities and Scheme of Financial Assistance or Modernisation of Madarsa Education as part of its revised Programme of Action (1992). Both these schemes were started nationwide by 1994. In 2004 the Indian parliament allowed an act which enabled minority education establishments to seek university affiliations if they passed the required norms.

Role of Central Government

As a part of the tenth Five year Plan (2002-2007), the central government of India outlined an expenditure of 65.6% of its total education budget of Rs. 438250 million, or (Rs. 287500 million) on elementary education; 9.9% (Rs. 43250 million) on secondary education; 2.9% (Rs. 12500 million) on adult education; 9.5% (Rs. 41765 million) on higher education; 10.7% (Rs. 47000 million) on technical education; and the remaining 1.4% (Rs. 6235 million) on miscellaneous education schemes. According to the United Nations Educational, Scientific and Cultural Organisation (UNESCO), India has the lowest public expenditure on higher education per student in the world.

Public Expenditure

In recent times, several major announcements were made for developing the poor state of affairs in education sector in India, the most notable ones being the National Common Minimum Programme (NCMP) of the United Progressive Alliance (UPA) government. The announcements are:

(a) To progressively increase expenditure on education to around 6 percent of GDP.

(b) To support this increase in expenditure on education, and to increase the quality of education, there would be an imposition of an education cess over all central government taxes.

(c) To ensure that no one is denied of education due to economic backwardness and poverty.

(d) To make right to education a fundamental right for all children in the age group 6-14 years.

(e) To universalise education through its flagship programmes such as Sarva Siksha Abhiyan and Mid Day Meal.

However, even after five years of implementation of NCMP, not much progress has been done on these promises or announcements. The public expenditure on education has actually declined from around 3.23 percent of GDP in 2000-2001 to 2.88 percent in the recent times. As a proportion of total government expenditure, it has declined from around 11.1 percent in 2000-2001 to around 9.98 percent during UPA rule. Due to a declining priority of education in the public policy paradigm in India, there has been an exponential growth in the private expenditure on education also.

Legislative Framework

Article 54, of the Constitution of India originally stated:

> "The State shall endeavour to provide, within a period of ten years from the commencement of this Constitution, for free and compulsory education for all children until they complete the age of fourteen years. "

This article was a directive principle of state policy within India, effectively meaning that it was within a set of rules that were meant to be followed in spirit and the government could not be held to court if the actual letter was not followed. However, the enforcement of this directive principle became a matter of debate since this principle held obvious emotive and practical value, and was legally the only directive principle within the Indian constitution to have a time limit.

Following initiatives by the Supreme Court of India during the 1990s the Ninety-third amendment bill suggested three separate amendments to the Indian constitution:

— The constitution of India was amended to include a new article, 21A, which read:
  - The State shall provide free and compulsory education to all children of the age of six to fourteen years in a such manner as the State may, by law, determine.

— Article 45 was proposed to be substituted by the article which read:

— Provision for early childhood care and education to children below the age of six years: The State shall endeavour to provide early childhood care and education for all children until they complete the age of sixteen years.

— Another article, 51A, was to additionally have the clause:

— ...a parent or guardian [shall] provide opportunities for education to his child or, as the case may be, [a] ward between the age of six to fourteen years.

The bill was passed unanimously in the Lok Sabha, the lower house of the Indian parliament, on November 28, 2001. It was later passed by the upper house-the Rajya Sabha-on May 14, 2002. After being signed by the President of India the Indian constitution was amended formally for the eighty sixth time and the bill came into effect. Since then those between the age of 6-14 have a fundamental right to education.

Article 46 of the Constitution of India holds that:

"The State shall promote, with special care, the education and economic interests of the weaker sections of the people, and in particular of the Scheduled Castes and Scheduled Tribes, and shall protect them from social injustice and all forms of social exploitation'."

Other provisions for the Scheduled Castes and Scheduled Tribes can be found in Articles 330, 332, 335, 338-342. Both the 5th and the 6th Schedules of the Constitution also make special provisions for the Scheduled Castes and Scheduled Tribes.

Content And Curriculum

School Education

The process of change in content of education and curriculum which was initiated as a aftermath of NPE, 1986 has made a significant impact on the teaching-learning process. The broad developments in this sphere has been on following lines:

— enrichment of curricula by cultural content;

— significant place to value education;

— use of media mid educational technology;

— integration of work experience in learning process;
— promotion of environmental consciousness;
— gearing science and mathematics teaching for promoting spirit of enquiry.

The 10+2+3 pattern of education introduced in the country envisages a broad based general education in respect of all pupils during the first ten years of school education. The curriculum at this stage is, therefore, undifferentiated and all the curricular areas are compulsory and no attempt is made to introduce diversified courses at this stage. The focus of the curriculum at the primary stage is on development of basic skills of literacy and numerary, study of environment in terms of physical and social phenomena, participation in activities which would develop productive skills, creative expression and habits of healthy living. In the initial years, the content and methodology are directed to achievement of excellence in communication and computational skills with a view to developing the basic tools of learning.

The content and process of education at the upper primary stage are directed to the consolidation of knowledge, skills, attitudes and values acquired at the lower primary stage and acquisition of wider knowledge base in the context of a broad-based general education. At this stage, the pupil is required to continue with the curricular areas introduced at the primary stage but in greater depth in terms of content and processes.

The curriculum at the secondary stage is designed to equip the children either to take up higher level courses of study to prepare for entrance into the first degree in a college or to equip them for vocational instruction at the higher secondary stage or to enter the work force. Since secondary education continues to be terminal for a large majority of children who are likely to enter the world of work, the emphasis is on bringing their education to a standard which would enable them to enter life with self-confidence along with useful knowledge and skills, proper work habits, attitudes and character which would contribute to their productivity and wellbeing.

There is a renewed emphasis on use of new technologies for improving education in schools. It has been envisaged that modem educational technology should reach out to the most distant areas and deprived sections of beneficiaries simultaneously with areas of comparative affluence and easy availability. Some of these programmes being implemented are described in the following paragraphs.

Educational Technology Programme

An Educational Technology Programme was started in the Central sector in the year 1972 during the Fourth Plan Period for widening access to and bringing about qualitative improvement in education. Under the scheme, a Centre for Educational Technology was set up in the NCERT and 100 per cent assistance was provided to twenty-one States for setting up Educational Technology (ET) Cells.

In view of expansion of broadcasting facilities with the advent of INSAT and concomitant demand for educational software, the Department of Education decided to take on the responsibility of production of educational television programmes for relay through satellites. Accordingly, a scheme was prepared by the Department for creating Educational Television (ETV) programme production facilities within the education sector on a decentralised basis by setting up a Central Institute of Educational Technology (CIET) in the NCERT and State Institutes of Educational Technology (SIETs) in six States, viz., Andhra Pradesh, Bihar, Gujarat, Maharashtra, Orissa and Uttar Pradesh and strengthening of ET Cells in other States.

The Educational Technology Scheme was revised in 1987 with the broad objectives of strengthening of both ETV and audio programme production capabilities and providing wider access to the same by supplying one lakh Colour Television (CTV) sets and five lakh Radio- Cum-Cassette Players (RCCPs) to primary schools during the Seventh Plan.

Programme production has commenced in CIET and all the six SIETs. In fact, from the academic year 1988-89, responsibility for programme production, which was until then being shared between CIET and Doordarshan on 50:50 basis, has been taken over by CIET and SIETs. The satellite based ETV service presently provides telecast of educational programmes for the children and their teachers at the primary level in the morning for 45 minutes duration in each of the five regional languages, namely Gujarati, Hindi, Marathi, Oriya mid Telugu on time sharing basis. The programmes for children are telecast from Monday to Friday and for primary level teachers on every Saturday. There are separate programmes for the children in the age groups of 5-8 and 9-11 years on each day.

The ETV programmes are relayed by all high and low power transmitters in the six INSAT States. The programmes in Hindi are relayed in the States of Haryana, Himachal Pradesh, Madhya Pradesh, Punjab and Rajasthan and the Union Territory of Chandigarh.

An ambitious programme of distribution of CTV sets and RCCPs was undertaken under the ET Scheme. Funds are also being sanctioned for audio programme production by State Governments and non-Government organisations. The CIET has also produced more than 1100 audio programmes on various educational themes at various levels of school education. SIETs have also geared efforts towards production of audio programmes either by themselves and/or through outside agencies. A list of about 40 video and audio programmes produced by the CIET have been identified for providing meaningful media support to the DIETs in their teacher training activities.

Computer Education in Schools

A pilot project on Computer Literacy and Studies in Schools (CLASS) was initiated in 1984-85 in 248 selected secondary/higher secondary schools jointly by the Department of Electronics and the Department of Education to acquaint students and teachers with the range of computer applications and its potential as a learning medium. Till 1989-90, 2,598 schools were covered under the project. Sixty-one resource centres were set up to train school teachers and provide logistic support to the participating schools. Installation of hardware and its maintenance is the responsibility of Computer Maintenance Corporation (CMC) and the NCERT is the nodal agency for software development, academic support and organisation of teachers' training. The Steering Committee for the project is jointly headed by the Secretaries of the Department of Electronics and the Department of Education. Upto 1986-87, the schools received a set of two BBC Micros. This number was increased to five BBC Micros from 1987-88 onwards. Since the last financial year, a decision has been taken to provide an additional three BBC Micros to those old schools which have so far only two computers each. Therefore, no new schools have been added since 1990-91. The project is currently under review for streamlining its implementation.

Higher Education

The University Grants Commission introduced the scheme of restructuring of courses with a view to making the first degree courses more relevant to environment and to the developmentai needs of the community and to link education with work/field/practical experience and productivity. The scheme has been conceived as a major programme for reforms in higher education at the undergraduate level. The programme aims at imparting training to every undergraduate student in the following areas:

i) A set of foundation courses designed to create an awareness of areas such as Indian History and Culture, History of the Freedom Struggle in India and other part of the world, Social and Economic Life in India including concepts and processes of development, scientific methods including the role of science and technology in development, alternative value systems and societies based thereon, Cultures of Asia and Africa (selected countries) and Gandhian thought.
ii) A set of core courses to give an opportunity to students to acquire broad familiarity with some chosen disciplines, including study of one or more of them in depth.
iii) Some applied studies/projects/field activity to form an integral activity of the course and to be carried out in the final year.
iv) Involvement in a programme of national or social service for the first two years.

Nine universities and 208 colleges have introduced restructured courses under the scheme upto March 1991. The Commission has also desired that the work of restructuring of courses may be undertaken on the pattern of Curriculum Development Centres.

Some of the important programmes launched to improve teaching- learning process include:

— College Humanities and Social Science Improvement Programme (COHSSIP).

— College Science Improvement Programme (COSIP).
— University Leadership Programmes.
— Special Assistance Programmes (SAP).
— Curriculum Development Centres.

Country-wide classroom programmes

The University Grants Commission has been allocated two hours transmission time daily for six days a week for telecasting 'Countrywide Class-room' programmes relating to higher education. The programmes are essentially enrichment programmes meant to take education to remote, rural and backward areas of the country.

Race to save the planet

The University Grants Commission, which was involved in collaboration with a premier public broadcasting Corporation, WGBH, Boston in producing a ten-part television series entitled 'Race to Save the Planet' is telecasting the series on Doordarshan network from 14th October, 1990 on Sundays. The programmes of the series have been shot all over the world including the Antarctica. The series analyses and presents the most important dilemma of our times, viz., how to reconcile the urge of growth and development with the need to preserve and improve the environment and enhance the quality of human living. The series also comes at a time when awareness of these problems is on the increase, both within the country and abroad. It also lends perspective to the story of the human happening on the planet and provides some wisdom to choose the specificities of our development agenda.

Educational Research

A large number of institutions across the country are involved in promotion and conduct of educational research in India. During the last 40 years, more than 4,000 research studies in the area of education have been completed. The bulk of these studies have been carried out at university departments and a majority of them are doctoral research studies. These doctoral studies are conducted by research scholars who receive fellowships for this purpose from University Grants

Commission, the Indian Council for Social Science Research and such other national bodies in order to ensure the competence and aptitude of the scholars for doing research, the University Grants Commission has been conducting a specially designed eligibility test at the national level for receiving Research Fellowships.

A major limitation of doctoral research work is that these studies have a relatively narrower conception and applicability as they are carried out by individual scholars working under constraints of time as well as resources. In order to overcome these constraints there has been a greater thrust during the recent years, to carry out research projects at institutional level with a long-term perspective and commitment. Towards this end, the national funding agencies have been specifying priority areas for promoting research so that the findings of die research can be effectively utilised for planning and policy making.

The University Grants Commission promotes educational research by providing funds for the purpose to universities and colleges. The Commission has been operating various schemes such as Centres of Advanced Studies, Departments of Special Assistance and Departmental Research Support. Under these schemes selected university departments which have capabilities in terms of qualified manpower are encouraged to pursue research vigorously and for this purpose necessary support is extended by way of providing equipment, consumable items, contingent expenditure, etc. The Commission also continues to support university/college teachers for undertaking research through such schemes as Minor Research Project, Major Research Project, Career Award and Research Scientist Schemes. In order to cater to the information needs of the researchers, the Commission has established National Information Centres in Science, Humanities and Social Sciences including Education. In fact programmes of strengthening them have received very high priority.

National Council of Educational Research and Training, promotes research on different aspects of school education through in house research projects as well as through funding of research studies taken up by outside individuals and institutions. The research activities of the Council are monitored by a specially constituted committee called "Educational Research and Innovations Committee" (ERIC).

The ERIC helps to identify priority areas in research and sanctions funds for research projects undertaken by the departments of the NCERT. Currently, the ERIC is encouraging national level researches in three priority areas, namely, universalisation of elementary education, vocationalisation of education and curriculum development.

The National Institute of Educational Planning and Administration also has been carrying out research studies in the field of educational planning and administration. Till recently, the research activities of the Institute were limited to in-house projects carried out by its faculty members. However, during 1987-88, the Institute initiated a research grant scheme for promoting research on various aspects of educational planning and administration by outside individuals and institutions.

SYSTEM OF ADMINISTRATION

India is a Union of States with a written Constitution. It enjoys a Parliamentary form of Government at the Union and State levels. According to the Constitution, Central Government is solely responsible for the subjects mentioned in the Union list of the Constitution. Similarly, the State Governments are responsible for the subjects mentioned in the State there is also a Concurrent List which is the joint List. responsibility of Central and State Governments.

By a Constitutional Amendment in 1976, education was placed in the Concurrent List. Prior to this Constitutional Amendment, the Central Government was directly responsible by virtue of entries in the Union List for several educational sectors including:

(a) co-ordination and determination of standards in institutions for higher education and research and scientific and technical institutions;

(b) union agencies and institutions for professional, vocational or technical training;

(c) promotion of special studies or research; and

(d) Central universities and any other institutions declared by Parliament as institutions of national importance.

In discharging this constitutional responsibility, the Governments at the Centre and the States have enacted legislation to govern the educational institutions and administer the programmes at various levels and in different fields. The statute books of the States, for example, cover legislations relating to: school education, State Universities, Boards of Secondary Education, Compulsory primary education, etc., while those of the Centre include University Grants Commission Act, Acts governing the Central Universities and the five Indian Institutes of Technology, Apprentices Act etc.

The Ministry of Education and Culture plays a major role in ensuring a coordinated development of education all over the country and in developing national programmes in some essential areas like elementary, adult and secondary education and research. State Education Departments share the major responsibility in administering education particularly at the school level.

The Union Ministry of Education and Culture is guided in the main by the Central Advisory Board of Education the members of which include the Ministers of Education in the States and educationists. There are a few advisory and expert consultative bodies like the All India Council of Sports and the All India Council for Technical Education, the National Council for Teacher Education, the National Council for Women's Education and the National Book Development Board.

To carry out its responsibilities, the Ministry during the years has built up a number of offices and organisations. The important amongst them are: The University Grants Commission, the National Council of Educational Research and Training, the National Institute of Educational Planning and Administration, Indian Institute of Advanced Study, Central Schools Organisation, Central Board of Secondary Education, Central Hindi Institute, Central Institute of Indian Languages, National Sanskrit Institute, Lakshmibai National College of Physical Education and Netaji Subhas National Institute of Sports. In the field of technical education there are five Indian Institutes of Technology, the Indian Institute of Science, fifteen Regional Engineering Colleges, three Institutes of Management, four Technical Teachers' Training Institutes, Indian School of Mines, School of Planning and Architecture, National Institute for Training in Industrial Engineering, and National Institute of Foundary and Forge Technology.

While scientific research is promoted in a chain of specialised research laboratories under the Council of Scientific and Industrial Research set up by the Central Government and in the Universities, three significant organisations viz. Indian Council of Social Science Research, Indian Council of Historical Research and Indian Council of Philosophical Research have also been set up to promote research in the social sciences, history and philosophy.

In every State there is an Education Minister, who is, in some States, assisted by Minister of State/Deputy Minister. The Secretary is the Head of the Education Department which has a Secretariat for Policy and Coordination and Directorate of Education that perform the functions of direction, regulation and inspection in various sectors of education. There are State Institutes of Education and State Councils of Educational Research and Training in the States to look after the academic aspects, which are replicas of the National Council of Educational Research and Training. Functional Inspectorates or Bureaux like Inspectorates for Physical education, Audiovisual education, Vocational guidance bureau, Evaluation units also function in the States.

Both at the Centre and in the States, educational programmes are looked after by a number of Ministries/Departments, besides the Ministry/Department of Education. Medical education is looked after by the Ministry/Department of Health and Agricultural education by the Ministry/Department of Agriculture. In some States technical education remains with a department other than Education viz. Department of Industries.

Educational Planning is the joint endeavour of the Central and State Governments. The Planning Commission in the Centre and the State Planning Departments decide the policy and approach in the field of national development. A Planning and Monitoring Division in the Central Ministry works in close liaison with the Education Division of the Planning Commission, on the basis of the broad guidelines issued by the Planning Commission, draft Five-Year and Annual Plans are prepared by the Central Ministries and the State Governments. These plan programmes are discussed and examined at various levels before they are finally approved for implementation. Joint consultation on educational planning between the Centre, the States and the Planning Commission is promoted in all India forums like the Central Advisory

Board of Education or State Education Ministers' Conference, Official meets and Annual Plan discussions.

Department of Education

On 29th August, 1947, the Department of Education became the Ministry of Education under a Cabinet Minister, Maulana Abul Kalam Azad. The Department of Education, which was created in 1910, acquired its new role after Independence. In the Post-Independence period, the Ministry of Education has undergone some metamorphosis both in its nomenclature and responsibilities. The Ministry of Education created 1947 continued until April, 1957, when for the First time two subjects "Education" and "Scientific Research" were brought under one Ministry named the Ministry of Education and Scientific Research.

A new Ministry of Education and Scientific Research was organised into three Departments, viz., Department of Education, Department of Scientific Research & Technical Education and Department of Culture Activities & Physical Education. In 1958, the Ministry of Education and Scientific Research was bifurcated into the Ministry of Education and the Ministry of Scientific Research and Cultural Affairs. The new Ministry of Education took over all the functions of erstwhile Department of Education in the erstwhile Ministry of Education and Scientific Research and the Subject of Physical Education from the Department of Culture.

In 1963 these two Ministries were unified with two departments, viz., Department of Education and Department of Science. These two departments were however abolished in March, 1964 and the Ministry was reorganised in five Bureaus. In 1969, the Ministry of Education was renamed as the Ministry of Education and Youth Services mainly with the objective of paying greater attention on the development of youth, especially those who were outside the educational institutions. In 1971, the Ministry was renamed as the Ministry of Education and Social Welfare. In 1979, the Department of Social Welfare became independent and the new Ministry of Education and Culture was born. Subsequently in 1984 the Department of Culture was separated from Education.

The present Ministry of Human Resource Development was created on 26th September, 1985 by clubbing five departments, VIZ., Department of Education, Department of Culture, Department of Arts, Department of Youth Affairs & Sports and Department of Women's Welfare. Thus, hitherto Ministry of Education now became a constituent Department under the new dispensation.

Organisation Structure

The Department of education is under the overall charge of the Minister of Human Resource Development. He is assisted by one Minister of State. The Secretariat of the Department is headed by the Secretary, who is assisted by an Additional Secretary and Joint Secretaries/joint Educational Advisors. The Department is organised into Bureaus, Divisions, Branches, Desks, Sections and Units. Each Bureau is under the charge of a Joint Secretary/joint Educational Advisor assisted by Divisional Heads.

Functions

Education is a concurrent subject. Concurrency implies a meaningful partnership between the Union Government and the States.

— Education Department deals with all stages of general and technical education, i.e. school and university.

— In addition it also deals with language development and book promotion and copyright

— Department of Education is the nodal department for two major UN Organisations.

— Department operates most of the programmes through subordinate offices and state government organisations.

Non-governmental Voluntary Organisations are involved in a large measure in Elementary Education (Non-formal Education), Adult Education and Language development besides to a lesser extent in handicapped education, minorities' education, etc. The most important advisory body, which helps for federal consideration, is the Central Advisory Board of Education (CABE). Minister of Human Resource Development is the Chairman of this Board. All State Education Ministers, elected members of Parliament and nominated academics are members of the Board.

Special programmes

On the occasion of the celebration of the Golden Jubilee of India's Independence, an allocation of Rs.200 crore has been provided in the budget grant of Department of Education, out of which Rs.50 crore is earmarked to the Department of Science &Technology. For the remaining amount, the Department. of Education is planning a series of activities to strengthen large number of scientific, technical, and educational institutions as well as specific activities synchronising the observance of the Golden Jubilee of India's Independence. A special package of Rs.9 crore for-Jammu & Kashmir and Rs. 7 crore for the North-East has already been approved in this respect.

University Grants Commission

The University Grants Commission (UGC) was established in 1956 by all Act of Parliament. Section 12 of the UGC Act provides that it shall be general duty of the Commission to take, in consultation with the universities or other bodies concerned, all such steps as It may think fit, for the promotion and coordination of university education and for the determination and maintenance of standards of teaching, examination and research in universities. For the purpose of performing its functions under the Act, the Commission may inquire into the financial needs of universities and allocate and disburse grants to them for the development and/or maintenance of such universities or for any other general or specified purpose. At present, UGC provides financial assistance to Central Universities both for maintenance and development purposes; development grants to 103 eligible State Universities; and development or maintenance grants, as the case may be, to the eligible Deemed Universities. UGC also provides development grants to 4,730 eligible colleges.

At present, there are 166 Central/State Universities, 37 Deemed Universities and 9,278 colleges, out of which only 4,730 colleges are eligible to receive grants from the Commission. The students enrolment in institutions of higher education is estimated to be approximately 64.26 lakh students. The teaching staff strength in universities and affiliated colleges stood at 3.10 lakh at the end of 1995-96.

Major programmes

A crucial element in the development of higher education is the promotion of research. UGC provides financial assistance on a selective basis, to such of the Departments which have credentials for undertaking quality research or are reputed centres of instruction and learning. Under the Special Assistance Programme, assistance is provided to the selected University Departments at three levels, namely:

1. Centres of Advanced Study (CAS)
2. Department of Special Assistance (DSA)
3. Departmental Research Support (DRS)

Indian Institute of Science (IIS)

The institute is basically a Post-Graduate and Research Oriented Institute and acts as a National Resource Centre. The Institute was established in 1909. It has close research links with Space and Defence Departments. It plays an important role in planning and execution of projects related to Power Sector, Civil Constructions, Communication and Environmental Planning. The Institute has several continuing education programmes that benefit a large section of students, teachers and scientists in the country. The Institute offers various Courses and programmes in all major disciplines of Engineering, Applied Science and Technology including those in emerging areas of engineering and technology. During 1995-96,1,537 students were getting training in various Scientific and Engineering disciplines in the Institute. Admission was offered to 447 students—176 in research, 21 students in Integrated Ph.D., 193 Students in M.E./M.Tech., 57 students in M.E. (integrated).

Super Computer Education and Research Centre

The Cabinet has approved during 1992-93, the installation of distributing Super Computer Facility and incurring an expenditure of up to Rs. 18.50 crore (Rs. 7.5 crore in Indian Rupees and Rs. 11.00 crore in foreign exchange) towards Capital expenses. The distributing Super Computer Facility consists of parallel computing, special purpose parallel computers, Numeric Vector and graphic Computer etc. The significant achievements are as under:

1. Creation of functionally distributed super computing environment;
2. High end super computing graphics;
3. Campus wide high speed fibre; optic network at fast access;
4. This facility is used by several scientists from other institutes;
5. Providing national and international trainings;
6. Undertaken sponsored and consultancy research ; and
7. Manpower training for Government and Industry personnel etc.

On 2nd March, 1997 the Super Computer Education and Research Centre was dedicated to the nation by the then Prime Minister. The Programme was dedicated as part of Golden Jubilee Celebrations of India's Independence.

National Council of Educational Research and Training

The National Council of Educational Research and Training (NCERT) was set up by the Government of India in 1961 as an autonomous Organisation for providing academic support to the school education system in the country. It functions as an academic adviser to the Ministry of Human Resource Development, Government of India. The main objectives of the NCERT are to assist and advise the Ministry of Human Resource Development, in implementing policies and major programmes in the field of school education. In the formulation and implementation of policies and programmes as well, the Ministry draws upon the expertise of the NCERT to a considerable extent. The Council is fully financed by the Government of India.

To bring about qualitative improvement in school education, the NCERT, has five Regional Institutes and Field offices in major States all over the country, and through them, the Council;

— conducts, aids, promotes and coordinates research in all branches of school education and teacher education;
— organises pre-service and in-service training of teachers, mainly at the advanced level;

— organises extension services for institutions, organisations and agencies engaged in educational reconstruction;
— develops and experiments with improved educational techniques, practices and innovations;
— collects, compiles, processes and disseminates educational information;
— assists the State/UT Governments and State/UT-level institutions, organisations and agencies in developing and implementing programmes for qualitative improvement of school education;
— collaborates with international organisations like UNESCO, UNDP, UNFPA and with national-level educational institutions of other countries;
— extends facilities for training and study to educational personnel from other countries;
— serves as the academic secretariat of the National Development Group (NDG) for the Asia and the Pacific Programme of Educational innovation for Development (APEID), UNESCO, Bangkok; and
— develops, prints and distributes textbooks.

Activities

NCERT proposes undertaking the following programmes as a part of the celebration of the Golden jubilee of India's Independence.

1. *National Seminar on 50 Years of Indian Educational Development:* The seminar will seek to bring together scholars to make research presentations on, and to critically discuss the development in every major area of school education, including teacher education, during the past 50 years.
2. *Publications for Students and Teachers:* A series of publications dealing with the Indian experience during the past 50 years, in the field of polity, economy, culture, science and technology. The publication varying in size from 64 to 80 pages, would seek to enhance teachers' and students' understanding of various dimensions of contemporary India.

3. *Study of Students' Perception of Freedom and India's struggle for freedom:* A study, based on an appropriate sample would be undertaken to assess students knowledge and understanding of the freedom struggle and its heritage, their perception of its relevance to contemporary India and their vision of the future development of independent India.

Financing of Education

Educational financing in India has developed to be a multisource system although the State has been taking an increasingly commanding position in this behalf since Independence. Education is now financed by the Central Government, State Governments, local authorities and through fees and other sources that include endowments, donations and voluntary contributions.

Educational financing by the Central Government and the State Governments is of two categories, viz., Plan and NonPlan. Plan allocations cover development expenditure while Non-Plan allocation provide for maintenance. The Central Government, however, is directly responsible for the development programmes in the fields within its purview. It also takes up schemes known as Centrally Sponsored Schemes and Central Schemes administered by the States which are of common interest and utility to the State Governments and represent nationally identified objectives. The Central Government has in the post-independence period, been extending increasing financial assistance to the State Governments besides incurring considerable direct expenditure on the Central and Centrally Sponsored Schemes.

References

Basu, AN (1947), *Education in Modern India, Orient Book Co.*, Calcutta.

Dayal, Bhagwan (1955), *The Development of Modern Indian Education,* Orient Longman, Bombay.

Gore, MS (1995), *Indian Education : Structure and Process,* Rawat Publication, Jaipur.

Haq, Ehsanul (1997), *Education, Polity and Society,* Shipra Publications, Delhi.

2

Objectives of Educational System

Ever since Independence, a major concern of the Government of India and of the States has been to give increasing attention to education as a factor vital to national progress and security. Problems of educational reconstruction were reviewed by several commissions and committees. A comprehensive review was made by the Education Commission (1964-66). which was appointed by the Government to advise on the national pattern of education and on the general principles and policies for the development of education at all stages and in all aspects. As a result of discussions mid deliberations on the Report of the Education Commission, a general consensus had emerged and a National Policy on Education was enunciated by the Government in 1968. Educational activities in India continue to be guided by the above-said policy.

Educational objectives, during these years, lay more stress on further democratisation of education, improving access to education, better educational opportunities for the disadvantaged, achieving more regional equity, increasing the range of educational opportunities, introducing increased vocational bias in the curricula, more relevance to socio-economic needs, developing alternate strategies, broadening the concept of continuing education, increasing access of women to all levels of education and awareness of environmental problems.

The most important problem in the field of education in India is the extent of illiteracy. According to 1981 Census although the literacy rate during the past 10 years has risen from 29.45% to 36.17%, the number of illiterates has also risen from 372 lakhs to 419 lakhs. Consequently our Sixth Five-Year Plan lays emphasis on minimum essential education to all citizens. Top priority has been given to the programmes of universalisation of elementary education and eradication of illiteracy. These programmes are also included in the new 20-Point Programme of the Government.

In the three decades of independence, there has been a tremendous expansion of educational facilities in the country. The number of institutions has gone up from 1,65,000 to 7,40,000. In the Sixth Plan, an attempt has been made towards consolidation of the facilities and improvement of quality in education.

Universalisation of Elementary Education

The Constitution of India directs that the State shall endeavour to provide free and compulsory education for all children until they complete the age of 14 years within a period of 10 years from the commencement of the Constitution. For various reasons, this goal has not yet been realised. For its developmental effort, India has adopted Five-Year Plans. So far, the country has gone through the process of 5 Five-Year Plans. Currently, the Sixth Five-Year Plan (1980-85) is in progress. According to the Policy frame of the Sixth Five-Year Plan, the main objective of educational development will be to ensure essential minimum education to all children up to the age of 14 years within the next 10 years. This objective has been reinforced by the 20-Point Programme announced by the Prime Minister of India on the 14th January, 1982. Point 16 of this Programme reads as follows:

> Spread Universal elementary education for the age-group 6-14 with special emphasis on girls, and simultaneously involve students and Voluntary agencies in programmes for the removal of adult illiteracy.

Elementary Education has been accorded a very high priority in the Sixth Five-Year Plan with a total plan outlay of Rs. 905 crores (Rs. 851 crores in the State Sector and Rs. 54 crores in the Central sector) or 36% of the total outlay of Rs. 2,524 crores for education. Besides, elementary education as a whole constitutes an essential component of the Minimum Needs Programme (MNP) of the Plan.

Universalisation of elementary education requires that education be made relevant and meaningful to specific communities. In context, experimental projects being implemented are providing worthwhile experiences. It is hoped that the approaches being developed will go a long way in reaching the goal of providing relevant and meaningful education on a universal basis. These Projects include the following:

(i) Comprehensive Access to Primary Education which aims at meeting the minimum educational needs of a large number of out-of-school children in the age-group 6-14. The main objective of the project is to develop and try out relevant and problem-oriented learning materials for use in the non-formal education centres. The programme is being implemented in almost all the States.

(ii) Primary Education Curriculum Renewal Project aims at decentralising the formulation of syllabus for 6-11 age-group with special reference to educational needs of children of rural, tribal and urban poverty areas. The main aim of this Projects to experiment with (a) the decentralisation of the process of curriculum development through involvement of teachers, (b) to evolve diversified curriculum through a detailed socioeconomic survey of the community leading to the attainment of a common core of competencies, (c) use of environment for meaningful learning, (d) involving local community in educational programmes and use of local resources for socially useful productive work.

(iii) Community Education and Participation Project aims at developing a package of educational programmes of encompassing the entire community drawing in the process on the resources already available in the community (such as the expertise and resources available with other development departments).

(iv) In the area of Early Childhood Education, various research and developmental projects have been undertaken for strengthening pre-school education as an important support to elementary education by strengthening motivation of students for schooling and by developing school readiness. It has been demonstrated that early childhood education helps in reducing the incidence of stagnation and drop-outs.

(v) Another Project which is being implemented is Nutrition Education, Health and Environmental Sanitation. Under this project textual materials are being developed on nutrition, health and environmental sanitation which are important concerns in all communities. Further, teachers and the communities are being trained in improved practices the adoption of which depends more on knowledge than on resources.

Education, particularly school education, continues to be the responsibility primarily of States/Union Territories. At present, education in classes I-VIII, in all the Government, local bodies, and aided schools in all States/Union Territories of the country, is free.

In the base year of the Sixth Plan i.e. 1979-80, the enrolment at the primary stage stood at 710.2 lakhs or 83.72% of 6-11 age-group Population and 194.01 lakhs at the middle stage or 40.16% of 11-14 age-group population. The targets of additional enrolment during the Sixth Plan are 180 lakhs of 6-14 age-group population-117 lakhs at the primary stage and 63 lakhs at the middle stage. If achieved, enrolment at the end of 1984-85 would rise to 95% and 50% respectively at the primary and middle stages based on the age-group population projections according to 1971 Census figures.

In addition to the enrolment position through the formal system indicated above, it is estimated that, for the country as a whole, coverage under the non-formal system is likely to be about 35 lakhs by the end of the current plan period. If achieved, the total additional coverage at the elementary stage is likely to be of the order of 240 lakhs.

The elementary age-group out-of-school children, more particularly primary age-group, belong to weaker sections including Scheduled Castes and Scheduled Tribes. Such children are concentrated in the educationally backward States and backward areas/pockets of each State. Further, about 70 per cent of the out-of-school children are girls including Scheduled Caste and Scheduled Tribe girls. The programme of Universalisation is, therefore, target-group-oriented with concentrated efforts in the educationally backward States and backward areas/pockets in a State. In this backdrop, the following steps have been, taken as part of the basic strategy:

(i) In the country as a whole, nine States have been identified as being educationally backward. They are: Andhra Pradesh, Assam, Bihar, Jammu & Kashmir, Madhya Pradesh, Orissa, Rajasthan, Uttar Pradesh and West Bengal.

(ii) Most of States/Union Territories have identified the backward areas/pockets for concentrated attention and have quantified the Sizes of non-enrolled scheduled caste and scheduled tribe children and fixed year-wise targets for enrolment.

(iii) Special efforts are being made by the States/Union Territories for accelerated coverage of girls including Scheduled Caste and Scheduled Tribe girls.

(iv) Efforts are also being made by the States to increase the coverage under the incentive programme like provision of free textbooks and stationery, free supply of uniforms particularly for girls, attendance scholarships particularly for girls and mid-day meals programme for the benefit of children of the weaker sections.

All the States and five Union Territories are having non-formal education programmes for out-of-school children including non-starters and drop-outs. Non-formal education is being developed as a massive alternate supportive system 'to, formal schooling. The main thrust and maximum extent of coverage is in the nine educationally backward States, which are receiving special Central assistance since 1979-80 under a centrally sponsored scheme of non-formal education for elementary age-group children.

Voluntary organisations in the nine educationally backward States running non-formal education centres on the State Government pattern and academic institutions, Government or private, in any State/ Union Territory taking up innovative and experimental non-formal education projects are given Central assistance.

In order to increase enrolment of girls in the Non-formal Education centres, enhanced (90%) Central assistance is being given for the establishment of NFE Centres exclusively for girls in the nine educationally backward States.

For production of teaching-learning materials, guide books ètc. for the massive non-formal education, programme for elementary age-group children in all the States/Union Territories, commodity assistance in the form of paper has been given.

To provide a further boost to the programme of universalisation of elementary education, and to give recognition for excellence in performance for the spread of girls' education, a scheme of incentives/ awards is being implemented.

With a view to increasing enrolment of girls which is a critical target group, a scheme of Central financial assistance for appointment of women teachers in primary schools in the educationally backward States has been formulated and put into operation.

In the context of universalisation of elementary education, Early Childhood (Pre-school) Education has assumed importance. While the pre-school child receives care in ECE Centre, his young caretaker, usually a girl, is free to join and attend school, thus removing one basic cause of drop-outs, particularly in the first two or three years of the primary stage. Realising the importance of the role of voluntary agencies in this area, the Union Ministry of Education has formulated and put into operation a scheme of financial assistance to voluntary agencies to run Early Childhood (Pre-school) Education Centres as adjuncts of primary/middle schools run' either by Government, local body or private management, particularly for the disadvantaged sections in rural/tribal/backward areas in the 9 educationally backward States.

Prior to the inception of Integrated Child Development Service Programme, Balwadis were being used for the Preschool education of children in the age-group 3 to 5 years. The Balwadis were located in the rural areas and were being run by voluntary organisations. The importance of pre-school education for the social and mental development of the Child has been recognised by the social scientists. When ICDS was formulated, informal pre-school education was introduced as one of its components. Non-formal pre-school education implies the Organisation of preschool activities for children in the age-group 3 to 5 years in Angawadis, which stimulate the children to learn from the environment and through play and creative activities,

Literacy Programmes

The problem of illiteracy is also being tackled through Adult Education Programme for the economically active age-group of 15-35. There are about 110 million adult illiterates in the age-group 15-35 in the country. The policies and strategies followed by the Government for removing illiteracy from this age-group are as follows:

(i) To cover districts having literacy below the national level and give priority to the target group of women, disadvantaged groups of Scheduled Castes and Scheduled Tribes;

(ii) To provide grants-in-aid to voluntary organisations working in the field of adult education for running adult education centres;

(iii) To enlist larger participation of students and non-student youth in the adult education programmes;

(iv) To strengthen post-literacy programmes to avoid relapse in illiteracy on neo-literates;

(v) To provide adequate resource support for needbased teaching-learning material;

(vi) To train the adult education functionaries at various levels;

(vii) To establish proper linkages with other development departments like health, agriculture, animal husbandry and social welfare;

(viii)To utilise the potential of traditional and electronic media for creation of learning environment.

All the State Governments have been instructed to prepare operational plans indicating year-wise physical targets, administrative and financial requirements to achieve the objectives of cent per cent literacy in the age-group 15-35 by 1990.

Rural Functional Literacy Projects have been opened in districts below the national literacy level. Each Project has 300 centres. This scheme is funded by the Central Government. However, the responsibility for its implementation rests with the concerned State Governments. At the end of June, 1983, 69,825 centres were running with an enrolment of 20,21,210 learners in the country. The State Governments have also opened similar projects in rural areas from the State Government funds and as on 30th June, 1983, 70,588 centres were functioning with an enrolment of 20,15,907 learners. Voluntary organisations have also been involved in the programme of 'Eradication of Illiteracy'. The role of voluntary agencies in adult education has several dimensions. The most important, of course, is the responsibility for organising adult education centres, including post-literacy and follow-up activities. Another area in which voluntary agencies have made an important contribution is resource development. Similarly, they also help in training of functionaries involved in adult education programme. In 1982-83 grants to 178 voluntary organisations were given for running 8,975 centres and enrolling 2,69,250 learners.

To enlist larger participation of students in the adult education programme, the University Grants Commission has prepared a detailed operational plan. India has a huge complex of 146 recognised universities and about 4.500 affiliated colleges. The University Grants Commission has decided to implement this programme in two phases. In the first phase, up to 1985, all affiliated universities and colleges are expected to organise 15 to 20,000 centres. In the second phase 1985-90, all universities and colleges are expected to be involved in this programme by opening at least 50,000 centres. It is felt that involvement of institutions of higher education in adult education will bring teachers and students in close contact with common people and their problems. Mobilisation of the vast energy of the students and of the academic community will impart great vitality to the adult education programme.

One of the major thrusts during 1982-83 has been initiating postliteracy and follow-up programmes at places where the regular adult education programme concluded. It was considered essential not only to prevent learners (who had acquired basic literacy skills in the 10-month adult education course) from relapsing into illiteracy, but also to make them selfreliant and induct them into a process of continuing education. With the programme of post-literacy and follow-up getting momentum it has been realised that graded materials that would be used by the neo-literate after the conclusion of the first phase of the programme should be available to them. The National Directorate of Adult Education has developed broad guidelines for the preparation on such material throughout the country.

Since adult education can contribute to the economic and social development of the community, it has to be recognised as an integral part of both the educational system and the development process. Through adult education programme, individuals and community of members acquired knowledge about the health status, modern agricultural techniques, fertilisers, animal husbandry etc. The global strategy of WHO indicates the value of literacy in promoting primary health care. There are some illustrations of close relationship between literacy rates and health status as in the State of Kerala in India. Thus the adult education programme performs an important role of integrating various elements of development.

The kind of learning the adult education promotes are skills and attitudes that are not limited to human sector. Efforts are, therefore, being made to include adult education as an integral part of development programmes, wherever possible. This would lead to the integration of adult education with health care, dairy development or development of children. Efforts are afoot to include literacy as a component in the Schemes of Rural Development like Integrated Rural Development Projects, Training Rural Youth for Self-Employment, Development of Women and Children in Rural Areas. In the year 1982-83, the Integrated Child Development Scheme of the Social Welfare Ministry had a component of Functional Literacy for Women where they have enrolled about 3.84 lakh women in literacy classes.

The census of 1981 showed that there were wide disparities between the male and female literacy levels in rural and urban areas. Nearly 3/4 of women in the country are illitrate. Out of 110 million illiterates in the age-group 15-35 approximately 68 million are women. Removing illiteracy amongst women has, therefore, been accorded high priority by the Government and adult education again is envisaged as a tool through which socioeconomic status of women and their quality of life can be improved so that they will be involved in the overall development process. Out of nearly 4.5 million learners enrolled in 1982-83, 41 per cent were women. The major thrust of the programme for women is to give them functional knowledge on subjects like health and hygiene, food and nutrition, civic education, vocational and occupational skills and home management and childcare. To encourage large participation of illiterate adult women, the Government of India proposes to introduce a Scheme of Incentives and Awards to the States which have done good work in this area.

To cover the target of 110 million adult illiterates in the age-group 15-35 by 1980, intensive efforts to create a demand for literacy are required in the coming years. Promotional strategies using mass media such as films and radios will have to be deployed. Ministries of Central and State Governments, wherever possible, will have to provide a part of their budget for educating the beneficiaries of their respective programmes. Further, significant efforts will have to be made to develop need-based literacy suited to the local needs in various States. Priority will also have to be given to postliteracy and follow-up activities by developing suitable reading material to motivate neo-literates to retain the self-learning habit. It is necessary that a spirit of self-confidence and optimism be instilled in the minds of the learners as welt as the functionaries. Indian society, with its long tradition of respect for learning, has to consciously build up the urgency for the creation of a new society where ignorance has no place.

Improvements in School Education

Apart from quantitative expansion of education as envisaged in the constitutional directives, the education policy has emphasised the need for bringing about qualitative improvement in education. The effort includes renewal and upgrading of curricula of elementary and secondary schools, environmental approach to teaching of different subjects, physical and moral education, art education including creativity and aesthetics.

For bringing about improvement of pre-service and in-service teacher education in the country both at the elementary and the secondary levels, the National Council of Teacher Educaton (NCTE) has been set up. Efforts are made to remodel teacher education on the curricular framework that NCTE has developed. Further, the other efforts undertaken by NCERT for improving teacher education include:

(i) implementation of innovative programmes of pre-service and in-service education of teachers including extension work of the centres of continuing education;

(ii) preparation of curricula and instructional material;

(iii) research into the problems of teacher education; and

(iv) collaboration with State Governments to improve teacher education programmes.

Centres for continuing education for elementary teacher educators and secondary school teachers have been set up in different States to provide facilities for in-service education on a continuous basis.

In the ten-year school curriculum, greater emphasis has been laid on science education to develop scientific attitude among the students. The curriculum content, textbooks, methods and techniques are not only up-dated but are related to the socioeconomic and cultural development of the country. Many more efforts are still needed so as to relate science education with agriculture, economic, cultural and scientific development in collaboration with the States. Several aids, gadgets and kits have been designed, fabricated and used for effective teaching-learning process. NCERT has organised various workshop-cum-training programmes to develop different training modules in collaboration with other developing countries. Publication of School Science Journal is a step towards the development and renewal of science education to improve cultural and technological standards of the masses.

In the field of school education, many programmes for improving the quality and content of education have been introduced. These include programmes for increasing the employability of students by programmes of Socially Useful Productive Work. Education for agriculture and industry and increasing the facilities for technical and vocational education at the secondary school stage are also included in these programmes. Socially Useful Productive Work has been recommended as an integral part of the 10-year school curriculum with the objective of familiarisation of children with the world of work. National Council of Educational Research and Training which is the apex body in India to advise the Government in matters relating to school education has formulated a comprehensive curriculum for the 10-year school which has been accepted by and large by all the State Governments. One of the highlights of this programme is the introduction of 10+2 System together with vocationalisation at the secondary stage which is also recommended by the National Policy on Education.

For the education of disabled children, a scheme of Integrated Education was launched in 1974 by the Department of Social Welfare as a Centrally Sponsored Scheme where handicapped children were sought to be integrated in the normal school system. For this purpose, certain resource facilities were made available and some financial incentives were given to the teachers and also to the children. These were mainly in terms of funding of salary of staff, special pay for teachers, allowance for books and stationery and initial equipment allowance.

The Scheme was revised in consultation with the experts and Planning Commission in 1981. The revised Scheme envisaged certain additional facilities such as the setting up of an assessment room, a resource room, enhanced salary of the staff and other incentives for the teachers and disabled children and provides 100% assistance. As the training of teachers in special education is special ingredient for the proper implementation of the Scheme, the NCERT has also started such a training course for the key personnel. Besides, the four National Institutes of the Handicapped are also expected to play a pioneering role in the training of teachers in special education and also in the preparation of equipment required by the disabled for education in integrated schools.

In India the cultural milleu is diverse as far as language, art, religion, caste, communities, etc. are concerned. There are also large scale disparities between different sections of the population, among regions etc. There is consequently an urgent need for bringing about social and national integration. ID education, therefore, various policies are being pursued to, achieve the goal of social and national cohesion. The National Service Scheme, social service and community education and community service scheme, labour and social service corps, NCC and Nehru Yuvak Kendra Camps are given priority in the: curricular and co-curricular activity in school curriculum.

Educational policies also stress the promotion of national consciousness, an understanding of cultural heritage and the creation of strong sense of nationalism. Hence, teaching of language and literature, philosophy, religion, history, painting, art, music, dance and drama have been included in the school curriculum. The ten-year curriculum frame work lays down stage-wise objectives of general education. Among the objectives listed are those that have a direct bearing on developing linkages between education and culture of the country.

Standards in Higher Education

Coordination and determination of standards in higher education is a special responsibility of the Central Government. This responsibility is discharged mainly through the University Grants Commission. Besides, the Government has established agencies for promotion and coordination of research efforts in specialised fields. There are three such national agencies at present, namely the Indian Council of Social Science Research, the Indian Council of Historical Research and the Indian Council of Philosophical Research. The Government has also been implementing a number of schemes in the field of higher education and research, including those relating to academic collaboration between India and other countries.

In the field of higher education, the growing facilities have attracted a larger number of people to universities and colleges. However, our economic development has not kept pace with this expansion. Consequently, unemployment among the educated, in particular, has been showing a rising trend. Although the ultimate solution to the problem of unemployment lies in the rapid industrial and economic development of the country, efforts arc afoot to make higher education more relevant to the needs of the people and to increase the employability of graduates.

Technical Education

The Technical Education System of the country is designed to meet the technological needs of economy both on short-term and long-term basis. The development of technical education is, therefore, regarded as an area of high priority in economic planning. In order to meet the urgent requirements of the nation, major emphasis has been on (a) optimum utilisation of existing facilities, (b) consolidation, (c) expansion of facilities in areas where weakness exists, (d) creation of infrastructure in areas of emerging technologies vital for the development of the country, (e) improvement of quality and standards of education, and (f) furtherance of national efforts to develop and apply science and technology as an instrument of country's socioeconomic progress. Besides the schemes instituted in the earlier years the following new plan schemes have been instituted:

National Manpower Information System: The main objective of the National Manpower Information System is to provide uptodate and meaningful manpower information on a continuing basis to enable the concerned authorities to anticipate areas of growth in the field of science and technology and consequently plan for technical manpower development on the proper lines. The system will help in many ways including collection, storage, updating, retrieval and analysis of manpower information to formulate necessary development plans on scientific lines to meet the national requirements.

Quality Improvement Programme: The programme of quality improvement was initiated with a view to improving the quality and standards of technical education system in India. The scheme continued to play its important role in the faculty development and curriculum development in the technical institutions. Quality improvement programme consists of (i) faculty development, and (ii) curriculum development which includes preparation of instructional material, textbooks and laboratory development.

Community Polytechnics: The scheme was instituted in the year 1978-79 under which 36 Polytechnics were selected to be developed as community polytechnics, in addition to offering diploma courses in different branches of engineering and technology, these polytechnics are also required to interact with the environment and serve as focal points to promote transfer of technology to the rural sector.

Advanced Technician Course: The scheme of Advanced Technician Course has been started from 1981-82. The main objective of this Scheme is to provide avenues of advancement to diploma holders and also to provide higher courses at advanced level to enable the technicians to advance professionally in their own lines.

Institutional Network Scheme: The Institutional Network Scheme, which was introduced in 1981-82, continued with vigour during 1983-84. Collaboration between the Indian Institutes of Technology and Regional Engineering Colleges continued in the areas of laboratory development and faculty exchange programme.

Expansion of Faculties in Areas where Weakness exists: The Scheme was instituted in 1981-82 to strengthen and expand facilities in the areas where weakness existed. The primary object of the scheme was to improve areas of Computer Science, Electronics, Maintenance Engineering, Instrumentation, Product Development and Bio-Sciences and Management Sciences etc.

Creation of Infrastructure in Areas of Emerging Technology The Scheme, which was introduced in 1981-82, envisages to create and develop facilities for research and education, and training in the areas of new emerging technology so important for the development and advancement of the country in this respect. These include Microprocessor application, Remote Sensing, User Technology Atmospheric Sciences, Environmental Engineering, Energy Sciences, and Water Resources Management. The strengthening and creation of facilities in these areas would be of immense help in accelerating the pace of development in the country.

REFERENCES

Limaye, PM (1945), *Education in India Today*, Deccan Education Society, Poona.

Premi, MK (1972), *Educational Planning in India,* Sterling Publishers, New Delhi.

Tilak, JBG (1992), *Educational Planning at Grassroots*, Ashish Publishing House, New Delhi.

Zellener, A. A. (1951), *Education in India*, Bookman Associates, New York.

3

Universalisation of Elementary Education

At the time of Independence, India inherited a system of education which was not only quantitatively small but also characterised by structural imbalances. Only fourteen per cent of the population was literate and only one child out of three had been enrolled in primary school. The low levels of participation and literacy were aggravated by acute regional and gender disparities. As education is vitally linked with the totality of the development process education being "the basic tool for the development of consciousness and reconstitution of society, " in the words of Mahatma Gandhi—the reform and restructuring of the educational system was recognised as an important area of state intervention.

The need for a literate population and universal education for all children in the age group of 6-14 was recognised as a crucial input for nation building and was given due consideration in the Constitution as well as in successive Five Year Plans. This has resulted in a manifold increase of spatial spread, infrastructural facilities, increased coverage of various social groups; but the goal of providing basic education to all could not be achieved. There has been a spectacular increase in elementary education during the post-Independence period. The elementary education system of India has expanded into one of the largest in the world. The number of primary schools increased from 209, 671 in 1950-51 to 572, 541 in 1992-93; the corresponding increase in upper primary.schools was from 13, 596 to 153, 921. These 726, 462 schools together with 2.7 lakhs non-formal education centres enrolled 150 million children as compared to 22.3 million in 1951.

Universal provision of education has been substantially achieved at the primary stage (classes IN).

According to the Fifth AR India Education Survey (1986), 94.5 per cent of the rural population had schools within a walking distance of 1 km. and 83.98% of the rural population have an upper primary school within a walking distance of 3 km. The survey estimated that there were 31, 815 habitations in the country which had a population of 300 or more but did not have a primary school within the walking distance of one kilometre. Most of these habitations are situated in educationally backward states such as Uttar Pradesh, Rajasthan, Madhya Pradesh, Bihar, Jammu and Kashmir, Assam and Arunachal Pradesh.

ENROLMENT

Since Independence, there has been a substantial increase in enrolment at all levels of education. Enrolment at the primary stage increased about five fold from 19.2 million to 105.37 million in 1992-93; the increase in the upper primary stage is far higher from 3.1 million to 38.7 million. The gross enrolment ratios of children in the age group 6-11 increased from 42.6 per cent in 1950-51 to 105.7 per cent in 1992-93. Likewise, the gross enrolment of 11-14 age group increased from 12.7 per cent in 1950-51 to 67.5 per cent in 1992-93. An analysis of the enrolment data reveals that the population of children moving up from the primary to upper primary stage has been increasing steadily, from 16.3 per cent in 1950-51 to 36.72 per cent in 1992-93.

While the gross enrolment ratios (GER) at the primary stage in the country as a whole and in most of its states exceed 100 per cent there are quite a few states where the ratio is considerably lower. These include Uttar Pradesh, Bihar, Rajasthan, Haryana, Jammu and Kashmir, and Meghalaya. At the upper primary stage these states and in addition, Andhra Pradesh, Orissa and Sikkim have GERs lower than the national average. Most of these states have literacy rates lower than the national average. There is thus a strong regional dimension of UEE.

The problem gets more complicated as the drop-out rates, though declining, continue to be high. Nearly half the children who entered Class I drop out before reaching Class V, and two-thirds of the children dropout before reaching Class VIII. Regional disparities also abound in rates of the dropouts.

Gender Disparities

As with any educational indicator, gender disparities are conspicuous in regard to enrolment and retention. Girls' enrolment has grown at the primary stage from 5.4 million in 1950-51 to 42.4 million in 1991-92 and at the upper primary stage from 0.5 million to 13 million. The rate of growth of enrolment of girls has been higher than that of boys but disparities still persist—girls still account for only 45.7 per cent of the enrolment at the primary stage and 37.73 per cent.

Dropping Out

The 42nd round of the National Sample Survey (July 1986-June 1987) provides valuable information on the reasons for non-enrolment and dropout. Nonavailability of schooling facilities seems to account for only about 10 percent of the "never enroled" in rural India and about 8 percent in urban India; the difference between the sexes is very small in rural areas but somewhat larger in the urban sector

However, nearly 30 percent of the persons surveyed, both in rural and urban India, gave the reason for "never enroled" as being "not interested". The difference between the sexes here is large: a larger proportion of "never enroled" females gave this reason in comparison with the males. The reason for being "not interested" could be considered as a demand side constraint to access: some authorities however, consider it as a supply side constraint rooted in poor facilities and quality of education.

Domestic Restraints

About 52 percent of urban males and 29 percent of urban females could not avail of the educational services because of participation in household economic activity and other economic reasons. Attending to domestic chores restrained around one percent of the males, both in rural as well as urban India, from ever enrolling as students. Nevertheless, this reason was one of the major demand side constraints on access to education for the females: for 9.9 percent of them in the rural and 10.7 percent of them in the urban sector Most of the young females are denied access to education because they look after their siblings besides performing a variety of domestic, housekeeping chores. Significantly, the proportion of currently "not enroled" decreases with the increase in per capita household income.

A little over one-fourth of all "drop-outs " in rural as well as urban India gave "not interested in education/further study" as the reason for discontinuance of education—with the proportion among females being somewhat higher—33.3 percent as against 26.5 percent for males in areas and 28.5 percent as against 23.6 percent for males in urban areas. Another 16.3 percent of rural and 20.3 percent of urban "dropouts" cited 'failure' to pass examinations as the reason for discontinuance. Again, it is a Moot point whether this is a supply side constraint due to the poor quality of eduction services or a demand constraint, or a combination of both.

Regional disparities are also conspicuous. High female literacy states (above 50 per cent) have by and large universalised primary enrolments among girls. Even in regard to upper primary enrolments Kerala, Goa, Pondicherry and Lakshadweep fare very well. In states with medium female literacy status (40-50 per cent) enrolment of girls appears to be satisfactory at the primary level. The situation in low female literacy states (20-40 per cent) causes concern. These states have more than half of the country's population, with just four of them (Uttar Pradesh, Bihar, Madhya Pradesh and Rajasthan) accounting for 40 per cent of the country's population.

Scheduled Castes and Scheduled Tribes

According to the 1991 census, the population of Scheduled Castes (SCs) was 138.2 million (16.33 per cent) and that of Scheduled Tribes (STs) 67.8 million (8.01 per cent) of the country's population. Both SC and ST populations are not homogeneous target groups in all respects. There are wide variations between different SC and ST groups regionally. Thus SC girls in Kerala are likely to be better placed than non-SC boys in some of the more backward states and districts. Because of the affirmative policies of the government, the enrolment of SCs and STs has increased considerably at the primary stage. The participation of SCs and STs is now more or less in proportion to their share in population at the primary level. Drop-outs, though declining over the years, are significantly large. Gender disparities are very conspicuous among SCs and STs also.

Handicapped Children

Handicapped children are a distinct target group where basic learning needs have to be catered to by special programmes. Handicapped children would include those who are orthopaedically handicapped, those with hearing impairments, visual impairments, the mentally handicapped and others. NPE, 1986 called for integration of "the physically and mentally handicapped with the general community as equal partners to prepare them for normal growth and to enable them to face life with courage and confidence."

The POA, 1992 estimates that about 10.39 million children with disabilities are to be provided education in the school system. Out of these, about half a million require vocational training. The statistics on participation of these children are not firm. At the end of 1991-92 about 30, 000 disabled children were availing of special benefits under the scheme of Integrated Education for Disabled Children (IEDC). In addition, about 60, 000 children with mild disabilities received resource support without special benefits. A large number of children with disability are also receiving education in 1, 035 special schools.

Learning Achievement

If the fact that half the children drop out before reaching Class V is shocking, far more shocking is the level of learning achievement of those remaining in school. A sample study of learning achievements of students was conducted in 48 districts as part of the DPEP. In the final year of primary schooling, in none of these districts the maximum average score for reading skills was higher than fifty two per cent; the achievements in arithmetic were worse.

Challenges Ahead

Inspite of the substantial accomplishments since Independence, India has the dubious distinction of having the largest number of illiterates and out-of-school children in the world—30 per cent of the world's adult illiterates and 21.87 per cent of out-of-school children. About 19 to 24 million children in the age group 6-14 are out of school of whom about 60 per cent are girls; about 121.3 million are adult illiterates in the age group 15-35 of whom 62 per cent are women. Given the demographic pressure the numbers are likely to increase further.

The benefits of investing in basic education, both for its intrinsic value in enhancing human capabilities, as well for its instrumental worth in contributing to social development and economic growth, greater efficiency and better functioning of democratic institutions are well established. Of equal significance is the ability of education to empower women and men to acquire greater control over the circumstances that dominate their lives. It is now recognised that fertility regulation cannot be a matter of mere promotion of contraception but has to strongly promote the socio-economic factors which strongly influence fertility behaviour such as female literacy and education. The low level of social indicators such as fertility rates, Infant Mortality Rate (IMR), sex ratio are related to the failure to achieve Universalisation of Elementary Education (UEE). If the East Asian experience has any relevance the criticality of UEE for the economic reform process cannot be over emphasised.

It is evident from the above that UEE has strong regional and gender dimensions. The Indian experience encompasses the entire Third World experience. At one end we have states such as Kerala which has achieved universal literacy as well as UEE in terms of school participation—though not in terms of learning achievement—with social indicators as good as the best among the Third World, if not the Scandinavian countries. On the other extreme we have states like UP, Bihar, Orissa and MP with indicators as worse as Sub Saharan Africa. To the extent that gender disparity is pronounced UEE is the problem of the girl child.

Teacher competence, motivation and performance are areas which require greater attention. These are crucial inputs in UEE. Whatever policies may be laid down, in the ultimate analysis, these have to be interpreted and implemented by teachers, as much through their personal example as through teaching-learning process.

Except in a few places where the ethos of Panchayati Raj system has been internalised the school remains rather isolated from the local community.

Experience in India and elsewhere has established that universal participation cannot be delinked from the operations of quality and relevance of education and from learning achievement. The challenge before the nation is to enhance universal participation and universal achievement of certain minimum levels of learning. In terms of numbers alone this is the greatest challenge that human society had ever faced—more so if one were to adhere to the goal set up in the National Policy on Education, 1986 of universalising elementary education before the commencement of the twenty-first century.

Legal Framework

Several articles in the Constitution of India bring into focus the general principles governing educational development in the country. These articles are rooted in India's struggle for independence. Basic education was one of the important goals of the freedom struggle and Mahatma Gandhi, even while leading the epic struggle against colonial power, evolved an alternative education system.

The Directive Principle contained in Article 45 of the Constitution enjoins that "the State shall endeavour to provide, within a period of ten years from the commencement of this Constitution, for free and compulsory education for all children until they complete the age of fourteen years." The expression "the State" which occurs in this Article is defined in Article 12 to include the Government and Parliament of India, the government and the legislature of each of the states and all local or other authorities within the territory of India or under the control of the government of India.

Article 29(1) of the Constitution provides that any section of the citizens, residing in the. territory of India or any part thereof having a distinct language, script or culture of its own shall have the right to conserve the same." Article 29(2) lays down that "no citizen shall be denied admission into any educational institution maintained by the State or receiving aid out of State funds on grounds only of religion, race, caste, language or any of them." Article 30(1) enjoins that "all minorities, whether based on religion or language, shall have the right to establish and administer educational institutions of their choice, " while Article 30(2) lays down that "the State shall not, in granting aid to educational institutions, discriminate against any educational institution on the ground that it is under the management of a minority, whether based on religion or language." Article 350-A lays down that "it shall be the endeavour of every State and of every local authority within the State to provide adequate facilities for instruction in the mother-tongue at the primary stage of education to children belonging to linguistic minority groups."

Special care of the economic and educational interests of the under-privileged sections of the population is laid down as an obligation for the State under Article 46. As per this Article, "the State shall promote with special care the educational and economic interests of the weaker sections of the people, and in particular, of the Scheduled Castes and the Scheduled Tribes and shall protect them from social injustice and all forms of exploitation."

Till the 42nd amendment of the Constitution when it was brought into the Concurrent List, education was in the State List except for certain specified items in the Union List like determination of standards in institutions for higher education or research, establishment and maintenance of central universities as well as specified institutions for scientific or technical education and research. The objective of incorporating education in the Concurrent List was to facilitate evolution of all-India policies in the field of education.

Though the parliament was thereby empowered with the authority to legislate on education, the Centre has been relying on a consensual process to promote educational development. The concept of concurrency was given an operational meaning by the National Policy on Education (NPE) 1986. This policy envisages concurrency as a "meaningful partnership between the Centre and the States" and placed on the Union Government a larger responsibility in regard to the national and integrative character of education, quality and standards, manpower planning, research and advanced study, and international aspects of education, culture and human resource development.

Policy Priorities

The late Prime Minister Rajiv Gandhi called for a comprehensive review of the existing educational system and the National Policy of Education (NPE) came into effect in 1986. Within the comprehensive framework enunciated by the NPE (1986), the developments and experiences since then were incorporated into the NPE in 1992 and a revised Programme of Action POA (1992) was formulated. Along with its Programme of Action (POA), the NPE provides a comprehensive framework to guide the development of education. Overall, the NPE is committed to:

— address all aspects of education: equity, efficiency, relevance, quality, content and process, linkages with culture, values, society, polity and economy, resources and management.

— emphasise the organic unit of early childhood education, primary education, non-formal education, adult education and post literacy and life long continuing education.

— tilt the balance away from quantitative expansion of institutions towards quality and equity.

— give unqualified priority to UEE, adult literacy and education for women's equality; this priority is reflected in the budget allocations during the current Five Year Plan (1992-97).

Shift the emphasis from enrolment per se to enrolment as well as retention and achievement.

NPE, 1986 also broke away from stereotyped confines of thinking and promoted thoughtful introspection and key strategies such as:

i) the shift from the States to the district as the unit of planning for implementation of elementary education and adult literacy;

ii) social mobilisation to promote basic eduction; and

iii) integration of adult literacy and non-formal programmes with socially relevant themes such as small population norms, health care, environment and nutrition.

Against the background of the demographic implications and the complex ground realities of the Indian scene, the goals of Education for All (EFA) in India constitute:

1. Expansion of Early Childhood Care and Development Activities especially for poor, disadvantaged and disabled children, through a multi-pronged effort involving families, communities and appropriate institutions.

2. Universalisation of Elementary Education (UEE) viewed as a composite programme of:-

   — access to elementary education for all children upto 14 years of age;

— universal participation till they complete the elementary stage through formal or equivalent non-formal education programmes;

— universal achievement of at least minimum levels of learning.

3. Drastic Reduction in Illiteracy, particularly in the 15-35 age-group, bringing the literacy level in this age group to at least 80 per cent in each gender and for every identified disadvantaged group, besides ensuring that the levels of the three R's are relevant to the living and working conditions of the people.
4. Provision of opportunities to maintain, use and upgrade education and provision of facilities for development of skills to a persons who are functionally literate and those who have received primary education through formal and non-formal channels.
5. Creation of necessary structures, and the setting in motion of processes which could empower women and make education an instrument of women's equality.
6. Improving the content and process of education to relate it better to the environment, people's culture and with their living and working conditions, thereby enhancing their ability to learn and cope with the problems of livelihood and environment.

Role of Voluntary Agencies

The NPE recognises that Voluntary Agencies or groups of public spirited individuals could provide a useful supportive framework for promoting universalisation of elementary education. After 1986, schemes are in place for enlisting NGOs in elementary education.

Voluntary agencies can contribute significantly to universalise elementary education through a number of measures such as:

— implementing non-formal education programmes and alternative school programmes in more people friendly and innovative ways in terms of pedagogy, instructional materials, training, organisation and management.

— providing resource support to teachers, schools and continuing education.

— training of teachers, local functionaries, Village Education Committee members and others.

— establishing linkages between education and other social services such as health, nutrition etc.

MAJOR INTERVENTIONS

Major interventions in the years since 1986 include :

Operation Blackboard

This programme is designed for improvement of primary schools and provision of support services. It envisages conversion of all single teacher schools into double teacher schools ensuring that at least one of the teachers is a woman and provide all such schools at least two reasonably large rooms.

Under this scheme 1, 10, 000 teachers (of them 57 per cent were women) have been recruited and 1, 36, 000 classrooms were constructed. This scheme has been expanded to cover upper primary schools and also provide a third teacher to primary schools with enrolment more than 100.

Non-formal Education (NFE)

This has become an important alternative channel for children who cannot attend full time schools. Although the focus of the centrally sponsored scheme of NFE is still on the ten educationally backward states, namely, Andhra Pradesh, Arunachal Pradesh, Assam, Bihar, Jammu & Kashmir, Madhya Pradesh, Orissa, Rajasthan, Uttar Pradesh and West Bengal, it covers urban slums, hilly, tribal and desert areas and areas with concentration of working children in the other states as well.

Financial responsibility is shared by the Central and state Governments in the ratio of 50:50 for co-educational centres and 90:10 for girls' NFE centres. Assistance to the extent of 100 per cent is provided to voluntary agencies for running NFE centres for experimental and innovative projects.

The number of NFE centres increased from 126, 000 in 1986 to 255, 000 by March, 1994 and the enrolment from 3.65 million to 6.4

million. During this period the number of girls centres has increased from 20, 500 to 96, 766. Over 425 voluntary agencies are participating in this programme. Alongside, around 50 experimental and innovative projects and 22 district resource units are in operation for in-depth work. Though the coverage has expanded a major challenge is the development and scaling up of effective NFE models that can help the learners to learn at their own pace.

Minimum Levels of Learning

The NCERT has developed the National Curricular Framework and within this framework the minimum levels of learning have been laid down for primary level and concerted steps are being taken to achieve these levels.

The strategy to improve learning acquisition in school focuses attention on what is happening in the class room, and seeks to bring the principles of equity, quality and relevance to bear upon it. The strategy aims to lay down learning outcomes expected from basic education at a realistic, relevant and functional level, prescribes the adoption of measures that would ensure that all children who complete a stage of schooling achieve these outcomes. These outcomes define the Minimum Levels of Learning common to both school and equivalent NFE programme.

The main steps by which MLLs are being introduced in schools are:

i) an assessment of the existing level of learning achievement;
ii) a definition of the MLLs for the area and the time-frame within which it will be achieved;
iii) reorientation of teaching practices to competency based teaching;
iv) an introduction of continuous comprehensive evaluation of student learning;
v) review the textbooks and revision, if required;
vi) the provision of inputs as necessary including provision of physical facilities, teacher training, supervision and evaluation, etc., to improve learning acquisition to the MLLs.

The endeavour is to monitor learning achievement, to direct greater resources where levels of learning are lower, and to consciously accelerate the pace of development in the needy areas, thereby to reduce disparities, equalise standards and govern inputs for quality improvement in the performance of the system.

Teacher Training

The NPE perceives teacher education as a continuous process and its pre-service and in-service components being inseparable have been incorporated in the new restructured programme of teacher education initated in 1987. Setting up of District Institutes of Education and Training (DIETs) is a significant institutional mechanism in this direction. Eventually DIETs are expected to provide academic and resource support to basic education and also to engage in action research and innovation. As of now, DIETs are being set up in 380 districts out of the 462 districts in the country; in 190 districts DIETs are already conducting training programmes. It is proposed to set up 425 DIETs by the end of the eighth plan (1997-98). Efforts are afoot to strengthen the SCERTs so that they can provide the resource back up.

The National Council for Teacher Education (NCTE) has been setup as a statutory body for determination and maintenance of standards of teacher education. This is expected to improve the quality of pre-service training, and upgradate the syllabi and curricula of teacher training programmes.

Distance Education

Distance education has a vital role to play in promoting basic education in high population countries as it can reach out to populations not served by the formal education system. Distance education also has the potential for making vast improvements in the educational system by offering training and skill upgradation opportunities to teachers and administrators dealing with education.

Several initiatives have been taken in India since the 1993 Summit to extend the scope and reach of distance education. A national component on distance education has been included in the District Primary Education Project. The National Open School has also formulated an innovative project aimed at providing alternative schooling to:

a) Neo-literates who have acquired functional literacy skills from the Total Literacy Campaigns.
b) Early school drop-outs with rudimentary literacy skills.
c) Drop-outs from the non-formal education system who have literacy skills.
d) Learners who have attended non-formal programmes and whose literacy skills are marginally better developed.

Resources

Education is funded largely by the central and state governments. Elementary education is funded almost wholly by the Government. After the inception of planning in 1950-51 spending on education as a proportion of GNP has steadily increased from about 1.2 percent to about 3.5 percent. While the increase is significant, because of financial constraints and competing priorities resource availability was not adequate. Nor was it possible to fulfil the aspiration articulated time and again from 1966 onwards, that the public expenditure on education should be at least 6 per cent of the GNP.

While public expenditure is below the articulated aspiration, at a macro-level, India's expenditure on education as a proportion of GNP compares favourably with that of the peer group of Asian developing countries. Public expenditure on elementary education has increased significantly during the post-independence period. Expenditure on elementary education increased from 0.46 per cent of GNP in 1950-51 to 1.72 per cent in 1989-90. During the 1980s alone, the public expenditure on elementary education increased 4.5 times from Rs.15, 373 million to Rs.68, 883 million in 1989-90. The share of elementary education in total public expenditure on education is about 45 to 46 per cent. A significant and welcome feature is the pronounced trend of a higher share of plan expenditure in the total expenditure on elementary education.

In the past, elementary Education in India was largely funded by the state government. NPE, 1986 gave an operational definition to the concurrency of education enshrined in the Constitution. With the launching of centrally sponsored schemes to promote non-formal education and the quality of elementary education, the central government's share in plan expenditure on elementary education has increased substantially. Education in India has been largely a budget-based system where efficiency is rated by ability to "consume" budget and to demand more. Performance at delivery point has not been an important criterion. The on-going economic reforms and structural adjustments would, therefore, demand a shift from inputs to performance and outcomes considerations of cost effectiveness should inform all levels of educational administration and planning.

Decentralisation

With the enactment of the 73rd and 74th Amendment Act (Panchayati Raj ACT), 1992, the focus is now on democratically elected bodies at the district, sub-district, Panchayat and municipal levels. These Panchayati Raj bodies, which are to have adequate representation of women, Scheduled Castes and Scheduled Tribes, minorities, representatives of parents, educationists, and appropriate institutions, will have the responsibility of preparing development plans and implementing educational programmes besides dealing with those subjects closely related to education such as health, social welfare and women and child development.

Detailed parameters for a decentralised management of education have been worked out by a CABE committee on Decentralised Management of Education. The committee's recommendations indicate how educational structures should be set up at the district, taluk/ mandal and village levels in pursuance of the Constitutional Amendments. The recommendations of the Committee have been endorsed by the CABE in its meeting held on 15 October, 1993.

State governments have initiated the process of establishment of structures for decentralised planning and management and are in the process of drawing up appropriate legislation which provides for Panchayati Raj Committees for Education.

The breadth and scope of the Panchayati Raj Act provides an exceptionally 'enabling' framework for viable strategies and interventions that would play a commanding role in promoting universal elementary education. The responsibilities vested with the district level body, for instance, cover planning, which includes, inter alia, area development, spatial planning, institutional planning, administrative and financial control and personnel management with respect to primary, middle, secondary and higher secondary schools and educational programmes.

The district level body will also implement, supervise and monitor all educational programmes, including non-formal and adult education. Besides, it will draw upon the expertise of DIETs and other institutions for substantive curricular and pedagogic inputs into district level programmes of Elementary Education (EE), Non-formal Education (NFE) and Adult Education (AE). From the district level, the process of decentralisation percolates down to the village level.

The Panchayati Raj Act envisages the formation of Panchayats for a village or a group of villages. These panchayats will have elected representatives. Each panchayat would constitute a Village Education Committee (VEC) which would be responsible for the administration of education programmes at the village level. The major responsibility of the VECs would lie in operationalisation of micro-level planning and school mapping in the village through systematic house to house surveys and periodic discussions with parents. Ensuring participation in primary education of every child in every family would be one of the prime aims of the VECs.

District Primary Education Programme

A major initiative, entitled District Primary Education Programme, was started in 1993 in the area of elementary education to replicate what the Total Literacy Campaigns (TLCs) have been accomplishing in the field of adult literacy. The DPEP seeks to operationalise the strategy of decentralised planning identified by the POA, 1992 to be the main strategy for achieving UEE.

It builds upon the national experience in the pursuit of UEE as well the experience gained in the implementation of projects like the Mahila Samakhya, a programme of women's empowerment, the Bihar Education Project, the Lok Jumbish and the UP Basic Education project. Central to DPEP are the following concepts:

(i) *UEE is contextual:* The contextuality varies widely across the country. Even in States like Kerala where participation is near-universal much requires to be done in respect of quality and achievement. In such States the pursuit of UEE would be mainly in the areas of quality, facilities and achievement. In other States participation and demand aspects need more attention.

(ii) Contextuality entails local area-planning with disaggregated targets and decentralised planning and management. Planning for UEE had hitherto been mainly at the national and state level. Barring some States and Union Territories, these entities are too large and heterogenous for effective planning; they cannot provide contextuality. Ideally the planning should be from below, right from the village upwards but given the objective conditions, a beginning has to be made with the district as the unit of planning. The district plans are to be prepared through an intensive process of interaction with the local bodies, teachers and NGOs so that it is "owned" by all who are to be associated in implementation and it refelects the ground-level realities.

(iii) Resources are an important but not sufficient condition for achieving UEE. A host of measures both financial and non-financial, both on the supply side and on the demand side, need to complement higher allocation of resources.

(iv) The strategies for UEE have hitherto emphasised mainly access in terms of construction of class rooms and appointment of teachers. This has been inadequate and needs to be augmented by:

(a) a holistic planning and management approach which goes beyond implementation of a disjointed set of individual schemes, perceives the task of UEE in its totality, integrates all the measures needed for achieving UEE in the specific context of the district;

(b) this holistic planning should incorporate a gender perspective in all aspects of the planning and implementation process and be an integral part of all measures needed to achieve UEE.

(c) addressing the more difficult aspects of access, particularly access to girls, disadvantaged groups and out of school children;

(d) improving school effectiveness;

(e) strengthening the alternatives to schooling, particularly the nonformal education system;

(f) stressing the participative processes whereby the local community facilitates participation, achievement and school effectiveness;

(g) toning up teacher competence, training and motivation;

(h) stressing learning competence and achivement;

(i) stressing the need for improved teaching/learning materials; and

(j) overhaul of planning and management in respect of both routine and innovative areas.

(k) Convergence between elementary education and related services such as ECCE and school health.

The programme would be implemented in a mission mode. A National Managment Structure is being set up on the lines of NLMA which would oversee the implementation of the programme through out the country and provide the necessary technical support to states and districts.

Implementation at the State level would be through registered autonomous societies with CMs as ex-officio Presidents of the General Council and Chief Secretary/Education Secretary as the Chairman of the Executive Committee.

NGOs, Teachers, Educationists and Women are represented in these Committees. VECs play a key role in the implementation of the programme at the village level.

The loftiness of the objectives, the nature and intensity of the planning process, the integration of professional inputs, participative planning and management, and the emphasis on capacity building have together rendered DPEP an exciting idea not only in the country but all over the world.

DPEP has broken new paths in international cooperation, in that it belongs to the new genre of developmental cooperation which emphasises sustainability, equity, local ownership and execution and is supportive of national policies in the education sector.

DPEP is a homegrown idea, in keeping with CABE guidelines, and its distinctiveness lies in that inspite of diversity of sources of funding, it is a national programme intending to achieve UEE in a contextual manner with emphasis on participation and capacity building.

The programme has been developed in 42 districts of the States of Madhya Pradesh, Assam, Haryana, Maharashtra, Karnataka, Tamil Nadu and Kerala. The objective is to gradually expand the coverage of the programme to all districts which satisfy the twin criteria of

(a) educationally backward districts with female literacy below the national average; and

(b) districts where TLCs have been successfully leading to enhanced demand for elementary education.

Five districts each in West Bengal and Andhra Pradesh are in the process of developing their district plans and would be ready for programme appraisal shortly.

The District Primary Education Programme has generated interest amongst several multilateral and bilateral funding agencies. The European Community has already committed approximately Rs.585 crores (150 million ECUs) as programme support for DPEP. Negotiations have been completed with the World Bank/IDA for a credit agreement amounting to US $ 260 million for six States.

The ODA of United Kingdom has pledged support for DPEP in Andhra Pradesh and West Bengal. In fact, DPEP appears to be emerging as the main vehicle in the development of elementary education in the country and is likely to develop at the national level as an intermediary technical and resource organisation for primary education development in the country on the lines of the IDBI of HDFC.

National Development Council (NDC)

The updating in 1992 of NPE, 1986 and its POA, the constitution of a National Development Council (NDC) Committee on Literacy which was later considered by NDC in 1993, the EFA Summit of Nine High Population Countries which was hosted by India in December, 1993, the meeting in February, 1994 of the Chief Ministers exclusively to consider elementary education and adult literacy, the subsequent meeting of the four Chief Ministers of Bihar, Madhya Pradesh, Rajasthan, and Uttar Pradesh in Bhopal in July, 1994 were all important events which helped renew the national commitment to universalisation of elementary education and to outline concrete steps to achieve that goal.

These have created a new political ambience. The Prime Minister stated at the EFA Summit that the country was determined to achieve the goal of allocation of six per cent GNP for education during the Ninth Five Year Plan. This was reiterated by the President in his address to Parliament in February, 1994.

The Delhi Declaration

The Delhi Declaration adhered by EFA to call for ensuring a place for every child in a school an appropriate education programme according to his or her capabilities, consolidate efforts towards the education for youth and adult education within the context of an integrated strategy of basic education for all people; to eliminate disparities of access to basic education; to improve the quality and relevance of basic education and in all actions to accord to human development, the highest priority at national and other levels so that a growing share of national and community resources is dedicated to basic education and improving the management of existing resources for education.

In the Chief Minister's Conference there was complete unanimity that EFA should be placed high on the country's developmental agenda and that achievement of the constitutional obligation of UEE brooks no further delay. It is a national challenge which transcends all political differences. The centre and the states would work together with a renewed sense of determination to further the national goals in their field.

It was suggested in the CMs meet that the Tenth Finance Commission should take note of the basic requirements of elementary education and that the exemption under Income Tax Act for donations to universities and institutions of national importance should be extended to elementary education.

It was also agreed by the CMs that along with higher allocation of resources it was necessary to ensure better utilisation of resources through effective implementation and monitoring of programmes in their States. CMs would periodically review the progress in this area. It was felt that special efforts are needed in educationally backward states like Bihar, Uttar Pradesh, Rajasthan, Madhya Pradesh and Andhra Pradesh.

The need to enlist the cooperation of NGOs, teacher's unions and socially conscious individuals came out very clearly in the discussions of the CMs. The shared perception was that without proper decentralisation of educational administration and greater community participation UEE cannot be achieved. The Chief Ministers felt that the 73rd and 74th Constitutional Amendments provide an opportunity to decentralise educational administration within the time span provided by the Amendments. The recommendations of the CABE committee on Decentralisation were endorsed and it was decided to appropriately implement the recommendations while enacting the State legislations to follow the Constitutional Amendments and framing the subordinate legislation in a time bound manner.

The Chief Ministers also agreed that special efforts would be made to promote convergence of primary education and related services like ECCE, ICDS, schools health and nutrition. It was felt that apart from improving efficiency such a convergence would promote enrollment and reduction of dropouts.

Following the CMs Conference a Group of Chief Ministers of low literacy and high population states was constituted for periodic review of EFA programmes. This group had already held one meeting in Bhopal on 1st July, 1994, reviewed their programmes and re-affirmed their resolve to achieve EFA by the turn of the century.

FUTURE PROSPECTS

Ever since planning began, India has been striving towards universalising of elementary education. Though the goal is still full of challenges, to miss what has been accomplished, in terms of spread of institutions, participation and equalisation of educational opportunities, is to "consider not the beam in thine own eye". The nation as a whole must keep on striving to complete the mission and erase what Mahatma Gandhi once called a national shame and curse.

The elementary education system has to bring into its fold areas and social strata more difficult to reach; what is ahead is a marathon race along a tortuous path strewn with socioeconomic barriers and impediments. That business as usual would not do is the moral of successful Total Literacy Campaigns. It is not the State apparatus alone but the whole civil society that needs to be mobilised for the cause of UEE.

Perhaps the greatest challenge before the country today as it strives to universalise primary education lies in this area of perceptional change. The common perception that the government alone must bear the sole responsibility for providing education needs to change. While the Union and the State governments have their full share of responsibilities, in the final analysis, it is people's involvement in educational reconstruction which will make the crucial difference in meeting the challenge of universalising primary education in India.

While the task and the challenges that confront India are formidable and daunting, they are achievable. The onus of action now rests both individually and collectively on teachers and educators, NGOs, the industrial sector, other sectors, the media, politicians, panchayat leaders, grassroots workers, on each and everyone. A grand alliance—an interactive combination of local, voluntary and state initiatives coupled with an assortment of productive, result oriented approaches and strategies holds the key to universalisation of primary education in India. That grand alliance needs to be sustained at least for a decade or so, if UEE in its entirety—access, retention and attainment—is to be achieved. Herein lies the challenge. As the experience with the Indian economy has shown, an overarching crisis can provide a fillip to reform.

The failure to achieve UEE is no less a crisis—the adverse impacts on demography, productivity and status of women and disadvantaged groups are too well known to bear repetetion—but it is a crisis with a difference, a silent crisis lacking the immediacy of a default on international commitments and as such devoid of that momentum to spur action. Therefore the National Will to achieve UEE has to be periodically renewed so that it does not flag and shrivel.

Educational administration has long tended to be too pre-occupied with provision of facilities — schools, school buildings and appointments of teachers to the neglect of the processes required to make the system work. There is enough empirical evidence on the mismatch between access and enrolment and to cast doubts on the propriety of this institutional pre-occupation.

This is said not to belittle the importance of such facilities to schools but to emphasise that the construction of school buildings and lower pupil teacher ratios are not the be all and end all of UEE. The education system, the state and the civil society at large should internalise a broader functional view of education, a view which conceives education as a dynamic, cumulative lifelong process, encompassing a wide diversity of learning opportunities, applying to all people, but laying stress on girls, children and youth, particularly those belonging to the disadvantaged groups. Strategies are needed to bring about the perceptional change. Innovation and dissemination are important components of any such strategy. Nothing can bring about the perceptional changes faster than the development and dissemination of viable and scalable models of non-formal education. Regional and international cooperation can facilitate innovation and dissemination.

The importance of financial resources cannot be exaggerated. As the economy is reformed, as state intervention gets re-focused and as public expenditure is restructured more budgetary resources will flow to education, particularly to universalisation of elementary education. To this end educational reform needs to be fitted into the "architecture that our (economic) reforms seek to create". The Prime Minister has already stated at the EFA Summit that the country was determined to achieve the goal of allocation of six per cent GNP for education during the Ninth Five Year Plan.

While economic liberalisation and the consequent financial restructuring can be expected to facilitate greater resource flow to education far more difficult is the management of change. The system, as of now, barely works and hardly discharges even the routine functions effectively. There is hardly any accountability. To transform such a system to one which can take on the unfinished task of UEE with elan and a new mindset is no mean task. There is no better way to ensure accountability than an awakened and "demanding" community, for the creation of which the 73rd and 74th Constitution Amendments hold great promise.

REFERENCES

Mehta, PL and Poonga, Rakhi (1997), *Free and Compulsory Education*, Deep and Deep Publications, New Delhi.

Naik, JP (1975), *Elementary Education in India : A Promise to keep,* Allied Publishers, Bombay.

Sharma, SN (1995), *Elementary Education : Experience and Expectations*, Kanishka Publishers, New Delhi.

Sharma Amita & Gopal Krishnan R (1996), Bringing *the People Back In : From Lok Sampark Abhiyan to Education Guarantee Scheme* (Document 3, Rajiv Gandhi Mission, October 1996).

4

Pattern of School Education

In India, the national education pattern is 10+2+3, with first 10 years devoted to general education, 2 years for diversification from general education to specialised academic or vocational courses and 3 years for degree programmes. In other words, first 12 years of education is called school education, which does not include pre-primary education comprising of nursery and kindergarten stages. At the +2 stage, a student is in a position to exercise a choice to select a stream (academic or vocational), keeping in view his interests and professional pursuit. Public examinations are conducted at the end of class X and class XII.

PATTERN OF 10+2+3 SYSTEM

The adoption of the common pattern of 10+2+3 for school and college classes has been an important reform whose implementation has long been overdue. The reform was first recommended, about 55 years ago, by the Calcutta University Commission (1917-19). At that time, the Matriculation Examination, which marked the end of the school course and also constituted an entrance examination to the universities, was held in different provinces at the end of 10-12 years of schooling. But in spite of this large variation of the duration of the school stage, these examinations, though conducted by different agencies, were regarded as equivalent to each other in all parts of the country. The Matriculation Examination was followed by a two-year intermediate course at the end of which another public examination, the Intermediate Examination was held. Then came a two-year period of undergraduate education after which the First Degree Examination was held. All these three examinations-Matriculation, Intermediate and First Degree-were held by the universities. The Commission examined in depth the content of education at the intermediate and the undergraduate stages and came to the following steps:

(1) That the intermediate stage was really a part of the school course and that the students at this stage could be more effectively taught by school methods than by those which were appropriate at the university stage; and

(2) That the standard of undergraduate education was so poor that the first degree in India was not really comparable to the first degree in the advanced countries.

The Commission, therefore, recommended that:

(1) The dividing line between the university and the secondary courses is more appropriately drawn at the Intermediate Examination than at the Matriculation;

(2) That the duration of undergraduate course for the First Degree should be increased to three years.

(3) A Board of Secondary and intermediate Education should be established for the purpose of reorganising high school and intermediate education on the lines recommended by it and for holding the matriculation and Intermediate Examinations. The universities would thus be left to their proper sphere, namely, the provision of undergraduate and post-graduate education and the holding of examinations for the first, second or research degrees.

This recommendation made a great impression on Indian educational thought and, for a time, it appeared to be on the verge of universal acceptance. But ultimately it was implemented only in one province, namely, the U.P. and that too, in a mutilated form. No steps were taken to increase the duration of the first degree course to three years; not were any effective steps taken to vocationalise the intermediate stage.

The University Education Commission (1948-49) under the Chairmanship of Radhakrishnan had, therefore, to take up the discussion of the problem once again. After examining the problem from all points of view, the Commission also came to the conclusion that it was necessary to adopt the uniform pattern of 10+2+3 for school and college classes. The Commission felt that this pattern would make it possible to vocationalise the secondary stage of education so as to divert students into different walks of life at the end of secondary school and thus reduce pressures on university admissions. It also felt that the lengthening of the undergraduate course to three years, preceded by an intensive preparation at the earlier stage of two years, would result in a considerable improvement of standards in higher education. Unfortunately, steps were not taken to implement these recommendations.

The problem came up for consideration once again when the Secondary Education Commission under the chairmanship of Dr. A. L. Mudaliar submitted its report (1952). The stage was now ripe to reorganise school and university education together, on the lines recommended by the University Education Commission and the Secondary Education Commission and to adopt a common pattern for school and college classes. At this time, throughout India, the duration of the post-Matriculation course leading to the first degree was uniformly four years and it was uniformly divided into two stages - two years of Intermediate and two years of undergraduate education. The simplest reform would, therefore, have been to add one year to the degree course and to transfer the two years of the Intermediate course to the school stage. But for various reasons, and mainly for financial considerations, this was not done. Instead the recommendation of the Sargent Report of an eleven-year higher secondary school followed by a three-year course for first degree was revived and the pattern of 8+3+3 was adopted. The Intermediate course was therefore broken up into two parts and the first year was either added to the school stage or converted into a pre-university course of one year and the second year was added to the two-year undergraduate course for the first degree to create the three-year degree course. This was an unfortunate decision dictated by the compulsion of economy rather than the logic of academic reform.

The entire position was reviewed once again by the Education Commission (1964-66). It found that, as a result of the decisions taken after the Report of the Secondary Education Commission, there were at least four different patterns of schools and colleges in the country which may be stated as follows:

(1) Kerala was the only State where the pattern of 10+2+3 had been adopted, with the two-year stage being located in junior colleges;

(2) The pattern of 10+2+2 prevailed only in Uttar Pradesh where a ten-year school was followed by a two- year intermediate course and a two-year course for first degree;

(3) The pattern of 11+3 prevailed in the Delhi Union Territory and the State of Madhya Pradesh where an eleven year higher secondary school was followed by a three year course for the first degree; and

(4) The pattern of 10 (or 11 or even 12 in some cases) + 1 + 3 was followed in the other States where a school stage of 10 to 12 years was followed by a year of pre- university course and a three-year course for the first degree.

The Commission examined this situation from all points of view and came to the conclusion that, on sound academic considerations detailed in its report, it would be highly desirable to adopt the uniform pattern of 10+2+3 for school and college classes in all parts of the country. The Commission was also definitely of the view that the school stage should consist of 12 years (10+2) and that every effort should be made to vocationalise the higher secondary stage so that, ultimately, 50% of the enrolments at this stage would be in the vocational courses. The Commission also recommended a detailed programme for bringing about these important changes.

These proposals of the Education Commission have found general support in the country. Even before the Report of the Commission was submitted, the National Integration Committee appointed by the Ministry of Education under the chairmanship of the late Dr. Sampurnanand recommended that, from the point of view of national integration, the uniform pattern of 10+2+3 should be adopted for school and college classes in all parts of the country. This recommendation was also supported by the Committee of Educationists and student leaders appointed under the directive of the National Integration Committee and also by several conferences of students organisations. The Central Advisory Board of Education has also unanimously supported the proposal and expressed the view that it should be implemented on a priority basis and that, at any rate, the programme should be completed in all parts of the country by the end of the Fifth Five Year Plan. The Resolution of the Government of India on the National Policy of Education also supports the uniform adoption of this pattern. The pattern has since been introduced in the States of Andhra Pradesh and Karnataka. Steps have been initiated to introduce the pattern in the States of Maharashtra, Gujarat and West Bengal. Several other States have set up committees to examine the issue and it is hoped that they will also follow suit in the near future.

The Education Commission of India (1966) emphasised that there is a direct link between education, national development and prosperity and stated that this can be vitalised only when the National system of education is properly organised, both qualitatively and quantitatively. This Commission also pointed out that the existing system of education was largely unrelated to the life, needs and aspirations of the people and there was a wide gulf between its contents and purposes as well as interests of National development. One of the major weaknesses of the present educational system is that secondary education fits students for college and almost unfits them for everything else.

In any well designed National system of education, secondary education must have two specific objectives:

(1) to prepare a student for the University, or

(2) to become terminal and prepare a student for some vocation in life.

Realising that the total period of education and the duration of its different stages have a direct bearing on the quality of education imparted for achieving the goal, the Education Commission recommended:

(1) Broadly uniform pattern of education;

(2) Extension in the total period of schooling to bring about a general rise in the standards of attainment; and

(3) Vocationalisation of education.

Bearing in mind the recommendations of the Commission, the Government of India issued in 1968 a National Policy statement on education for the country. In this statement, the Government of India stated that it was convinced that a "radical reconstruction of education on the broad lines recommended by the Education Commission, is essential for economic and cultural development of the country, for national integration and for realising the ideal of a socialistic pattern of society. This will involve a transformation of the system to relate it more closely to the life of the people, a continuous effort to expand educational opportunity, a sustained and intensive endeavour to raise the quality of education at all stages, and emphasis on the development of Science and technology and cultivation of moral and social values".

The policy statement also stated that it would be advantageous to have a broadly uniform educational structure in all parts of the country. The ultimate objective should be to adopt the 10+2+3 pattern.

The conference of Education Secretaries and Directors of Public Instruction held on 15th and 16th September, 1972 passed the following resolution:

> "Adoption of a uniform pattern of school and College classes (10+2+3).
>
> (1) A uniform pattern of education of 15 years, duration, leading to the first degree, should be adopted by all the States.
>
> (2) There should be very close co-ordination between the vocational courses attached to the higher secondary stage, the Industrial Training Institutes and the Polytechnics. Courses selected should have close affinity to the skills and services in demand in the locality. This will involve man-power studies and production centres as well as financing of the skilled personnel on cooperative or institutional pattern for self-employment or employment in production centres.
>
> (3) The scheme of Vocationalisation of Education as well as work experience deserves the highest priority in the Plan and should be assisted fully.
>
> (4) Vocational courses prescribed in the Institutions would need constant review and replacement as technology, materials and demands change. They would have to keep pace with development of local industries also, particularly the small scale, cottage and consumer industries".

The recommendations of the Conference of the Education Secretaries and Directors of Public Instruction were endorsed by the Central Advisory Board of Education in its 36th session held on 18th and 19th September, 1972, in New Delhi.

Almost simultaneously the Government of India, Ministry of Education and Social Welfare appointed a National Committee under the chairmanship of Dr. P. D. Shukla, with the following terms of reference;

(1) To suggest practical steps to be taken for-the implementation of the uniform pattern of 10+2+3 for the school and college classes in all States and Union Territories of the country.

(2) To estimate the cost of implementing the programme.

In view of the overwhelming national importance of this matter the Central Board of Secondary Education set up a special committee to suggest ways and means to implement the 10+2+3 pattern in the member schools of the Board and advise it on the educational innovations which should be introduced. With this Committee were associated eminent educationists and the experts from sister agencies like Directorate of Education, Delhi, Kendriya Vidyalaya Sangathan, National Council of Educational Research and Training and other such bodies. This committee favoured the introduction of the change for the following reasons:

(1) It will provide an opportunity and a means to revitalise and rationalise school curricula and to structure them on more scientific lines so as to serve the social and economic needs of the adolescent in a better manner.

(2) It will help initiate other educational reforms such as modernisation of teaching methods and evaluation techniques, essential to raise the general standard and quality of education, particularly at the school stage.

(3) A broadly uniform pattern in all States and Union Territories will facilitate the Board to share its resources and experience with other such bodies, in the areas of production of books and reading materials, teaching aids, training of teachers and their movement, reconstruction of syllabi and improvement in examination practices.

(4) It will do away with the present practice wherein a student is required to take a decision at too early an age about the particular stream of education to be taken up by him for future studies. At the same time it will help reduce pressure for admission on Universities and other centres of higher education.

(5) The improved academic and intellectual equipment of the student will provide him with an edge to face the challenges of modern life.

(6) A broadly uniform pattern of education all over the country will strengthen national integration.

(7) It will remove difficulties in the matter of education of children of the mobile population, to which this Board specially caters.

(8) It will serve as a vehicle of social transformation.

From what has been detailed heretofore it is apparent that this change has been long overdue to give a new direction to education.

Syllabi and Courses

In keeping with the objectives set by the National Policy on Education, The Central Board drafted syllabi and courses for classes IX and X, the first stage of the 10+2+3 structure, on modern lines incorporating latest pedagogical techniques. A large number of seminars of teachers and educationists were held in which the draft syllabi and courses with particular reference to their coverage and feasibility, were discussed. The courses aim at the promotion of higher intellectual capacities as also the harmonious development of the physical, emotional and other aspects of the pupil's personality. They seek to provide a wide range of knowledge to develop students into well-informed citizens and train them for democratic living and community service; at the same time to imbibe a scientific outlook for modern living.

A few of the salient features of the courses are mentioned below:

(1) They provide a comprehensive general education with work experience as an integral component.

(2) Science and Mathematics—formerly denied to almost 50% of the students, are now available to every student, which are so essential for the day-to-day life in the existing context.

(3) These envisage compulsory Health and Physical Education.

(4) They aim at Optimum relevance to the current life situation.

(5) Through community service, a sense of involvement in national reconstruction is planned to be generated in the student.

(6) Work experience makes learning possible by the use of hand and pave the way for vocational education at the subsequent stage.

(7) These aim at the development of the student upto the stage when he can successfully branch off into the academic stream or the vocational channel in accordance with his aptitude.

Evaluation Procedures

Educationists all over the world are unanimous on the inherent drawbacks in the prevailing system of assessment through examination. In actual practice, the entire system of education tends to focus on the score in the examination. The scheme of assessment, therefore, aims at rationalisation and imbibes the following features:

(1) Internal Assessment along with external examination.
(2) System of Grading instead of marks.
(3) Standardisation of raw scores.
(4) Question Banks.
(5) Improving quality of question papers.
(6) Improving evaluation procedures.

Basic Academic Considerations

While due weight must be attached to this series of weighty recommendations of important Commissions and Committees and the steps already taken to implement them, it is also necessary to examine these proposals on academic grounds and to satisfy ourselves that they are in the best interests of the country.

The first point to be decided, on academic grounds, is the stage or age at which a student should be deemed to be fit to enter the university system. In all the advanced countries of the world, a student entering the universities is expected to be 18 years of age or more. It is only then that he can be adequately prepared for entering upon a course of higher education and also be mature enough to study on his own and to profit by, the methods of teaching which are appropriate to the university stage. This necessarily implies a total duration of at least 12 years for the school stage (including elementary and secondary education), because the age of admission to the school system is generally six years. At present, when the total duration of the school stage is sometimes only 10 or 11 years, and the age of admission to the school system is five years or even less, very young students aged 14-17, often enter the university system. They are really children who deserve to remain at school and continue to be taught by methods appropriate to the school stage rather than young persons who are mature enough to profit by a course of higher education. This is bad for the schools that lose in their stature by a cut in their total duration. It is bad for the universities because it adversely affects their standards. What is even more important, it is not good for the students themselves. If this situation is to be improved, it follows that the total duration of the school stage (including elementary and secondary education) should be not less than twelve years.

The duration of elementary education is eight years in some States such as Uttar Pradesh, and seven years in others such as Maharashtra. If the total duration of school stage is to be twelve years, it follows that the duration of the secondary course would be four years in some States and five years in others. The Education Commission had an open mind on this issue and did not insist on a uniform pattern of seven or eight years for elementary education. It was, however, very emphatic on one point: secondary education should not form an integrated continuous course, but should preferably be broken up into two sub-stages: the lower secondary and the higher secondary. It further recommended that the elementary and lower secondary stage should cover the first ten years of school and that the higher secondary stage should cover the last two years. It is necessary to understand the reasons which led the Education Commission to make these recommendations.

The Education Commission found that whenever the course of secondary education is made continuous and unbroken, as in the higher secondary schools of Delhi or Madhya Pradesh, two undesirable consequences follow. The first is that the expansion of secondary education is much larger than necessary or desirable. This is because the principle of selective admissions cannot be introduced at the beginning of the stage (Class IX) when the students are too young and because every student who enters the stage has to continue till the very end because of the continuous character of the course. Such a system therefore prevents the students from leaving the school at the end of

Class X, although they would be eligible for admission to many vocational courses at this point. Secondly, the continuous character of the course compels the student to decide upon his future career at a very premature stage when he is entering Class IX and is about 13 or 14 years old. This is academically undesirable and in fact, Dr. D. S. Kothari has condemned it as a system of "child marriage". The Education Commission was therefore strongly of the view that the secondary stage should be broken into two parts at the end of Class X, that the students should continue to receive general education till the end of this stage, and that in the next higher secondary stage of two years, two distinct streams should be introduced, one stream preparing the students for admission to universities and the other preparing them for different vocational courses which would be terminal in character. The Commission also felt that the enrolment in courses of a vocational or terminal character should be as high as 50 per cent of the total.

It must also be pointed out that the Education Commission was not happy with the existing higher secondary pattern of 8+3 which provides seven different streams-Humanities, Science, Technical, Commercial, Agriculture, Fine Arts and Home Science and requires every student to join one stream of his choice. The vocational courses provided in this pattern have one major weakness their vocational content necessarily remains weak because the total time available is limited. These courses, therefore, do not become terminal and do not prepare the students for the pursuit of a vocation at the end of the secondary stage. In fact, they do not even prepare them for admission to the corresponding vocational courses at the university stage. The vocational courses in this stream have therefore never become either popular or terminal. Since the programme of vocationalisation of secondary education is extremely important and since it is obviously urgent to divert a fair proportion of students into different walks of life at the end of the secondary stage and thus reduce the pressures on university admissions, the Education Commission rightly came to the conclusion that the existing higher secondary pattern of 8+3 should be replaced by the proposed higher secondary pattern of 10+2.

Two important points must be mentioned in regard to the proposed reorganisation of school education:

(1) In the old days, and even in the multipurpose system introduced by the Secondary Education Commission, science and

mathematics tended to be neglected. They were studied only till the end of Class VIII, and thereafter the student had the option to omit them if he so desired. In many secondary schools, even the provision for the teaching of these subjects did not exist. The net result was that more than 50 per cent of the students at the secondary stage were deprived of basic education in science and mathematics. Adequate teaching of science and mathematics is essential in the modern world based on science and technology. It is equally necessary to improve the quality of education and to avoid the dangers resulting from a dichotomy of the "two cultures" of science and of humanities. Above all, a society like ours, which is committed to the ideals of socialism, has to ensure vertical mobility to the manual workers, whether engaged in industry or agriculture. For this purpose, it must provide the necessary grounding in science and mathematics to every person as a part of his school education because, without this, vertical mobility is not attainable.

(2) While a student should ordinarily be expected to decide whether he will go in for a vocational course or into the university stream at the end of Class X (when he is about 16 years of age), it goes without saying that such decisions would be tentative and that some young persons may like to change from one stream to the other at a later stage. The Central Advisory Board of Education, therefore, specifically recommended that such later transfers from one stream to the other should not only be permitted but also facilitated by due provision for transfer of credits on this account. The importance of this recommendation is obvious.

Even as early as 1919, the Calcutta University Commission had recommended that the course leading to the first degree should have a duration of three years. With the passage of time, the opinion on the subject has now become even stronger for three main reasons. Firstly, there is now a much greater demand for specialisation on account of the explosion of knowledge and, at the same time, there is also a demand for greater general education to enable the young persons to face successfully the complex societies of the modern period. Secondly, there is now a much greater demand for inter-disciplinary courses and for the provision of greater elasticity to the students to choose subjects of study to match their individual capacities and interests. Thirdly, there is also a greater emphasis on providing practical experience, opportunities for field work and project-oriented studies at the undergraduate stage to improve the standards of education and to bring the system of higher education in close contact with the community around, through programmes of social and national service. If these important purposes are to be satisfactorily achieved, it goes without saying that a two-year duration is extremely inadequate for the undergraduate stage and that the courses for the first degree will need a minimum duration of three years.

The pattern of 10+2+3 for school and college classes is an educational reform of great significance, that it is based on several important academic considerations, and is vastly superior to the alternative patterns that now prevail and that its universal adoption in all parts of the country will bring in several advantages among which the following may be mentioned:

(1) The school stage will be strengthened and its standards will improve because of its lengthening to twelve years and because of the inclusion, within it, of the intermediate stage which will bring in better teachers and better facilities.

(2) The two-year higher secondary stage will have several advantages. It will enable us to control expansion to some extent because an element of selective admission can be introduced at this point. The students will also be mature enough, when they enter Class XI to make a tentative decision about their future career and to embark upon some programmes of prespecialisations. It will enable the schools to prepare their gifted students intensively for the University and also to provide remedial action for any shortcomings arising from weaknesses in earlier education. Above all, it will be possible to vocationalise this stage intensively so that a fair proportion of students can be diverted into different walks of life, thus reducing the pressures on university admissions. An important and necessary innovation at this stage would be to provide for transfer of credits to a student who may desire to change from one stream to another.

(3) The standards in higher education will also improve as the students going into the university stream will now be better prepared and more mature.

(4) The three-year degree course would be a definite improvement on the existing two-year course for the first degree. With this longer duration, it will be possible to meet the demands of specialisation as well as of a broad based general and interdisciplinary education and to make adequate provision for practical experience, field work and project-oriented studies. The introduction of problem-oriented interdisciplinary courses at the Master's degree level would also be greatly facilitated with the adoption of 10+2+3 formula.

10+2+3 System: An Analysis

The Central Board of Secondary Education has introduced the pattern of education, commonly known as 10+2 in all its schools beginning with IX class, with effect from May 1975. The first course leading to the examination at the end of X class will include three languages, Mathematics, Physical Sciences, Life Sciences and Social Sciences, also work experience and Health and Physical Education-a general undiversified education for all.

The second stage to end with the 12th year is an improved Higher Secondary course with more accent on vocationalisation, involving diversification and specialisation in subjects best suited to the genius of the pupil. For Most Students, this will be the terminal stage of education and stepping-stone to careers in life. After that the academically disposed scholars could go in for the three-year degree course.

A radical feature of this scheme is that it makes work experience or community service compulsory. The pupil can choose from a long list of subjects like electric gadgets-their servicing and repairs, electronics, agriculture, photography, leather work, typing and tailoring. This part will consist of practicals only, no theory or written paper, and the assessment will be internal and cumulative at school. The traditional system of evaluation will also be reformed. There will be no pass or failure as such. There will be Grades for each subject-5 Grades in all: G-1, Outstanding; G-2, Very Good, G-3, Good; G-4, Fair and G-5, Poor; and this will be a surer guide for employers who look for special proficiency in their one special trade and also for admissions to higher professional or technical courses.

Forty years ago, Mahatma Gandhi advocated Basic education or work-centred education or learning through doing. He said that in a poor country like India, where 80 per cent of the population is agricultural and another 10 per cent industrial, it is a sin to give a purely literary or liberal education. The traditional education has a negative role, it makes pupils more unemployable: a farmer's son who passes B.A. and M.A. becomes unfit for unsophisticated farming; the housewife's daughter who passes M.A. looks down on housewifery and is all for a white collar job, which is in such short supply. It is anti-national to continue such a system.

The work-centred education will develop self-reliance and self-confidence through earning capacity instead of a feeling of helplessness without a routine job. It will instil dignity of labour found in all advanced countries but absent in India; it will produce the spirit of initiative and enterprise that will create openings and opportunities where there are seemingly none. Of course, mere education will not end unemployment; that depends on economic development and many other factors. But it will make our young men and young women fit to face new challenges in life and to transform both our society and its economy through innovations and unsuspected adventures.

System of Evaluation

The system of evaluation reflects also the new needs of a fast changing society. To declare a pupil as a failure in any class at so early an age will give him an inferiority complex for life and stunt his growth. Gandhi, Tagore, Edison, Einstein and Ramanujam all did poorly at school examinations but later became world figures. Why dub a child as a failure if he does badly in one or two subjects that he is compelled to study with or without his will? His interests may lie elsewhere. Give him a poor Grade in that and a good Grade in subjects in which he shines. That is simple justice to the young.

The system is the first step towards revolutionary changes in the educational scene. And there is the rub. Everyone clamours for a wholesale change in the system of education and examination. There are no two opinions that the present system has out-lived whatever limited utility it once had. It produces neither employment nor character nor discipline. Laymen look on schools and colleges as time-filling institutions. The experts express their dissatisfaction with it. Yet as soon as there is a real prospect of a radical change some members of the intelligentsia fiercely rally to the Support of the system of which they themselves have been critics. Our main problem seems to be that our radical thinking is not matched by radical action.

Soundness of School System

The current school system has got overwhelming support from expert educational opinion. It was recommended by the Kothari Commission, it conforms to the National Policy Resolution on Education (1968), it has been approved by the Central Advisory Board of Education and by various all-India forums and seminars. If such massive commendation is not enough to launch it into practice, nothing can be. Let the dissenters not wince before the challenge of change which they have been advocating so frequently. The system seems to be the best under the circumstances and deserves an honest and sincere trial.

The no-changers warn us that the 10+2+3 system will encounter many difficulties. Nothing great was ever achieved without surmounting huge difficulties. But that is no reason for not making education for self-reliance a beginning in the right direction. If men remained confined within the safe familiar limits, there would have been no aeroplane, no space travel, no adventurous inventions. A verse in the Panchtantra says, "Low men do not start any venture for fear of meeting obstacles; the middling ones do make a start but leave off when there are obstacles but the high-minded persist in the right course, though again and again beset with difficulties".

India has over-abundance of human resources and acute scarcity of finance. Our policies should be man-power centred and not money-centred. Human effort and human ingenuity work wonders, while mere money power proves a non-starter. Indian education would have been in a far happier position today, if Gandhiji's ideas of developing education around work experience had been adopted 2 to 4 decades ago. But then the no-changers had their day and Gandhiji was too busy with more urgent programmes to secure independence for India, to devote his whole time and attention to educational reform.

Work Experience

Of all the changes contemplated under the 10+2+3 pattern of education recently adopted by the Central Board of Secondary Education in its member-schools, the introduction of work experience as a compulsory part of the school curriculum is the most vital. This however, has raised doubts and misgivings in the minds of some people, which is not unnatural, considering that this change envisages a drastic departure from the age-old conception of education which kept learning and earning strictly apart. In all societies, when education was first started in an organised manner, it was confined to a selected few. We have travelled far from those days and we are in an era when education is not for the selected few but is sought to be made universal. It is now universally agreed that education should be relevant to life and should not only train the mind, refine the intellect, and culture the emotions, but it should also improve the productive capacities of the individuals.

The change has been received very enthusiastically by most people who have hailed it as a reform long overdue. There are however, some isolated voices of resistance which mainly arise because of lack of proper awareness about the nature and scope of work experience at the school level. Work experience has been introduced to provide a corrective to some of the deficiencies of the present system of education, and to make it more relevant to life. In fact, it provides one of the most essential dimensions to education which has been missing so far and which has been acutely felt by all right thinking persons.

The present system of education, except for a few good exceptions, has been producing young people who are not found easily employable and what is worse, who themselves are lacking in self confidence because they have not been trained in any skill or creative activity which could enable them to face the challenges of life. The introduction of work experience is a step to remove this handicap, not because it will create jobs for everybody but because it will make the products of education relatively more employable and it will imbue them with greater self-confidence because of their experience of having produced something.

It has, therefore been decided to adopt a very simple concept of work experience meaning thereby inculcation of skills and knowledge through creative and productive activities which may result in the students acquiring ability to produce goods and services which are marketable. A creative activity and its productivity in terms of its market value are the two essential characteristics of the concept of work experience. It is hoped that some important values will be inculcated as automatic by-products. The courses have been so designed as to accelerate the realisation of educational values, like inculcation of dignity of labour, capacity to work hard, love of aesthetics, innovation and experimentation and greater confidence to face challenges.

The concept of work experience will in future be more and more sharply defined and the curriculum and courses will be redesigned to realise the educational values in a much more direct and explicit manner. Long years of teaching-learning process have more or less fixed the contours at various levels of most traditional subjects and the instructional ritual has almost got fixed with little incentive or encouragement to explore unchartered areas. This has generated a rigidity and inflexibility about the whole process which makes routine practices safer and more acceptable to all concerned because of their familiarity. There is left not much scope for innovation on the part of the teachers although some imaginative persons have tried experiments and innovated ideas even in these areas with very fruitful results.

Routinism in any sphere is harmful to real progress, but in education it is more so because it leads to sterility of thinking and offers no way out of the dreary desert sands of dead-habit. Fortunately work experience at least does not suffer from this handicap and offers to teachers full scope for their imaginative experimentation and innovation. It is hoped that the teachers, while actually implementing the programme, will enrich this simple concept of work experience through their dynamic thinking and practical efforts. They will bear in mind that they are pioneers in this field and can legitimately feel proud that it has fallen to their lot to work out this revolution in educational thinking which seeks to liberate us from centuries of inertia which has kept earning and learning delinked from each other.

This does not, however, mean that the teacher is left entirely on his own without any directions or guidelines. After a good deal of deliberations, a list of about 40 work experiences has been suggested by way of illustration and a student is free to choose any one out of these in accordance with his own aptitude and facilities provided by the school. For most of these suggested work experiences, broad syllabi have also been prepared to make the level of proficiency in each work experience as unambiguous as possible.

The teacher has also been given a four-week training in various areas of work experience during the summer recess. About 1,000 teachers, at the rate of one teacher for each affiliated school, have been put through this practical training. For this purpose the facilities and expertise available in our Engineering Colleges, Technical Teachers Training Institutes, Polytechnics and Regional Colleges of Education have been utilised.

Work experience will be no blind alley for the students because it will be followed by vocational stream in the XI and XII classes. The students doing very well in work experience will have the choice of joining the vocational stream, which will be all integrated programme of academics and vocations. Even at the University level, some Universities are already thinking of starting some vocational courses.

Teachers acquiring workshop skill will be mostly done in the school itself and that obviously would restrict to some extent the choice of work experience on the part of the schools. The use of community facilities in the neighbourhood or making arrangements with a factory or workshop or productive centre in the neighbourhood is not precluded. In fact the latter has to be encouraged and large scale co-ordination will have to be developed with other agencies concerned with productive activities.

Importance of Science Education

In an age when education is sought to be made universal it would be incongruous to continue with the legacies of the elitist traditions of education evolved mostly in the context of the requirements of leisured classes. Education cannot continue with its ivory tower approach and cannot go on merrily oblivious of the changes in the social and economic scene. Education has to assume a dynamic role and has to become meaningful, purposeful, useful and relevant to life. This necessarily involves appropriate changes in the curricula and content of courses as also methods of teaching, apart from the overall change in the general approach which has to permeate throughout under the

10+2+3 pattern of education. It is a pity that in the popular mind the structural aspect of change as reflected in the years to be spent for various stages of education under the 10+2+3 pattern, has received great attention to the almost exclusion or the very great changes in contents and methods of instruction.

Education is not only to stimulate thought but also to inculcate skills for improved action. This coordination between thought and action is sure to generate a two-way process resulting in improvement in both. Whereas work will be improved with the application of knowledge itself will benefit and become more purposeful and realistic when put to use in refining and improving action.

Teaching of science in this country has been becoming more and more theoretical and getting away from the realities of ordinary life resulting in loss of popularity. It is essential to evolve a new methodology of teaching science which will make the subject more interesting, more readily assimilable by the students and also restore to various science disciplines their fading vitality and popularity. Any subject which is not constantly reviewed in the matter of its contents as well as methodology of instruction in order to retain its relevance to the changing life situation, is likely to get fossilised and suffer the fate of the classics. Science can be a discipline for specialised and sophisticated action, or its applicability to life situations can be underlined for the benefit of the citizens. Science, if it is to help any country in ushering in an era of science and technology, cannot ignore the needs of the citizens and has to be reoriented to help in solving problems of daily life.

The new change sought to be introduced in the method of teaching science through the scheme of project technology seeks to give a more practical bias to science teaching, pointing out at every step the relevance of science to various life situations and the way it can help to solve various problems. The whole idea is to develop science teaching around some chosen projects allied to technology. This will stimulate innovative thinking among students and will inculcate among them the scientific temper, originality, creative and improvisational abilities, which are so necessary in a society, which is trying to become increasingly technological. It also involves doing things with the hands by the student and this naturally develops greater interest and eliminates some of the passivity and boredom which are associated with the class-room situation.

Inter-disciplinary Approach

Another advantage of the project technology is that it very often encourages the interdisciplinary approach which develops a wider understanding of the unity underlying all knowledge and also brings people from various disciplines together fostering a team spirit which in these days is most essential for any significant achievement in any field. This method also eliminates the isolation of science from the community by creating an awareness of the social, economic and moral problems.

Recently the method of project technology was tried by the Central Board of Secondary Education in a Workshop at Lawrence School, Sanawar, which was attended by 21 teachers from schools in different parts of the country and was guided by experts from India and abroad. This quiet workshop away from the maddening crowds, generated tremendous interest among the participants.

As a matter of fact their absorption in their work all the day long was to be seen to be believed. Their complete concentration through long hours indicated the strong motivating effect of project technology. If the introduction of this programme in schools results in the same motivation and the development of the same interest among students, it will be a breakthrough in solving many of the ills of the present-day education. This small workshop has thrown up very fruitful ideas and has shown the great potentialities of the project technology for more purposeful teaching of science.

It has been decided that suitable follow-up action will be initiated with the help of these 21 teachers and it would be possible to generate a snow-ball movement in order to cover all the thousand schools affiliated to the Central Board of Secondary Education in about a couple of years. Some of the projects designed and completed at Sanawar were very interesting and useful. The chief characteristic of these projects was that very cheap and improvised material had been used. It is hoped that the habit of improvisation, experimentation and innovation when properly developed and emphasised would become a life-long asset and for our socio-economic development this type of asset is most urgently needed.

Examination System

It is common knowledge that examinations have dominated education. The curriculum framers keep the examination as the ultimate aim while drawing up courses. The time-table of the school is prepared in such a way that the students can be best prepared for the examination. The quality of the school is judged on the basis of the Board's results. Not only that, even the teacher's assessment is based upon the performance of his students in the Board's examinations.

According to the Secondary Education Commission of India, the educational system in our country was examination-ridden and that the dead weight of the examination tended to curb the teacher's initiative, to stereotype the curriculum, to promote mechanical and lifeless methods of teaching, to discourage all spirit of experimentation and to place stress on wrong or unimportant things in education. It is, therefore, not surprising that any move for a change in the curriculum, teaching methods and evaluation practices should be met with resistance.

The National Policy on Education, issued by the Government of India in 1968, mentioned that the major goal of examination reform should be to improve the reliability and validity of examinations and to make evaluation a continuous process, aimed at helping the student to improve his level of achievement rather than "certifying" the quality of his performance at a given moment of time. Earlier, the Education Commission too had stated that the crippling effect of external examination on quality of work was so great that examination reform had become crucial to all progress and has to go hand in hand with the improvements in teaching. Two main things have, therefore, to be done if the existing examination system has to be reformed. First, its domination over the educational system has to be minimised and secondly, the quality of examination has to be improved so as to make it more valid and reliable. In both these directions the Central Board of Secondary Education has taken appropriate steps while introducing the new pattern of education from the current academic session in its member schools.

One radical change that has come about, is the introduction of the system of Grades instead of marks. Under the existing system, the result is declared on a 101 point scale of marking. The marks obtained by a candidate in different subjects are totalled up and the result worked out on the basis of the aggregate. There is hardly a case where a student offering subjects which are considered to be less scoring is able to get higher aggregate marks than the one who offers subjects like Sanskrit and Mathematics for higher Secondary Examination.

The concept of high scoring and low scoring subjects has therefore, to be given up. It only leads to anomalous situations. A candidate getting 56% aggregate marks is regarded today as superior to a candidate getting 55.9% marks irrespective of the nature of the subject offered and gets admission to either higher courses of study or gets a chance for being interviewed for a post. The Plan of Action on Examination Reform, circulated by the Government of India recently, rightly points out that this kind of situation causes a considerable measure of frustration. It also points out that the 101 point scale of marking together with the arbitrary minimum for a first, second or pass class is scientifically unsound. The system was adopted when our scientific knowledge about examinations was inadequate. It is no longer relevant and is, in fact, doing harm to the student population.

As is done in several other countries, the students will be given five Grades:

— Grade 1: Outstanding,

— Grade 2: Very Good,

— Grade 3: Good,

— Grade 4: Fair,

— Grade 5: Poor,

Instead of totalling up the marks of different subjects, the grades will be awarded subjectwise and if any student wants to improve his grade in any subject or subjects he will be allowed to do so. Today he is asked to repeat ail the subjects notwithstanding his satisfactory performance in some of the subjects. This in fact, is a reform which was long overdue. It was in 1966 that the Education Commission recommended that a student should not be branded as a total failure if he passes in certain subjects but is unable to make the grade in others. There is no reason why he should carry with him the stigma of being declared an unsuccessful candidate if he has partially succeeded in his educational effort.

The system of grading, of course, raises an important question as to what will be the criteria for admission to higher courses of study. The Central Board of Secondary Education is seized with this problem and is formulating guidelines for the schools for the purpose. The CBSE has taken various measures in the past such as training of paper-setters, doing away with overall options and introducing internal options in question papers so as to eliminate selective study by pupils, introducing short answer questions to have a wide coverage of syllabus, providing marking schemes to the examiners and the standardisation of scores etc. Several other measures are in the offing. Greater emphasis is being laid on testing application of knowledge and understanding.

References

Department of School Education, Government of Madhya Pradesh, Bhopal, *Annual Administrative Report* (1996-97).

Directorate of Public Instruction Madhya Pradesh, Bhopal, *Basic Educational Statistics* (1997).

Jolly, KG (1992), *Literacy for All by 2001 : Strategies at District Level,* D.K. Publishers, New Delhi.

Sinha, Amarjeet (1998), *Primary Schooling in India*, Vikas Publishing House, New Delhi.

5

Higher Education System

From time immemorial India has attached importance to a search for higher knowledge and its diffusion. We had in ancient India universities such as those at Nalanda and Takshila. According to Heuan Tsang, Nalanda University alone had 12,000 students. Knowledge, both temporal and spiritual, was imparted in these institutions of higher learning and it is well known that the ancient Hindus had made significant advances in mathematics, astronomy, medicine and philosophy. Before the advent of British administration in this country and particularly during the Mughal period, this country had a magnificent system of 'Madarasas', 'Makhtabs' and 'Pathshalas' where higher education was imparted in the literatures and the sciences of those days.

The British advent in India made a change in the pattern of the educational system followed by our country. In its early years the East India Company took hardly any interest in helping the foundation of any educational institutions in this country. The Regulating Act of 1773 passed by the British Parliament made considerable changes in the government of this country as it provided it with a Governor-General who had an Exeçutive Council to assist him for managing the administrative affairs of Bengal and other parts of the country which had come under the control of the East India Company. The earliest institution founded by Warren Hastings, the first Governor-General of this country, was the Calcutta Madarasa in 1781. It was followed by the establishment of the institution known as the Sanskrit College at Banaras by the acting Governor-General Mr. Jonathan Duncan. These institutions, however, concentrated on oriental learning. It was under the persuasive-eloquence of Lord Macaulay, helped and aided by Raja Ram Mohun Roy and other Indians of progressive and modern outlook that the decision to introduce in India education on western lines was taken in 1835 by the East India Company. Whatever may have been the motives guiding the British administrators of those days, the decision must be regarded as a landmark in the history of this country in evolving a system of education suited to modern requirements. Soon after the first War of Independence and the transfer of power from the East India Company to the British Crown, the Calcutta University war, established in 1857. Universities were also established in Madras and Bombay in the same year. Colleges sprang up in various parts of the country where English education was imparted. Progress in this direction was slow but the efforts of government were aided in this respect by Christian missionaries and non-official Indian agencies.

The question of education in all its aspects was reviewed by the Commission of 1882. A university was established in the Punjab in 1882. It must be made clear that the system of Government, in which the people of the country had hardly any share, evolved by the British was completely unitary-the so-called provinces being subject to the control of the Governor-General who had to take orders from the Secretary of State, who as a Member of the British Cabinet was responsible to the British Parliament for the good government of this country. Advantage was taken of a few facilities offered for higher education by some Indians belonging to the well-to-do classes.

The period saw the growth of public opinion and the rise of the national movement. The British administrators of those days were alarmed at the rise of an educated class saturated with national ideas which they looked upon as a source of potential danger to their interests as an alien power in India. They had no love for the new middle class which was springing up as a result of contact with modern thought. In 1902 a Universities Commission was appointed by the Government of Lord Curzon, to go into the question of university education, which, it was felt, was producing a class of elements discontented with British administration.

Ostensibly with the object of improving the administration of the universities and the education imparted by them, the Indian Universities Act was passed in 1904 in the teeth of strong opposition from Nationalist India, for its effect was to officialise the university bodies which were controlling the universities and colleges in this country. In 1909 the Minto-Morley Reforms were effected but while expanding the Councils and recognising a system of elections with separate special electorates for Muslims and admitting Indians in the Executive Councils of the three Presidencies and Constituting Executive Councils for the provinces and the Centre, it did not bring about any change in the relationship of the Government of India to the provinces or of the Government of India to the Secretary of State. This position continued until the advent of the Montague-Chelmsford Reforms in 1919. India continued to be governed from the White Hall but during this period the Banaras Hindu University which represented a great effort at providing this country with a University, basically non-official in character, was established. In 1877 or thereabouts the Anglo-Muhammadan Oriental College had been established by Sir Syed Ahmed but it was not until 1920 that the Aligarh Muslim University came into existence.

The period of the first world war (1914-18) was marked by considerable unrest in this country. There was an insistent demand for what was in those days called Home Rule and in a memorandum presented on behalf of 19 Members of the Viceroy's Legislative Council, a plan was put forward for a type of diluted autonomy for this country. On the 17th August, 1917, a statement was made in the British Parliament declaring the objectives of British policy by Mr. Montague the then Secretary of State for India. The statement declared the goal of British policy to be the gradual development of self-governing institutions with a view to progressive realisation of responsible government in India and the increasing associations of Indians with every branch of administration in India as an integral part of the British Empire. The goal was, however, to be achieved in successive stages and Britain reserved to herself the right of deciding the pace of each advance, the criterion for which was to be the cooperation received from the people working the Constitution.

The Montague-Chelmsford Reforms and the Government of India Act, 1919, based upon them, while visualising at some unforeseeable future a self-governing India which would achieve Dominion Status, as an integral part of the British Empire did not establish what might be called a federal or even quasi-federal system of government. The Montague Act, however, introduced a system of diarchy in the provinces and while reserving many major subjects including law and order in the hands of Governors vested with complete powers of affirmative and negative legislation in respect of reserved subjects, transferred education to the control of Ministers responsible to Provincial Legislatures. What was done by the Act was devolution of authority subject to the reserved powers of Governors and their responsibility in the ultimate analysis to the Secretary of State remaining unimpaired.

The transfer of education to Indian hands led to many changes in the Acts governing the universities in many States. Courts or Senates were made more representative of educational and public opinion and in some of the universities, a system of Vice-Chancellors elected either by the Court or by the Executive Council, subject to the approval of the Governor who was to be the Chancellor and Visitor, was introduced. As a result of the Montague Act, the Government of India ceased to have any direct responsibility for education and it became a provincial subject. One of the members of the Viceroy's Executive Council, however, had charge of education for the Centrally administered areas and the education department was expected to keep in touch with educational systems in the provinces and supply them with such information as they required. This position continued until the Government of India Act, 1935, which envisaged, subject to reservations and safeguards, a federal system of government in this country to which the Indian States would accede by duly executed instruments of accession.

The Simon Commission (1927-1929) which was a purely Parliamentary Commission, considered the question of future constitutional advance. Nationalist India withheld its co-operation with it on the ground that it was a completely British Commission. The Commission had a special Committee presided over by Sir Philip Hartog to advise it on education. It is not necessary to make any reference to the recommendations of this Committee, but it may be mentioned that previous to it an important event in the educational history of this country was the report of the Sadler Commission on the Calcutta University (1917-19). Though the Commission was appointed to enquire into the affairs of the Calcutta University, its recommendations were of a far reaching character and it continues to be a classic on educational matters even to this day.

In 1921, the Central Advisory Board of Education was appointed. It was dissolved after two years but revived in 1935. The function of this Board was to offer expert advice on all important educational matters that were referred to it and to conduct educational surveys, whenever required.

The first Conference of Indian Universities was held in Simla in May, 1924. One of the recommendations of this Conference was the creation of a Central Agency in India (a) to act as interuniversity Organisation and bureau of implementation, (b) to facilitate the exchange of professors and students, (c) to assist in the co-ordination of university work and the promotion of specialisation of functions, (d) to assist Indian universities in obtaining recognition for their degrees, diplomas and examinations in other countries. As a result of this recommendation, the Inter-University Board of India was set up.

Educational Provisions in Indian Constitution

Immediately after the attainment of Independence in 1947, the Constituent Assembly, set about the task of framing a constitution for India. When the Constitution was being framed, the role of the Government of India in education came up for discussion and it was decided that education including universities, subject to certain provisions, should be a State responsibility. While deciding to include education in the State List, the Founding Fathers were anxious to safeguard the interests of higher education including research and scientific and technical education. Accordingly, the following Entries relating to education are included in the Seventh Schedule of the Constitution:

List I-Union List

The institutions known at the commencement of this Constitution as the Banaras Hindu University, the Aligarh Muslim University and the Delhi University, and any other institution declared by Parliament by law to be an institution of national importance.

Institutions for scientific or technical education financed by the Government of India wholly or in part and declared by Parliament by law to be institutions of national importance.

Union agencies and institutions for-

(a) professional, vocational or technical training, including the training of police officers; or

(b) the promotion of special studies or research; or

(c) scientific or technical assistance in the investigation or detection of crime.

Co-ordination and determination of standards in institutions for higher education or research and scientific and technical institutions.

List II-State List

Education including Universities, subject to the provisions of Entries 63, 64, 65 and 66 of List I and Entry 25 of List III.

List III-Concurrent List

Vocational and technical training of labour. There is no reference to the co-ordination and determination of standards in the Government of India Act of 1935. It is thus clear that the Founding Fathers took a far-sighted view of the future of higher education in this country. Their aim was that the country should maintain the highest possible standards in higher education and research and that they should not be lower than international standards. The co-ordination of facilities and determination of standards in institutions of higher education is thus exclusively a Central responsibility. This makes it incumbent on the Government of India to take a direct interest in the affairs of all universities. To discharge these functions efficiently and effectively, the Government of India constiuted a University Grants Commission in 1952. Later, the Commission was converted into a statutory body, by an Act of Parliament, in 1956. Attention may be invited to Section 12 of the University Grants Commission Act, 1956, which provides, inter alia, that:—

> "it shall be the general duty of the Commission to take, in consultation with the Universities or other bodies concerned, all such steps as it may think fit for the promotion and co-ordination of University Education and for the determination and maintenance of standards of teaching, examination and research in Universities."

The Commission is empowered to inquire into the financial needs of universities and allocate and disburse out of its funds grants for the maintenance and development of Central universities and also for the development of State universities or for any other general or specified purpose. Section 29(1) of the University Grants Commission Act, 1956, lays down that :

> "in the discharge of its functions under the Act, the Commission shall be guided by such directions on questions of policy relating to national purposes as may be given to it by the Central Government."

Guiding Principles of Higher Education

Obviously, as the Robbins Committee on Higher Education observe that "the growing complexity in the developing branches of knowledge in many cases requires a better foundation of fundamental studies than can be provided in the present first degree course, and it is in this respect that arrangements in some other countries are superior". Expenditure on higher education cannot be regarded as unproductive. It is basically an investment from which future generations will benefit. Higher education must not become the monopoly of the rich. Children of poor persons must not be debarred from types of education for which they are fitted. Obviously universities will have to choose scholars from those who will profit from higher education. But in so doing, in-as-much as the State is contributing towards their functioning, they must ensure that they devise a machinery which will not prevent any person who is capable of benefiting from the education given on the ground that he is too poor to pay for it. Education must be regarded as the most important investment of all, to use the language of Prof. A. C. Pigou, in the health, intelligence and character of the people. Indeed, to advocate, as that eminent economist puts it, economy in this regard should be regarded as a criminal offence.

The quality of higher education is dependent to a large extent upon that of the higher secondary education imparted in our schools or colleges. Unless there is an improvement in the quality of candidates turned out by our secondary schools, the quality of higher education and research, whether fundamental or applied, cannot be high. The quality of teachers and teaching has to be improved, not only in our colleges and universities, but also in our schools which act as feeders to our universities. Our higher educational institutions must be so equipped as to meet the demands of progress for every type of higher education, literary and scientific, technical and professional. They must help us in fighting poverty, disease, ignorance, superstition and all that accompanies it.

Education is a subject that concerns the common man. No central agency can be effective in exercising administrative authority or supervision over the vast field covered by education in a large country like India. For the purposes of national integration it was essential to have a unified control over all aspects of education. Any attempt to centralise education may lead to serious complications between the Union and the States and it will be unfortunate if education is dragged into the arena of regional controversies. The administration of universities will not improve necessarily by any provisions which would substitute for direct relationship of the States with that of the Centre. The University Grants Commission exercises vast influence over university education. It has helped to improve university standards. The power of giving financial aid to universities and colleges in a country where the springs of private charity are drying up gives to the Commission an authority which, if properly utilised, can help it to maintain and improve standards and coordinate educational activities.

The second alternative is to convert education particularly university education into a Concurrent subject. Our Constitution envisages three Lists. So far as the subjects enumerated in List I of the Seventh Schedule are concerned, Parliament has, in respect of them, exclusive power of legislation. State Legislatures have also power to make laws enumerated in List III in the Seventh Schedule and this is known as the Concurrent List. Subject to clauses (1) and (2) of Article 246 of the Constitution a legislature of any State has exclusive power to make laws enumerated in List II of the Seventh Schedule for the territories comprising the States. The Constitution further lays down that in the case of a conflict between a law made by Parliament and a law made by a State Legislature, the former shall prevail whether the law made by Parliament is prior or later being immaterial. The administration of the law will, however, remain vested in the State Government.

The Central Government is already exercising an appreciable degree of influence over higher education by the system of financial grants which are given to universities and higher institutions by it. This system has the merit of respecting the autonomy of the universities. The University Grants Commission is a body of eminent educationists and in making grants no considerations other than those of an academic or educational character are ever entertained.

STATUS OF TERTIARY EDUCATION

Higher education in India has evolved in divergent streams with each stream monitored by an apex body, indirectly controlled by the Ministry of Human Resource Development and funded jointly by the state governments. Most universities are administered by the States, however, there are 18 important universities called Central Universities, which are maintained by the Union Government. The increased funding of the central universities give them an advantage over their state competitors.

Apart from the several hundred state universities, there is a network of research institutions that provide opportunities for advanced learning and research leading up to a PhD in branches of science, technology and agriculture. Several have won international recognition. 25 of these institutions come under the umbrella of the CSIR - Council of Scientific and Industrial Research and over 60 fall under the ICAR - Indian Council of Agricultural Research. In addition, the DAE - Department of Atomic Energy, and other ministries support various research laboratories.

The Indian Institutes of Technology were placed 50th in the world and 2nd in the field of Engineering (next only to MIT) by Times Higher World University Rankings. Earlier, an Asia Week study had ranked them (Along with Birla Institute of Technology and Science - Pilani), among the top 20 technical universities in Asia. Indian Institute of Science is the premier research institute in the field of science and engineering. There are several thousand colleges (affiliated to different universities) that provide undergraduate science, agriculture, commerce and humanities courses in India. Amongst these, the best also offer post graduate courses while some also offer facilities for research and PhD studies.

Technical education has grown rapidly in recent years. With recent capacity additions, it now appears that the nation has the capability to graduate over 500,000 engineers (with 4-yr undergraduate degrees) annually, and there is also a corresponding increase in the graduation of computer scientists (roughly 50,000 with post-graduate degree). In addition, the nation graduates over 1.2 million scientists. Furthermore, each year, the nation is enrolling at least 350,000 in its engineering diploma programmes (with plans to increase this by about 50,000). Thus, India's annual enrollment of scientists, engineers and technicians now exceeds 2 million.

2008 data from Maharashtra's Higher Secondary Board reveals that .87 million passed the school leaving exam and enrolled in college for undergraduate studies. Adding enrolment in polytechnic programmes and graduates from other boards puts Maharashtra's total at close to a million and its college enrolment ratio at roughly 39%. States like Tamil Nadu, Haryana and Kerala also have comparably high tertiary enrollment ratios. In Andhra Pradesh, the tertiary enrolment rate is now approaching 25%.

Across the country, tertiary enrollment rates have been increasing at a rate between 5-10% in the last decade, which has led to a doubling of the tertiary enrolment rate to near 20%. (However, outdated government data does not yet capture this trend, which can be seen from analysing individual state data.)

International league tables produced in 2006 by the London-based Times Higher Education Supplement (THES) confirmed Jawaharlal Nehru University (JNU)'s place among the world's top 200 universities. Likewise, THES 2006 ranked JNU's School of Social Sciences at the 57th position among the world's top 100 institutes for social sciences.

The University of Calcutta was the first multi-disciplinary university of modern India. According to The Times Higher Education Supplement's survey of the world's top arts and humanities universities, dated November 10, 2005, this university, ranked 39, was the only Indian university to make it to the top 50 list in that year. Other research institutes are the Saha Institute of Nuclear Physics, the Asiatic Society, and the Indian Statistical Institute.

The National Law School of India University is highly regarded, with some of its students being awarded Rhodes Scholarships to Oxford University, and the All India Institute of Medical Sciences is consistently rated the top medical school in the country. Indian Institutes of Management (IIMs) are the top management institutes in India.

The private sector is strong in Indian higher education. This has been partly as a result of the decision by the Government to divert spending to the goal of universalisation of elementary education. Within a decade different state assemblies has passed bills for private universities, including Birla Institute of Technology and Science, Amity University and Xavier Labour Relations Institute.

Accreditation for universities in India is required by law unless it was created through an act of Parliament. Without accreditation, the government notes "these fake institutions have no legal entity to call themselves as University/Vishwvidyalaya and to award 'degree' which are not treated as valid for academic/employment purposes". University Grants Commission Act 1956 explains,

"the right of conferring or granting degrees shall be exercised only by a University established or incorporated by or under a Central Act carlo bon tempo, or a State Act, or an Institution deemed to be University or an institution specially empowered by an Act of the Parliament to confer or grant degrees. Thus, any institution which has not been created by an enactment of Parliament or a State Legislature or has not been granted the status of a Deemed to be University, is not entitled to award a degree."

Accreditation for higher learning is overseen by autonomous institutions established by the University Grants Commission:

— All India Council for Technical Education (AICTE)
— Distance Education Council (DEC)
— Indian Council of Agricultural Research (ICAR)
— Bar Council of India (BCI)
— National Assessment and Accreditation Council (NAAC)
— National Council for Teacher Education (NCTE)
— Rehabilitation Council of India (RCI)

— Medical Council of India (MCI)
— Pharmacy Council of India (PCI)
— Indian Nursing Council (INC)
— Dental Council of India (DCI)
— Central Council of Homeopathy (CCH)
— Central Council of Indian Medicine (CCIM)
— Veterinary Council of India (VCI)

Role of The Union Government

Before 1947, the part played by the Central Government in the expansion and development of university education was not such as it could be proud of. In 1857, the Universities of Calcutta, Bombay and Madras wore established on the pattern of the University of London. From 1870, Provincial Governments began to play a greater part educational matters, though of course, they remained subject to the control of the Government of India and the Secretary of State. By about 1900, only two more Universities, namely, the Punjab University in 1882 and the Allahabad University in 1887 were added to the three mentioned above by us. Both of them owed their creation to the Acts of the Central Legislature.

The appointment of the Education Commission of 1882 and the Universities Commission of 1902, the Resolution of the Government of India of 1904 on educational policy, the Indian Universities Act, 1904 empowering, inter alia, the Governor-General in Council to determine the territorial limits of the Universities, the Resolution of the Government of India of 1913, the establishment in 1915 of the Bureau of Education, under the Educational Commissioner with the Government of India, with a view to collect and collate educational information in India and abroad and to arrange for the publication of educational reports and a quinquennial review on the progress of education in India, and the appointment of the Calcutta University Commission, 1917-1919 were about the only contributions that the Government of India made to the advancement of higher education in this country.

The Governor-General in Council was, as Lord Morley described him, the agent of the Secretary of State who was responsible to the British Parliament for the good government of this country. Control of education, therefore, remained completely under British hands until the year 1919 when the Montague Chelmsford Act introduced a system of diarchy in Provincial Administrations and transferred education to the control of Ministers responsible to largely elected provincial legislatures. The education imparted in our universities was generally of a literary type. Scientific and technical education was neglected. The Sadler Commission, that is to say, the Calcutta University Commission emphasised the need for an Organisation to keep local governments in touch with one another and- their observations on this point are quoted below:

> "The Government of India can perform an invaluable function by defining the general aims of educational policy by giving advice and assistance to local governments and to universities, by acting as an impartial arbiter in cases of dispute, by protecting disregarded interests, by supplying organised information as to the development of educational ideas in the various provinces, and also elsewhere than in India, by helping to obtain the service of scholars from other countries, by coordinating the work of various universities, and by guarding against needless duplication and overlapping in the provision of the more costly forms of education".

This recommendation was accepted by the Government of India and in August 1920, a Central Advisory Board of Education was established. The main function of the Board was to offer expert advice on important educational matters referred to it and to conduct educational, surveys, whenever required. The Board, however, was abolished on grounds of economy in 1923 but it was revived again in 1935. It was this Board which was responsible for the drawing up in 1944 a Plan of Post-War Educational Development in India generally known as the Sargeant Scheme.

Indian universities started meeting in conferences in 1924. Their first conference was held in Simla in May 1924. The conference recommended that a central agency in India should be created (a) to act as inter-university organisation and bureau of implementation, (b) to facilitate the exchange of professors and students, (c) to assist in the coordination of university work and the promotion of specialisation of functions, (d) to assist Indian universities in obtaining recognition for their degrees, diplomas and examinations in other countries. As a result of this recommendation, the Inter-University Board of India was set up. The Board has, since then, acted as a forum for discussion of University problems.

In 1935, the Government of India Act gave a new Constitution of a quasi-federal character to this country. One of its distinguishing features was that it divided the subjects of legislation into three lists, List I which was to be the Union List, List II the State List and List III the Concurrent List. In List I, two noticeable entries were (i) Entry 12 and (ii) Entry 13.

(i) *Entry 12:* Federal agencies, and institutions for the following purposes, that is to say, for research, for professional or technical training, or for the promotion of special studies.

(ii) *Entry 13*: The Banaras Hindu University and the Aligarh Muslim University.

With the exception of these two Entries, education remained an entirely Provincial subject in terms of Item 17 of List II of the Seventh Schedule to the Government of India Act. It may be noted that the functions of the Government of India in the field of education were of an extremely limited character under the Government of India Act, 1935. Indian opinion too did not want the interference of the Central Government as education was a transferred subject and there was a natural reluctance on the part of Ministers and Provincial legislators to allow the Central Government to influence their policies.

Role of Ministry of Education

The first act of the Ministry was to appoint a high-powered commission on university education under the chairmanship of Dr. S. Radhakrishnan to report on Indian university education. The Commission surveyed the entire field of university education in the country and submitted its Report in 1949. One of the recommendations of this Commission was that university education should be placed in the Concurrent List. While agreeing with the view that in a large country like India, good government is only possible if wide powers are conferred by the Constitution upon the Provincial Governments, the Commission went on to observe that the all India aspects of university education, the repercussions and interchanges necessary and desirable between universities and the need for a national guarantee of minimum standards of efficiency, make it impossible for university education to remain a purely Provincial subject. They went on to observe that the necessary safeguards can be achieved by Concurrency and they, therefore, recommended that education should be made a Concurrent subject.

The Constituent Assembly had before it the Report of the Radhakrishnan Commission. It appears to have felt that the purposes that the Radhakrishnan Commission had in mind would be met by vesting the Union Government with powers such as are to be found in Entry 66 of List I of the Seventh Schedule. They also seemed to have been of the view that the further points made by the Radhakrishnan Commission would be met by authorising Parliament to declare certain institutions of higher education to be institutions of national importance. It was on this basis that the Constituent Assembly appears to have proceeded.

The Radhakrishnan Commission was itself careful to observe that it was not in favour of superimposing on, or substituting central control for the existing measure of provincial control of universities. They recognised that many of the evils present in our universities arise from the fact that they have "no real autonomy whatever, and have proved incapable of resisting pressure from outside". They were of the opinion that while "universities should be sensitive to enlightened public opinion, they should never let themselves be bullied or bribed into actions that they know to be educationally unsound or worse still, motivated by nepotism, faction and corruption." Their view was that the right public policy is "to give a university the best possible constitution, securing among other things the inclusion, of wisely chosen external members of its governing body and then to leave it free from interference." They went on to elaborate the directions in which the constitution of the universities should be framed.

The Constituent Assembly did not accept their recommendation that university education should be a Concurrent subject. The question is whether the Education Ministry of the Government of India has taken the initiative that was intended to make our universities real centres of higher learning. For an answer to this question, we must examine the work that the University Grants Commission which has been established by an Act of Parliament in 1956 has done in the field of university education. We may mention that even prior to 1956, the

Education Ministry had taken steps to establish a University Grants Commission. It consisted of nine members including five vice-chancellors of universities, two officers of the Central Government and two other educationists of repute. Its functions were to (i) to advise Government on the allocation of grants-in-aid from public funds to Central Universities, (ii) to advise Government on the allocation of grants-in-aid to other universities and institutions of higher learning whose case for such grants may be referred to the Commission by Government; and (iii) to advise the universities and other institutions of higher learning in respect of any question referred to the Commission by the Government.

The University Grants Commission Act has as many as 26 Sections. Its Preamble enacts that it is intended to make provision for the coordination and determination of standards in universities. The word "University" as defined in Section 2 of the Act has been given a wide meaning and includes any institution recognised by the Commission in accordance with the regulations made by it. According to the Act, the Commission is a body corporate having perpetual succession and a common seal. It consists of nine members selected as follows —

(a) Not more than three members from among the vice-chancellors of universities ;

(b) Two members from among the officers of the Central Government to represent that Government; and

(c) The remaining number from among persons who are educationists of repute or who have obtained high academic distinctions.

The further proviso is that one-half of the total number so chosen shall be from among persons who are not officers of the Central Government or of any State Government. The appointing authority is the Central Government and members hold office for a period of six years, but one-third retire on the expiration of the third year in accordance with the procedure prescribed and their vacancies are filled up by fresh appointment. The office of the Chairman is a whole-time salaried one. The Commission has been empowered to associate with itself any person in such manner and for such purposes it may desire in carrying out any of the provisions of this Act.

Whereas the Commission can grant funds for the maintenance and development of Central universities it can allocate and disburse grants to other universities only for the purpose of development. Their maintenance is not its concern. The Commission has been further empowered to recommend measures necessary for the improvement of university education and advise a university upon the action to be taken for the purposes of implementing such recommendation, advise the Central Government or any State Government on the allocation of any grants to universities for any general or specified purpose out of the Consolidated Fund of India or the Consolidated Fund of the State, as the case may be; advise any authority, if such advice is asked for, on the establishment of a new university or on proposals connected with the expansion of the activities of any university; advise the Central Government or any State Government or university on any question which may be referred to the Commission by the Central Government or the State Government or the university, as the case may be; collect information on all such matters relating to university education in India and other countries as it thinks fit and make the same available to any university; require a university to furnish it with such information as may be needed relating to the financial position of the university or the studies in the various branches of learning undertaken in that university together with all the rules and regulations relating to the standards of teaching and examination in that university respecting each of such branches of learning, and perform such other functions as may be prescribed or as may be deemed necessary by the Commission for advancing the cause of higher education in India or as may be incidental or conducive to the discharge of the above functions.

The most important power which has been given to the Commission is that it can under Section 13 for the purpose of ascertaining the financial needs of a university or its standards of teaching, examination and research and after consultation with the university, order an inspection of any department or departments thereof to be made in such manner as may be prescribed or by such person or persons as it may direct. It will be obligatory on the Commission to communicate to the university the data on which such inspection is made and the university shall be entitled to be associated with it. It will be open to the Commission to communicate to the university its views in regard to the results of any such inspection and it may after ascertaining the opinion of the university recommend to the university the action to be taken as a result of such inspection.

Section 14 of the Act authorises the Commission to withhold grants after taking into consideration explanations offered by the university for failure on the part of the university to comply with its recommendations. The Central Government has, as required by the Act, to pay to the Commission such sums as may be considered necessary for the purpose of its functions and the Act makes it clear that the Commission shall have its own funds.

The University Grants Commission has helped to maintain standards and by far the most valuable service that it has done is to raise salary scales of university teachers and research scholars. But it has not been able to solve fully the problem of affiliated colleges, for it has no direct connection with them. Steps have to be taken to improve further the scales of the salaries of hundreds of teachers who are to be found in our aided colleges and institutions. The consolidated grant to the University Grants Commission for the period of the Third Five Year Plan was Rs. 37 crores. The number of universities has increased from 16 in 1947-48 to 55 at present. It cannot be said that the grant that the Commission is getting is at all adequate for the purposes of improving the needs of university education and higher research.

Maintenance of Standards

We shall now consider the question of the steps which the Union Government must take to ensure that minimum standards of efficiency and uniformity in the sense of equivalence of standards in all the universities and institutions of higher education in such matters as courses of study, examinations and standards of teaching are maintained. Courses of study are obviously matters for universities to decide. There can or should be no all-India courses of study, for, if the courses of study were prescribed by an outside body such as an All-India Council for Higher Education, the principle of university autonomy which we regard as vital for a free competition of ideas will be impinged. But the phrase "courses of study" has not been used in any narrow sense here

A uniform pattern of examinations cannot be set for the entire country. It is desirable that in the interests of higher education itself there should be some diversity in our educational system. But what should be aimed at and what can be achieved is a minimum standard of attainment in the examinations conducted by our Universities. Though the syllabus or the textbooks prescribed may differ to some extent in various universities it is possible to work out schemes which will enable anyone who wishes to familiarise himself with our educational system to say that, broadly speaking, there is an equivalence in the minimum standards demanded from those who leave our universities.

Both courses of study and examinations are dependent upon the standard of teaching in our universities. Obviously all universities will not be able to have the highest standard of teaching in every subject that a candidate can offer for various examinations. Some universities will have in particular subjects teachers of greater repute than those to be found in others. Possibly, a few of the universities in the country will reach a higher degree of efficiency both in basic learning and research than others.

But nevertheless there will be a minimum standard which at all events all will endeavour to reach. In order that this minimum might be achieved, it is essential that our universities should have a supply of good teachers. It is not difficult to lay down minimum standards for members of our university staff. It is not, however, possible to achieve or attain these minimum standards unless there is a determined effort on the part of those responsible for higher education to ensure that the best type of the young men and women turned out by our universities take to an educational career.

As educational standards are dependent upon the quality of teaching it follows as a matter of logic that our university men and women should be made to regard education as an attractive career. The question of the pay scales of our teachers has thus a direct bearing upon the quality of teachers employed in our higher educational institutions. The scales should be such as will not compare unfavourably with those sanctioned for our administrative services serving either under the Union or the States. An educational career has a charm of its own for the scholarly type of young persons. It provides them with opportunities of keeping themselves informed of the latest developments in their subjects and other allied branches of knowledge and contributing, if they have the will and the skill to do so to the sum total of human thought in various branches of knowledge. Even from a monetary point of view, a teacher or a professor who writes qualitative books should be able to make, as education advances in this country and the demand for books increases, a good income from his writings and lectures. Teachers have the leisure to engage themselves in a study of the branches of knowledge that interest them. Their contact with youth should act as spur to activity.

There has been a continuous increase in the number of students in our universities and higher institutions. It is neither possible nor essential for raising the cultural level of the community or efficiency in higher education to insist upon, subject to certain minimum conditions being fulfilled, uniformity of standards in our higher educational institutions. Some are bound to excel others; that is inevitable. It is not in every discipline that a university can reach the highest standard. There will be variations in the standards reached by our universities and higher institutions in the various disciplines. Some will specialise in particular branches of knowledge or, even for that matter, in particular aspects of branches of knowledge than others.

Some universities and higher institutions in our country reach much higher standard than others in the quality of their staff, libraries, laboratories and general equipment. This lack of uniformity of standards will, no doubt, grow less with time. In the United States, there are over 2,000 institutions of higher learning with varying degrees of efficiency. This lack of, what may be called for want of a better word, uniformity of standards has not prevented that country from providing equality of opportunity to its young people and building up enviable traditions of scholarship and research in some institutions which have come to acquire worldwide reputation as centres of learning. Highly efficient as the new civic universities in Britain are, few will be prepared to go as far as to claim for them that they are in every respect equal to Oxford, Cambridge or London or some of the older Scottish and Irish universities.

We need in our country various types of universities and colleges, viz., teaching, unitary and residential, federal and affiliating or even purely affiliating and examining with proper supervision and control over colleges affiliated to them. Clearly, our resources do not permit us to have universities and institutions which will specialise in all branches of knowledge in all our regional centres.

Role of University Grants Commission

The University Grants Commission has an impressive record of work to its credit for promotion and coordination of university education and for the determination and maintenance of standards of teaching, examination and research. To put it briefly, the Commission has from time to time, constituted Review Committees consisting of eminent university teachers, to examine the existing facilities for teaching and research and the current syllabii in various subjects of study. Thus, it can be truly claimed for the Commission that the Committees appointed by it have helped to improve and modernise our educational system. The reports of some of the Committees so appointed have been forwarded to universities for their consideration and action. The question of standards in our universities has received special attention at the hands of the Commission.

For encouraging the pursuit of excellence in teaching and research and for accelerating the attainment of international standards, Centres of Advanced Studies in selected subjects in some universities have been established by the Commission. One of the most important services which the Commission has rendered is to revise the scales of pay of the teaching staff of the universities, so that it might become possible for them to recruit and retain some of their best products in the universities. The practice of the Commission is to share the additional expenditure required for the introduction of these scales to the extent of 80% provided the universities or State Governments concerned contribute the balance and give a reasonable assurance that the revised scales will be maintained on a permanent basis even after the Commission's assistance ceases.

Seminars and summer schools which provide opportunities to teachers and research workers to acquaint themselves with the latest developments in their various fields of knowledge have been encouraged by the Commission. By so doing, the Commission has endeavoured to improve the professional competence of teachers and contributed towards raising the standard of teaching in universities and colleges.

Another activity in which the Commission has taken interest is examination reform. An Expert Committee whose report was published in 1962 has examined this question which appears to have evoked widespread and searching interest in the subject. Many universities have expressed their general agreement with the recommendations of the Committee and some are even contemplating to introduce certain measures of reform recommended by it.

Tutorial classes in selected institutions have been encouraged by the Commission. Assistance has been given for this purpose and the Commission has helped by financial assistance the provision of additional accommodation and expansion of libraries in universities and colleges. In order to bring about rationalisation and modernisation of general education, the Commission has, from time to time, taken steps to promote re-orientation of undergraduate courses of study.

Universities are provided with grants by the Commission for the improvement of physical facilities, recruitment of additional staff, purchase of books and scientific equipment, the development of libraries and laboratories, the construction of hostels and staff quarters and the provision of other essential amenities necessary for a better academic atmosphere for students and teachers.

It has been the endeavour of the Commission to stimulate research and attract suitable personnel to the teaching profession. For this purpose, the Commission has instituted a number of research scholarships and fellowship. It has also provided special grants to teachers to enable them to carry on research and other learned activities.

Attention may be drawn to the fact that for improving existing conditions of study and work, the Commission makes grants, inter alia, for the following purposes:

(i) Travel grants to teachers and research scholars.

(ii) Assistance to retired teachers to enable them to continue their teaching and research work.

(iii) Publication of doctoral theses and learned works of high standard.

(iv) Printing presses.

(v) Extension lectures.

(vi) Gandhi Bhavans.

(vii) Hobby workshops.

The Chairman, University Grants Commission, in his interview with the Committee pointed out that the most serious difficulty which faced them was the pausity of funds necessary for raising standards and implementing approved schemes effectively and particular reference was made by him to the need for improving teacher-pupil ratio from 1: 17 to at least 1:10.

The existing provisions of the University Grants Commission Act do not enable the Commission to give recurring grants to State universities. Necessarily this leads to difficulties and retards the pace of development. It may not be possible to go as far as to suggest that the Commission should make itself responsible for the maintenance grants of State universities but certainly the grants for development purposes should not only be increased but also given without the condition of a matching grant attached to it.

In the new era which we have entered, a wider conception has to be taken of the duties and responsibilities of our universities. Their task is to provide leadership for all our national activities. It is their job to ensure, that the country possesses a sufficient supply of statesmen, parliamentarians, diplomats, judges, jurists, scientists, engineers, technologists, physicians, surgeons and men capable of giving a new lead in agriculture, industry and business. Our universities must be so equipped as to meet the challenge which is bound to increase as we advance along the lines of progress for every type of higher education, literary and scientific, technical and professional. Our places of learning have to help us in fighting poverty, disease, ignorance, superstition and all that goes with it. They have to enrich our society by bringing it into accord with notions of that justice upon which emphasis has been placed in the Preamble of our Constitution. In order that they might be able to accomplish the vast task, they need teachers and researchers, inspired by a zeal for advancing knowledge and determinately loyal to definite social purposes. It should be the endeavour of our universities to secure for their staffs a sufficient supply of teachers dedicated to the pursuit of knowledge.

References

Brennan J., Kogan M. and Teichler U., (eds.), (1996). *Higher Education and Work*, Jessica Kingsley, London.

International Finance Corporation. 2005). "India's Issues and Challenges for Future Private Investment in Higher Education." Unpublished presentation, IFC, Washington, DC.

Chen, D. (2001). "Restructuring through Amalgamation in China." *International Higher Education* Fall.

Elzkowitz, H., and L. Leydesdorff, eds. (1997). *Universities and the Global Knowledge Economy: A Triple Helix of University-Industry-Government Relations*. London: Cassell Academic.

Clarke, B. R. (1998). *Creating Entrepreneurial Universities: Organizational Pathways of Transformation*. Oxford, UK: IAU Press, Pergamon.

6

Secondary Education System

Secondary education serves as a bridge between elementary and higher education and prepares young persons between the age group of 14-18 for entry into higher education or work situations. The population of children in this age group has been estimated to be 88.5 million as per Census, 2001. Enrolment figures show that only 31 million of these children were attending schools in 2001-02, which means that two-third of the population remained out of school. Given the liberalisation and globalisation of the Indian economy, the rapid changes witnessed in scientific and technological world and the general need to improve the quality of life, it is essential that school leavers acquire a higher level of knowledge and skills than what they are provided in the eight years of elementary education. The average earnings of secondary school certificate holders are significantly higher than those with primary school education.

Paras 5.13 –5.15 of the National Policy on Education (NPE), 1986 (as modified in 1992) deal with Secondary Education. Para 5.13 of the NPE, inter alia states that access to Secondary Education will be widened with emphasis on enrolment of girls, SCs and STs, particularly in science, commerce and vocational streams. Boards of Secondary Education will be reorganised and vested with autonomy so that their ability to improve the quality of secondary education is enhanced. Efforts will be made to provide computer literacy in as many secondary level institutions as possible so that the children are equipped with necessary computer skills to be effective in the emerging technological world. A proper understanding of the work ethos and of the values of a humane and composite culture will be brought about through appropriately formulated curricula. Vocationalisation through specialised institutions or through the refashioning of secondary education will, at this age, provide valuable manpower for economic growth.

It is universally accepted that children with special talent or aptitude should be provided opportunities to proceed at a faster pace, by making good quality education available to them, irrespective of their capacity to pay for it. Pace setting residential schools, Navodaya Vidayalas, intended to serve this purpose have been established in most parts of the country on a given pattern, but with full scope for innovation and experimentation. Their broad aim will continue to be to serve the objective of excellence coupled with equity and social justice (with reservation for the rural areas, SCs and STs), to promote national integration by providing opportunities to talented children from different parts of the country, to live and learn together, to develop their full potential, and, most importantly, to become catalysts of a nation-wide programme and school improvement.

Steps have been taken in the last few years to universalise elementary education. Towards that end Sarva Siksha Abhiyan (SSA) is being implemented all over the country in collaboration with the State Governments. Mid-day Meal Scheme is a part of this programme. As a result of these steps, the number of "out of school" children (6-14 years) has come down to less than 5% of the total population in that age group. The Sarva Shikha Abhiyan at the elementary level to universalise elementary education for the age group 6-14 has already set the stage for an exponential growth of demand for secondary education. While the growth of enrolment in the secondary school, had increased at an annual rate of 2.83 per cent during 1990s, it increased at 7.4 per cent, per annum between 2000 and 2003. The full impact of SSA is likely to be reflected during the terminal years of the Eleventh Plan. If the goal of universal retention at the elementary level is achieved by 2010, steps will have to be taken to expand facilities for secondary education in a big way.

Central Board of Secondary Education

A trail of developments mark the significant changes that took place over the years in shaping up the Board to its present status. U P Board of

High School and Intermediate Education was the first Board set up in 1921. It has under its jurisdiction Rajputana, Central India and Gwalior. In response to the representation made by the Government of United Provinces, the then Government of India suggested to set up a joint Board in 1929 for all the areas which was named as the ' Board of High School and Intermediate Education, Rajputana. This included Ajmer, Merwara, Central India and Gwalior.

The Board witnessed rapid growth and expansion at the level of Secondary education resulting in improved quality and standard of education in institutions. But with the advent of State Universities and State Boards in various parts of the country the jurisdiction of the Board was confined only to Ajmer, Bhopal and Vindhya Pradesh later. As a result of this, in 1952, the constitution of the Board was amended wherein its jurisdiction was extended to part-C and Part-D territories and the Board was given its present name 'Central Board of Secondary Education'. It was in the year 1962 finally that the Board was reconstituted. The main objectives were those of : serving the educational institutions more effectively, to be responsive to the educational needs of those students whose parents were employed in the Central Government and had frequently transferable jobs.

Jurisdiction

The jurisdiction of the Board is extensive and stretches beyond the national geographical boundaries. As a result of the reconstitution, the erstwhile ' Delhi Board of Secondary Education' was merged with the Central Board and thus all the educational institutions recognised by the Delhi Board also became a part of the Central Board. Subsequently, all the schools located in the Union Territory of Chandigarh. Andaman and Nicobar Island, Arunachal Pradesh, the state of Sikkim, and now Jharkhand, Uttaranchal and Chhattisgarh have also got affiliation with the Board. From 309 schools in 1962 the Board today has 8979 schools on 31-03-2007 including 141 schools in 21 countries. There are 897 Kendriya Vidyalayas, 1761 Government Schools, 5827 Independent Schools, 480 Jawahar Novodaya Vidyalayas and 14 Central Tibetean Schools.

Decentralisation

In order to execute its functions effectively Regional Offices have been set up by the Board in different parts of the country to be more responsive to the affiliated schools. The Board has regional offices in Allahabad, Ajmer, Chennai, Guwahati, Panchkula and Delhi. Schools located outside India are looked after by regional office Delhi. For detailed jurisdiction of regional offices of CBSE click here. The headquarter constantly monitors the activities of the Regional Offices. Although, sufficient powers have been vested with the Regional Offices. Issues involving policy matters are, however, referred to the head office. Matters pertaining to day-to-day administration, liaison with schools, pre and post examination arrangements are all dealt with by the respective regional offices.

Financial Structure

CBSE is a self-financing body which meets the recurring and non-recurring expenditure without any grant-in-aid either from the Central Govt. or from any other source. All the financial requirements of the Board are met from the annual examination charges, affiliation fee, admission fee for PMT. All India Engineering Entrance Examination and sale of Board's publications.

Major Activities and Objectives

The Central Board of Secondary Education was set up to achieve certain interlinked objectives:

— To prescribe conditions of examinations and conduct public examination at the end of Class X and XII. To grant qualifying certificates to successful candidates of the affiliated schools.

— To fulfil the educational requirements of those students whose parents were employed in transferable jobs.

— To prescribe and update the course of instructions of examinations

— To affiliate institutions for the purpose of examination and raise the academic standards of the country.

The prime focus of the Board is on:

— Innovations in teaching-learning methodologies by devising students friendly and students centred paradigms.

— Reforms in examinations and evaluation practices.
— Skill learning by adding job-oriented and job-linked inputs.
— Regularly updating the pedagogical skills of the teachers and administrators by conducting in service training programmes, workshops etc.

Organisational Setup

The Board functions under the overall supervision of the Controlling Authority which is vested with the Secretary Education, Government of India, Ministry of Human Resource Development. The Board has various statutory committees which are advisory in nature. The Governing Body of the Board is constituted as per its rules and regulations. The recommendations of all the committees are placed for approval before the Governing Body of the Board.

Structure of the Board

Chairman is the Chief Executive of the Board assisted by five Heads of Departments: the Secretary, the Director (Academic), the Controller of Examinations, HOD (Edusat, R & D and vocational Education) and the HOD (Spl. Exams., Projects & Training). The Secretary (Education), Ministry of Human Resource Development, Government of India is the Controlling Authority of the Board, and appoints the Chairman and Heads of Departments.

The Secretary CBSE is the Chief Administrative Officer responsible for the matters relating to Administration, Audit and Accounts, Public Relations, Legal and grant of Affiliation to schools.

The Director (Academics) is the head of the Academic Unit. The major functions of the unit include developing the curriculum for all the subjects in academic and vocational streams at the secondary and senior secondary levels, to organise teacher training workshops, to develop support material for the guidance of the teachers and students, to publish text books for secondary and senior secondary classes and monitoring the academic projects.

The Controller of Examinations is responsible for all matters concerning examinations and administration of examinations, the major areas being pre and post examination work, coordination with regional offices for conducting annual secondary and senior school certificate examinations and All India Pre-Medical/Pre-Dental Entrance Examination.

The HOD (Edusat, Research and Development and vocational Education) is responsible for all matters concerning Distance Education through Education Satellite launched by ISRO and designing of curriculum for vocational subjects.

The HOD (Special Exams, Projects & Training) is responsible for all matters concerning the All India Engineering Entrance Exams. And Jawahar Navodaya Vidyalaya Selection Test etc.

KENDRIYA VIDYALAYAS

Kendriya Vidyalaya is a system of Central government schools under the Human resources ministry of the Government of India. The system came into being in 1965, named as "Central Schools", and has been affiliated to CBSE since then. It served the children of people in the defence services who were often posted to remote places. With the army starting its own Army Public Schools, the service was extended (but not restricted to) to all central government employees. The uniform curriculum followed by these schools all over India ensured that the children of government employees do not face educational difficulties when the parents are transferred. The name was later changed from "Central School" to "Kendriya Vidyalaya".

There are 981 Kendriya Vidyalayas at present including 4 outside India, having 10,18,581 students (as on 30.09.2008) and 48,262 employees (including outsoursed) on rolls (as on 01.03.2009). These have been divided amongst 21 regions each headed by an Assistant Commissioner. A body known as the Kendriya Vidyalaya Sangathan (Central School Organisation) oversees the schools.

Kendriya Vidyalayas try to promote egalitarian values among children of various socio-economic backgrounds.

Objectives

— To cater to the educational needs of the children of transferable Central Government employees including Defence and Para-Military personnel by providing a common programme of education;

— To pursue excellence and set pace in the field of school education;
— To initiate and promote experimentation and innovativeness in education in collaboration with other bodies like the Central Board of Secondary Education and National Council of Educational Research and Training etc.
— To develop the spirit of national integration and create a sense of "Indianness" among children.

Salient Features

— Common text-books and bilingual medium of instructions for all Kendriya Vidyalayas.
— All Kendriya Vidyalayas affiliated to Central Board of Secondary Education
— All Kendriya Vidyalayas are co-educational, composite schools.
— Sanskrit is taught from class VI to VII and optional as main subject in IX & X.

Schools Outside India

There are 4 K. V. schools outside India in Kathmandu, Moscow, Tehran and Kuwait. These are intended for children of Indian Embassy staff and other expatriate Indian central government employees. One K.V., located in Tshimalakha, Bhutan was transferred to Bhutan authorities thus ceasing to be a Kendriya Vidyalaya (then known as Indo-Bhutan Central School (IBCS)) in 1989, after one of the major Indo-Bhutan project (The Chukhha Hydal power project) was near completion and Indian government employees were gradually transferring back to their home country.

Management

The Kendirya Vidyalaya Sangathan is registered as a society under the Societies Registration Act (XXI of 1860). The primary aim of the Sangathan is to provide, establish, endow, maintain control and manage the Central Schools (Kendriya Vidyalayas) located all over India and abroad. The Sangathan has three tier management structure with its (I) Headquarters (II) Regional Offices managing a cluster about 45-50 schools and (III) Kendriya Vidyalayas spread all over the country and abroad each having their Vidyalaya Management Committees.

General Body

The general body of the Kendriya Vidyalaya Sangathan is the apex body. The Minister of Human Resource Development, in-charge of the Kendriya Vidyalayas scheme, is the Chairman of the Sangathan. The Minister of state in the Ministry of Human Resource Development is the Deputy Chairman and an Officer of the Ministry of Human Resource Development, specified by the Government of India for this purpose, is the Vice Chairman of the Sangathan. Other members are appointed by the Government of India from amongst senior officers of the Ministries of Finance, Defence, Works and Housing, Health and department of Personnel and Training as well as distinguished educationists including representatives of the Central Board of Secondary Education. National Council of Educational Research and Training and State Governments besides Members of Parliament, Women representatives and Members of Schedule Castes and Schedule Tribes.

Standing Committees

Finance Committee, Works Committee and Academic Advisory Committee are the Standing Committees of the Board of Governors of the Sangathan. The functions and powers of these Committees in brief, are as under:

— *Academic advisory committee:* To advice about the academic and co-curricular programmes of Kendriya Vidyalayas—to help prepare guidelines for implementation of these programmes—to help Kendriya Vidyalayas realise, among others, the objectives of the Sangathan, vis., to develop the Vidyalayas as "School of Excellence" in the context of the National goals of education—to promote national integration and to review publication programmes and suggest improvements.

— *Finance committee:* To scrutinise the accounts and budget estimates of the Sangathan—to consider and make recommendations to the Board for new expenditure on account of major work—to scrutinise re-appropriation statement and audit notes and to review the finances of the Sangathan besides getting concurrent audit conducted.

— *Works Committee*: To recommend the work policy of the Sangathan—to consider and approve the work programme—to prescribe norms for issue of administrative approval and expenditure sanction—to review the progress of construction work to advice the Board on policy matters relating to works programme.

VOCATIONALISATION OF EDUCATION

Education in our country was generally identified with liberal education and it was the Wood's Despatch (1854) which for the first time highlighted the need for introduction of occupational education for a sizeable segment of student population. But evidently this report did not make any noticeable impact until Hunter Commission was set up in 1882 to examine the problems of education as a whole especially of technical and vocational education. It recommended that at the high school stage there aught to be two distinctive streams first for preparing the students for entrance examination to the university courses and the second for practical occupations. These recommendations of the Hunter Commission, however, were not implemented.

Thirty years later the Calcutta University Commission recommended that "the intermediate colleges must be regarded as fulfilling a double purpose. In the first place, it must provide training such as will qualify its students for admission to the university, in different faculties or in other institutions of higher or technological training. In the second place it must provide training suitable for students, who after completing the courses will proceed directly into various practical occupations. As the system develops we should expect to find an increasing number of students entering upon the intermediate courses solely with a view to preparing for various practical careers".

The Hartog Committee (1929) and Sapru Committee (1934) both emphasised the vital role of vocational education in the country's economic development. The Hartog Committee recommended diversified courses in the schools to enable the students to prepare for industrial and commercial careers at the end of middle school stage, as preparation to special instruction in technical and industrial schools. The Sapru Committee recommended 11 years of school education (5 years for primary, 3 years for lower secondary and 3 years for higher secondary) with vocational studies commencing after 11 years of education. The main purpose of the Sapru Committee was to find ways and means of solving unemployment problem through diversified courses at the secondary stage. But it too made little impact on the educational administration.

Again Wood-Abbot Commission (1936) examined certain problems of education, specifically the vocational problem, and it was on the basis of this Report that a net-work of polytechnics was created in the country. The duration of polytechnic courses was two or three years depending upon the courses offered in such institutions. These courses were offered in Engineering or Technical Schools. The Sargent Report restated more or less what the Sapru Committee had recommended. It further recommended that the first year of the intermediate should be transferred to the high school and the second year to the university and also to introduce two streams: (a) academic (b) technical with the objective "to provide good all round education combined with some preparation in the later stages for careers which pupils will pursue on leaving the schools".

The Radhakrishnan Commission (1948) recommended that in order to direct the students to vocations at the end of Class X, a large number of intermediate colleges should be opened. "The aim of these colleges would be to meet a variety of needs of our youngmen and women by giving a vocational bias to their courses by retaining at the same time their value in a system of general education as preparation for university courses". Here again the stress was on preparation for higher studies rather than making some of them terminal.

The Mudaliar Commission (1952) reiterated that "the secondary education is a complete unit by itself and not merely a preparatory stage, that at the end of this period the student should be in a position, if he wishes, to enter into responsibilities of life and take up some vocations". It also recommended diversification of the courses at the secondary stage. This resulted in the Creation of multipurpose schools, Unfortunately, for various reasons including lack of proper appreciation of the scheme, inadequate preparation in terms of infrastructure and teaching staff and over-emphasis on preparation for university courses, the multipurpose schools were reduced to shadows of what were intended to develop.

Again in 1955, the All India Council of Technical Education was set up to advise the Union Government on all aspects of technical education at the diploma as well as degree levels. It was about the same time that a net-work of Industrial Training Institutes to train the base level industrial workers was started. To bridge the gap between the I.T.Is and Polytechnics. Junior or Technical schools were started with a view to continuing education with technical training for certain types of operational jobs in industries. This scheme also gradually suffered neglect and at present only 200 schools are in existence.

Some basic academic considerations again compelled the Government to appoint the Education Commission of 1964 under the Chairmanship of Dr. D. S. Kothari to re-examine the entire educational system of the country keeping in view the national goals, improvement of quality and standard of education.

The Kothari Commission considered the undesirable effects of uncontrolled admissions to the universities on the one hand and the resulting unemployment problem of the graduates on the other. It came to the firm conclusion that for majority of the occupations which the university graduates seek, the university degrees are not necessary and those jobs can be competently performed by well trained higher secondary students. Therefore, the Commission suggested that at the higher secondary stage there need be two distinctive streams: one preparing students for advanced education in the universities and the professional colleges and the other preparing for a variety of occupations immediately after completion of vocational studies which fit them into those vocations. In keeping with this recommendation the Commission suggested that for college preparatory general education courses the duration may be two years and the duration of studies and training for the vocational stream may range from one to three years or more.

Given the proper planning, cooperation, coordination and implementation of the scheme, the Commission felt, it should be possible to divert at least 50 per cent of the students who successfully complete 10 year education to the vocational stream thus reducing the pressure on the universities on the one hand and preparing the students for employment including self-employment on the other. For a majority of vocational higher secondary students it would be a terminal stage in a sense although further educational facilities should be made available on a large scale so that those in jobs may benefit through part-time or evening studies.

The National Policy of Education Resolution agrees with these recommendations of the Education Commission on vocational education. To quote :

> "There is need to increase facilities for technical and vocational education at secondary stage. Provisions of facilities for secondary and vocational education should conform particularly to requirements of the developing economy and real employment opportunities. Such linkage is necessary to make technical and vocational education at the secondary stage effectively terminal. The facilities for technical and vocational education should be suitably diversified to cover a large number of fields such as agriculture, industry, trade and commerce, medicine and public health, home management, arts and crafts and secretarial training."

The Central Advisory Board of Education, which is the highest body concerned with educational policy in the country, has also been exercised about this problem. While deliberating at its 37th Session held in November 1974, the Board observed that the amount of Rs. 10 crores provided in the draft Central Plan for the introduction of vocational courses at the higher secondary stage was inadequate and recommended that the provision should be substantially increased. The Board also observed that the new courses should be started after taking into account the existing facilities to meet the demand for middle level persons in the concerned district/State. They also suggested that the National Council of Educational Research and Training may work out model curricula and syllabi for such courses and provide guidelines to the State Governments.

The Central Advisory Board of Education at its 38th meeting held in November 1975, while noting with satisfaction the adoption of the educational pattern of 10+2+3 by most of the State Governments, deemed it necessary to stress the crucial importance of the 2 year stage between the school and university stages of education. It reiterated that this stage should be regarded not merely as college preparatory but as a period for preparing an increasingly larger number of school leavers for different vocations in life. The Board was also of the view that guidance and financial assistance by Central Government would enable State Governments to take quick and effective action in this direction and recommended the same.

The Conference of Ministers of Education of the States and Union Territories held at New Delhi in August, 1977 recommended that the new pattern (10+2) be implemented all over the country before the end of the Sixth Plan. It also urged reorganisation of higher secondary education, especially its vocationalisation, by providing for suitable internal restructuring and modification of content and by developing strong links between education and the various development departments such as industry and commerce, agriculture, health and community development.

Scheme for Vocationalisation

To ensure countrywide acceptance of the concept of vocationalisation and to assist the State Governments in establishing the relevance and importance of this concept to our socioeconomic needs, the Government of India launched during 1977 a centrally sponsored scheme of vocationalisation of higher secondary education. The main objective of the scheme is to encourage the State Governments to initiate the vocationalisation of education at plus 2 stage and to expand and consolidate it on a regular basis as a State Scheme in the Sixth Plan. The scheme has the following main components:

(i) District Vocational Surveys in 150 districts

(ii) Introduction of vocational courses in 40 selected districts.

The central assistance will be provided for the following items

(i) Conduct of district vocational surveys;

(ii) Appointment of District Vocational Education Officers;

(iii) Purchase of equipment for vocational courses; and

(iv) Salary of teachers for vocational courses.

The other allied expenses were to be met by the State Governments themselves. Rupees 2 crores were sanctioned for implementation of this scheme during the Fifth Five Year Plan. The scheme itself was cleared only towards the end of February, 1977 for implementation.

Till the end of financial year 1977-78, financial assistance has been released for the conduct of vocational surveys in 55 selected districts of Assam, Gujarat, Jammu and Kashmir, Karnataka, Madhya Pradesh, Maharashtra, Nagaland, Orissa, Rajasthan, Sikkim, Tamil Nadu and Tripura. Under the scheme vocational courses have been introduced in three districts of Karnataka and one district of Sikkim from the academic year 1977-78. To strengthen the efforts of the Government of West Bengal which has already introduced the vocational courses financial assistance under the scheme was released for the purchase of equipment only. The Government of Maharashtra has also decided to introduce vocational courses in 5 districts from the academic year 1978-79 under the scheme. Financial assistance for making preparatory work has been sanctioned. The other States have been requested to identify districts for conduct of surveys and apply for financial assistance under the central scheme. It has been decided to continue the scheme during the year 1978-79. No doubt several States/ Union Territories have introduced programmes of vocationalisation, but most of them are experimenting on a pilot basis in their own way. It is too early to assess the impact and ultimate usefulness of this programme at this stage. However, a brief account of the working in some of the States may be of interest.

According to the National Pattern of Education, Central Board of Secondary Education (CBSE) has provided two streams-academic and vocational at plus 2 stage. The vocational courses have been designed to be terminal in character, but at the same time vertical link is provided both with the courses of academic nature as well as vocational and technical nature. The courses have been designed for a duration of 2 years coinciding with the duration of academic courses in the transitional stage as it is difficult to locate the facilities in or out of school for the extended courses. The CBSE adopted the scheme of studies and the courses prepared by the NCERT.

The courses offered by CBSE as under:

Agricultural vocations

— Inland Fisheries

— Agriculture

Commerce and business related vocations

— Office Management and Secretarial Practice

— Stenography

— Accountancy and Auditing

Engineering and technical vocations

— Basic Electrical Technology

— Electronic Technology

— Air-Conditioning and Refrigeration Technology

— Furniture making and designing

Vocations related to home science

— Nutrition and Food Preparation

— Canteen Management

— Dress Making and Designing

— Textile and Designs

Miscellaneous

— Photography

However the enrolment to these courses are not satisfactory. Some of the reasons for luke-warm response to the vocational courses are:

(i) A great majority of the students wish to seek employment in organised sector; therefore, very few students like to take risk with the career unless one is sure that a particular course would lead him to a specified job.

(ii) The climate for self-employment is still not encouraging so that the students with the type of training provided in the schools could feel themselves confident to risk a heavy investment;

(iii) A heavy investment is needed by the school in terms of equipment and teachers which can be rendered useless by the changing demands of the employment market. This factor has discouraged several institutions to come forward for vocational courses; and

(iv) Owing to geographical distances, particularly with reference to CBSE schools, it has not been possible to share the limited resources available. This has further increased the cost of investment.

In order to make courses more attractive, experience suggests that these courses need be designed at the grass-root level, particularly by the schools themselves. This is all the more necessary owing to the fact that the students who have to terminate their studies to enter main stream of life would settle by and large in the same area where they have grown up. Their employment market, therefore, lies in their own districts or the States. The courses, therefore, should be relevant to the local requirements and be acceptable to the industry, trade or any other organised sector in the area.

Basic Principles

Vocationalisation of education is a major thrust in the reconstruction of present educational system. While it is recognised that modern education cannot sacrifice its liberal content totally, its principal aim should be to equip the youth with such manual skills founded on basic scientific principles as would be needed in today's society and with capacity to adapt to ever changing scientific and technological developments. The vocationalisation of education has to be looked from the point of view of the country's special needs and the goals set by the Government. Thus the new education envisages an appropriate blend of training in practical arts for the fulfilment of these goals, the requirements of employing agencies in terms of attitudes, competencies, skill excellence and adaptability to change. Education itself does not produce jobs but vocationalised education makes an individual more employable.

Our economy being a developing one, there must be an adequate supply of personnel for higher administrative and professional levels, as also unskilled and semi-skilled manpower for the lower levels. But there are also crucial middle level supervisory and other positions without which neither production can be increased nor services improved. Through vocationalisation of education we can prepare middle level manpower who would not merely be superior to skilled workers but who would work with their brains as well as their hands. They would interact with others to produce new goods and services, which may satisfy a long felt need of the Community.

The accent on self-employment is an index of anxiety that all those who qualify in vocational studies are unlikely to secure gainful jobs of their choice. Further vocational education at no stage can be a guarantee for jobs. Millions of jobs cannot be created year after year whatever be the growth rate. One of the chief aims of vocational education is to produce entrepreneurs with special emphasis on agriculture including agro-based and small and cottage industries who through adventurous efforts and abilities, become creators of jobs for themselves and also for others. But entrepreneurship and self-employment are not meant for all.

There may be a small but a significant percentage, who will dare to embark upon their own enterprises. They require not only first class skill mastery but the art and science of management of money, machines and men. Specialised entrepreneurship courses must be offered by experts and experienced entrepreneurs or business managers. These will be the future captains of new industries, banks, medical practitioners on whom the society will depend for its needs and progress. Financial assistance, adequate training, apprenticeship in big concerns and continued interest in solving their problems at the initial stages should be provided until they succeed and this requires an imaginative investment policy and administrative set-up.

Schools for Vocational Studies

There are academic and sociological reasons to impart vocational training in the same school where general education is imparted to destroy the unhealthy mental barriers of status, means, intellectual abilities etc. among the students who are admitted to academic and vocational streams. It would also result in economising initial investment by making use of the existing facilities of classrooms, laboratories, library, play grounds, etc. The academic and vocational streams will be controlled by the Higher Secondary Boards and therefore, the question of recognition will present no special problems.

On the other hand there are equally weighty arguments for offering vocational courses in separate institutions. In such institutions there is a greater possibility that the academic as well as vocational teachers will devote all their attention to the students and better cohesion between theory and practice is likely to be achieved. If both the streams are located in the same school the students of one stream will necessarily work for longer hours than the other to acquire practical skills. The academic stream being essentially college preparatory it is necessary that duration of the course is rigidly for two year. On the other hand, the vocational courses will have to be conducted for varying durations and the instruction should follow modular system. Therefore, the evaluation system, the methods of instruction and duration of courses will have to be different.

The Vocational Courses will have to be affiliated to the Councils of Vocational Education for purposes of National and State recognition. Naturally, the school administration will not be happy to be controlled by multiple agencies. The past experience in certain States of the Country where academic and vocational streams were conducted under one roof provides clear indications that psychological factors that were expected to diminish with time, instead, became more acute. Experience cannot be expected to be different for some years to come.

Therefore, even if any school has a capacity to run both the streams it is essential that the school has a separate wing or set-up to conduct the vocational courses. But the choice of such schools will have to be made very carefully and continuous supervision will have to be maintained.

To economise on the initial investment all industry-oriented courses should be added on to the existing polytechnics and ITIs. Some schools in the neighbourhood of industries could be attached to the industries with their cooperation and assistance. The paramedical courses should be provided in selected schools close to the hospitals and medical colleges. Vocational schools in commerce and home science will have to be equipped properly. The investment on them may not be prohibitive. The resources of the new defunct Junior Technical Schools and Multipurpose Schools lying unused should be fully harnessed and supplemented. As far as possible new facilities in selected schools on pilot basis should offer those vocational courses for which the existing institutions cannot provide adequate facilities and the demand for supply of new skills are evident.

Since adequate facilities for vocational education in rural areas are not available, all the new schools to provide vocational studies should be constructed in rural areas only and should be adequately equipped. It is recommended that at least 500 new schools may be constructed in a phased manner.

Existing Facilities

Many of the existing technical and vocational schools have either reverted to academic instruction or deteriorated on account of neglect, inadequate supply of raw materials, and poor pay-scales to teachers. These institutions should be revitalised with appropriate inputs and attractive pay-scales for instructional staff. New vocational courses for which there is good demand should be added to these institutions and adequate facilities should be provided in them.

There are 327 polytechnics, which offer about 42 diploma courses in technical subjects and 13 in Commerce subjects. The durations of these diploma courses vary from two to three years. Some polytechnics also offer post diploma courses. About 80% of them offer traditional courses in civil, mechanical and electrical engineering. To make optimum use of the existing facilities, it is recommended that new courses in these major areas may be added to the polytechnics wherever necessary, strengthening the existing facilities if necessary.

There are 365 Industrial Training Institutes offering training in 53 trades mostly industry-oriented. Of them about a dozen require pass in 7th Standard and the rest pass in 10th Standard for admission. The durations of courses vary from 6 months to 2 years. Apprenticeship facilities with stipends are offered to those having courses of one year's duration or more. At present 103 trades are listed for apprenticeship, but many trades which have been designated do not have training facilities so far. It is, therefore, recommended that such courses may be identified for introduction in ITIs if the job potential is good for them.

Some high schools should be converted wholly into craft schools if there is good scope for employment and offer a variety of craft training. Besides, the existing facilities of the craft schools should also be expanded to accommodate new crafts as warranted by the vocational surveys. If the craft schools have deteriorated or have become defunct in the past it is on account of the non-availability of raw materials required for continuous work, inadequate physical facilities in terms of equipment and building space, poor scales of pay for the craft teachers and general apathy of the administration towards craft schools. If these institutions are to be revitalised it is necessary that these bottlenecks will have to be removed and steps taken to make the schools attractive. Since mostly the students from low income groups will be opting for these courses, adequate incentives in the form of scholarships should be offered to them. For the disposal of the finished products adequate marketing facilities will have to be created through cooperative ventures. All craft courses, as far as possible, should be so designed that they should lead to advance training in these disciplines through vocational higher secondary courses.

Teachers

The role of teachers is crucial in the scheme of implementation. It is the teacher who translates the scheme into action through well thought out instructional plan in the classrooms, laboratories, agricultural fields, workshops, hospitals, banks, cooperative stores, hotels, etc. There is perhaps sufficient expertise available in the basic subjects but very little in the new vocational subjects which may be selected for introduction. To prepare or train the adequate number of teachers requires time and the scheme cannot wait until then. On the other hand, half-baked or ill-trained teachers may destroy the whole scheme because of their poor understanding or incompetence. These are mutually irreconcilable aspects.

For a vocational subject a teacher has to be one who has first class practical competence; he must also possess the comprehensive knowledge of scientific principles underlying the practicals. But a person who has a good background in theory only in our context will not be able to impart the practical skills. A compromise is needed at least in the initial stages. It is, therefore, necessary that a practitioner from the particular vocation is invited to participate in the instructional work and arrange for his training in instructional methods through short term courses-perhaps summer institutes. Simultaneously regular staff in certain areas may be appointed and trained. There is an advantage in having persons from the field to instruct the students. Not only the latest practices will be imparted and through his influence regular on-the-job training can be arranged but it may even ensure employment to the students ultimately resulting in a good collaborative arrangement.

Part-time teachers on suitable remunerations from the vocational fields should be employed. Many private agencies have training centres from which we can draft the instructors. Many retired defence service personnel with appropriate skills can also be appointed on short-term basis. But certain percentage of teaching complement must be appointed in each school on regular basis. Periodical re-training of teachers, to keep them abreast of their knowledge in appropriate trades, should be arranged. The Technical Teacher Training Institutes, the Regional Colleges of Education, the Central Training Institutes and Small Scale Service Institutes should be involved in the teacher training programmes. To ensure the success of this programme it is recommended that where vocational courses are imparted either the Head or deputy-head of the institution should possess vocational qualification.

Curriculum Preparation

A curriculum generally indicates the framework of aims and objectives of a course, the syllabus, instruction in the classroom, laboratory or workshop, teaching materials and evaluation. The main aim is to design appropriate curricula for vocational courses to attract a sizeable section of student population to vocational streams and to provide alternative avenues of training which prepare them for gainful vocations in their future careers.

The curriculum should be so designed as to develop skills of the levels and quality acceptable to the employing agencies; for, the test of effectiveness of the curriculum lies in the employability of the student. To integrate appropriate components of education and skill acquisition in the curricula, it is most desirable to bring together the experts from the employing agencies and academics and entrust them with the task. Preparing curricula centrally should be done away with. In preparing the curricula broadly the following is considered to be most appropriate :

1. Language 15% of total instructional time
2. Basic subjects relevant to vocations 20%
3. Vocational studies and Practice 65 %

Since a variety of courses of different durations are likely to be offered it will be highly advantageous to offer them in terms of well connected units or modules which are complete in themselves. A student may be permitted to receive instruction in as many modules as he desires to go through and on the completion of each module his performance shall be evaluated and certificate issued. For admission to any advanced courses later, completion of certain number of modules may be prescribed which he will be required to complete before seeking admission to a selected course. Revision of curricula must be a continuous process to help identifying shortcomings and making modifications in the light of student and teacher performance.

Textbooks

As teachers, the good textbooks and teaching aids are indispensable prerequisites. Well illustrated books with good practical details without sacrificing the underlying scientific principles have to be ready before the courses are introduced.

The production of suitable textbooks for a large variety of vocations will be a formidable and time consuming job. It is, therefore, recommended that in the initial stages suitable publications may be procured from the countries where similar courses are conducted and be made available to teachers and students for consultations and study. Simultaneously, if publishers are encouraged to find knowledgeable authors who can write well illustrated books in clear and simple language with authentic practical details on the models of the foreign publications, keeping the local conditions in view, it will help solve our problems more expeditiously and also provide incentives to the publishers. Simultaneously, Teacher guides based on the textbooks should be got prepared to help the teachers to modify their methods of instruction.

Courses for Rural Sector

At present the vocational schools are located mostly in the cities and towns and all the rural students who desire to benefit from vocational studies have no option but to move to urban centres. The courses invariably have urban leanings and a majority of the rural students seldom return to the villages after completion of their education as the urban set-up offers easier life, and several attractions. This is a great loss to the families who derive nothing out of their sacrifice. To combat these Problems imaginative steps will have to be taken not only to offer the type of education of their choice but also to create such conditions in their own surroundings which may provide them with a fairly decent living. If this could be achieved the problem of migration from rural to urban areas can be arrested.

The women population in rural areas have to be given even greater attention. In villages the family structure and age old practices are stronger than in towns and the system of education and training will have to eliminate the prejudices systematically and surely by offering congenial atmosphere in schools and opportunities of employment or self-employment. Social barriers are breaking down but not fast enough. The working group, therefore, feels that the solution to the rural problems would require much greater care and attention than the urban sector and it is the right time to tackle the problems without further delay.

Vocational Courses generally with agricultural bias should be introduced in rural areas. Vocationalisation of education may be linked with the new strategies for rural development and village uplift through various programmes like small and marginal farmers development, integrated tribal development, drought prone area development, community area development and integrated rural development etc. These programmes will generate enormous opportunities for various types of skills and competencies and will broaden the scope of vocationalisation in rural sector.

Courses on modern methods of crop production through mechanised farming, use of appropriate types of fertilisers, methods of irrigation etc. should be offered to those who are likely to benefit from such education and training and possess land holdings of 3 hectares and more. On the other hand vegetable and fruit culture and seed production may offer lucrative proposition to small and marginal farmers. Cash crops such as mulberry, areca, coffee, coconuts, spices etc. can be raised when good irrigation facilities and climatic conditions favour. These courses should provide the special knowledge and techniques required for such cultivation.

Courses of various durations on animal husbandry, dairying and dairy products, poultry farming etc. should be offered for gainful self-employment.

Courses on repairing and maintenance of farm machines like tractors, power tillers, pumping sets, plant protection equipment, threshers and others relevant to the rural needs should also be provided.

These courses will provide opportunities for self-employment and wage employment in their own neighbourhood. Cold storage of vegetable, milk processing, knitting and embroidery, designing and weaving of carpets, food preservation etc. will be equally attractive courses for girls.

Courses for Urban Sector

Most of the industries, business enterprises, administrative offices, higher educational institutions and health organisations are located in cities and towns, and the living patterns are essentially dictated by the activities in them. The middle-level employment opportunities will be mostly in the industries, public works departments, offices, hospitals, business centres, banks, educational institutions and many social service organisations. For most of the engineering and technological jobs adequate training facilities are available in the polytechnics and industrial training institutes.

Trade and commerce offer a fertile field for a variety of jobs and require minimum financial inputs. When the plan targets for the export reach 10 thousand crores, as it is expected to reach in a year or two, middle level services such as stenographers, office assistants, accountants, import-export assistants etc. will be needed in large numbers. The demand cannot be met with the present institutional training facilities. Good Commercial Schools will then have to be started at the higher secondary stage as an advance preparation.

Textile printing, garment making, knitting, banking and confectionery and cosmetics are areas quite fertile and offer vast scope for self-employment. Handicrafts have good export potential. Khadi and Gramudyog Commission has big plans for expanding its activities which are expected to throw up large employment potential. For all these vocations facilities will have to be created.

In view of the large shortage in paramedical forces, especially in rural sector, creation of new facilities should be given priority. Since paramedical courses cannot be conducted in every vocational school, it is recommended that a certain number of new schools should be developed in the neighbourhoods of medical colleges and hospitals and offer suitable courses by utilising the services of the qualified staff and on-the-job training facilities available there. This will help to meet the needs of these institutions and also the requirements of the society.

Repair, maintenance of common domestic appliances such as electrical gadgets, refrigerators, scooters, motorcycles etc. have very good self-employment potential. Adequate training facilities are worth creating in big cities like Delhi, Calcutta, Bombay, Madras, Bangalore, Hyderabad and Kanpur.

A variety of other occupations which have bright job opportunities but for which no training facilities available are likely to increase with the development of small scale, tiny and cottage industries. Ancillary industries around big manufacturing centres will also spring up. The existing instructional facilities will hardly be able to cope up the demand for new skills especially in non-industrial areas. Therefore, adequate facilities will have to be provided.

In view of the revolutionary changes in science and technology and the contemplated social transformation, the training in narrow job specifications or in over specialised employment in other areas might become obsolescent with changing pattern of production. It is therefore recommended that the vocational courses should be designed with good knowledge in basic subjects so as to help the student adapt to changing developments or easily undergo retraining in an allied skill.

The aspirations of the students for superior positions on the employment ladder cannot be ignored and this can be done when the system permits him to secure further qualifications for vertical and horizontal mobility whenever they desire or opportunities occur. While most of the students of the Vocational Courses will enter into the world of work either through self-employment or by taking up a job, for those who wish to continue and improve their qualifications, there should be a provision for allowing them admission in technical and professional institutions in specialised areas of their interests. Similarly universities should not close the doors for those who wish to pursue further studies by suitably offering package courses in different subjects.

Further Educational Facilities

Learning is a continuous process, therefore, part-time, on-the-job vocational and technical training should be made available for those who have entered employment and wish to improve their professional competence through further education. Such courses may be of varying duration and may include part-time courses, correspondence courses, sandwich courses, etc.

The industries mostly have developed on the imported technologies and know-how. These industries demand higher level skills to cope with the operation of sophisticated machinery and equipment. It is likely that as the present industrial practices go obsolete and more advanced techniques are adopted and newer machinery installed, the workers and supervisory staff also need updating their skills and knowledge. Therefore, advanced specialised training facilities have to be planned. Besides, those engaged in farming and agro-based industries, small entrepreneurs and those working in small scale and cottage industries, paramedical technicians, secretarial staff and the like may desire to improve their professional status through further education. It is very necessary, therefore, to plan in specialised advanced diploma courses whose standards are equivalent to university degrees. These advanced courses must be distinctly different from the traditional university courses and be indicative of the levels of specialisation. Even if these diplomas are awarded in the traditional colleges they must bear the stamp of professional excellence and acceptance.

The Education Commission in its wisdom felt that in modern world whose activities are so comprehensively and completely controlled by the fantastic developments in science and technology, every child must be equipped to meet the challenges it will have to face in its life span and for such a preparation the first ten-year education should be general for all the students and include comprehensive studies in elementary science, mathematics, social sciences and humanities.

Socially useful productive work should be integrated with the general education to equip the students with certain elementary skills that will enable them to take care of simple functions such as repair and maintenance of domestic appliances and vehicles, care of garments, raising vegetables, rendering social services etc. These not only are productive in a sense but inspire self-confidence and self-dependence among the children. The student may also gain some special proficiency in a particular skill. Since a segment of students drop out at the end of ten-year schooling, the elementary exploratory experiences in general would hardly be sufficient to help him to enter life. This opinion is held by some educationists. In a way this may however, serve as pre-vocational training for those who may opt for vocational studies later.

An important factor that controls and promotes the pre-vocational training is the availability of means of training for a variety of student interests, aptitudes and inclinations. In this the practice of socialist countries can be profitably emulated. Creative work centres can be established in chosen localities with facilities and equipment which the schools cannot provide for on-the-job practice or production of goods. They can be kept open for long hours of the day for all students, say, of age-group 14 to 16. The finished products prepared by the students, if of good quality, can be sold and the sale proceeds may be able to bring revenue to meet the raw-material cost and also some earning to the students. But this assumes that well-qualified training personnel are available and the creative work centres are equipped with a variety of equipment.

Recruitment Policy

While the largest proportion of job-opportunities relate to middle level employment it has been observed that advertisement concerning 80 % of such jobs prescribe a university degree as an essential qualification irrespective of the job-requirements. What is needed in most of these positions is adequate skill and proficiency to perform duties efficiently and not a university degree. This could be secured through suitable vocational education/training without the university education.

In view of this there is full justification that employment policy of the Government as well as public undertakings should be so revised that wherever vocationally qualified persons are available they should be preferred to graduates and they should be entitled to the pay scales and promotional avenues available to the graduates, so long as the jobs performed are the same or similar. They should also be given opportunities for superior positions when they improve their qualifications through correspondence or evening courses or block time training. Such a recruitment policy will provide the greatest incentive to, the really intelligent students to join the vocational streams especially those coming from low income groups and would go a long way in creating a favourable reaction among the students and more so among their parents. This factor alone in due course will make vocational institutions more popular than academic institutions.

National Council of Vocational Education

At present different Vocational Courses are controlled by different Ministries and organisations, statutory or otherwise, having professional control over certain vocations. The Indian Council of Agricultural Research is responsible for agricultural education at university and polytechnic levels; the All India Council for Technical Education at the Centre and the State Boards of Technical Education in the States control Polytechnic education while the Industrial Training Institutes are controlled by the Directorates of Employment and Training in the Ministry of Labour; all the paramedical schools are under the control of statutory councils, such as the Nursing Council, the Pharmacy Council and Dental Council. Since all these organisations are functioning independently there is no co-ordination or cooperation. There is replication of efforts and financial investment. Each of these organisations is functioning in isolation safeguarding its interests jealously even though each is offering education and training for middle level jobs. To avoid the wastage of resources and to bring cooperation and co-ordination among various agencies there must be an Apex Body in a Department of the Government.

All the agencies imparting vocational education in the fields of paramedical, agriculture and technical etc. shall be affiliated to the State Councils of Vocational Education in the States and to the National Council at the national level. The constitution, membership and its functions have to be worked out in clear terms. These councils should ensure, quality and standard of vocational education, co-ordination and cooperation among all agencies which are at present offering vocational education and those connected with employment.

Strengthening of Education Department

Vocationalisation of education falls under the purview of school education although the programmes in vocational streams may extend beyond two years of study at the higher secondary stage. The responsibility of planning, co-ordination, monitoring and evaluation of the programmes, therefore, naturally belongs to the Department of the Government which is dealing with the school education at the higher secondary stage.

Naturally, the experiment being new and of considerable magnitude with the attendant complexities, it should be headed by very senior officer of the Ministry, not in any case lower than that of a Bureau-Head, who will be supported by adequate competent staff and other facilities. The Bureau of School Education will be responsible for ensuring proper implementation of the policies laid down and the schemes set by the NCVE through the appropriate State Government Bodies.

The Bureau will also be responsible for ensuring provision of infrastructural facilities, appointment of competent instructional staff-full time and part time-purchase of equipment, periodical inspection of schools etc. Most importantly the Bureau will co-ordinate the work of the different Ministries insofar as the vocational programmes are concerned and will work out the guiding principles for implementation of the scheme efficiently and economically, scheme of execution, control and monitoring.

Obligation of Government and Private Sector

The Government have a great obligation to the present and future generations in offering a system of education relevant to the vital needs of the nation and the urgent requirements of the masses. Political will, enlightened and imaginative administration and daring to learn from mistakes committed in the past and the present, a will to identify the causes of failure and to find solutions are the major tasks before the Government. However, this huge task, cannot be accomplished without the willing cooperation of all concerned.

The country should encourage private voluntary organisations and also the patriotic individuals to participate in this national venture by offering incentives to start new schools and allowing certain autonomy to run them. Incentives may also be provided by allowing certain Tax exemptions in lieu of Training facilities provided to the students of vocational stream. Investment in vocational education is an investment for the future generation. The country should find necessary resources to make this investment lest the coming generations should hold the present one responsible for all their miseries and problems.

Issues in Secondary Education

The key issues relating to secondary education highlighted in the Tenth Plan are: greater focus on improving access; reducing disparities by emphasising the Common School System; renewal of curricula with emphasis on vocationalisation and employment-oriented courses; expansion and diversification of the Open Learning System; reorganisation of teacher training and greater use of ICT. The Tenth Plan objectives for secondary education are in consonance with the broad parameters and strategy of the National Policy on Education (NPE) of 1986 and the Programme of Action of 1992. These include: Extending access in un-served areas and educationally backward areas with concentration of SC/ST population. A uniform educational structure of 10+2+3, with the first 10 years envisaged as a stage of general education with undifferentiated courses providing basic knowledge in languages, science (including social and natural science) and mathematics.

The higher secondary stage to provide for diversified courses with emphasis on vocationalisation. Vocational education is to become a distinct stream, intended to prepare students for identified occupations spanning several areas of activity, at the +2 stage. The social, gender based and regional disparities need to be addressed. Educationally backward districts should receive greater support for school infrastructure. Besides providing new schools need-based up-gradation of upper primary schools will have to be given greater priority. The quality of education needs to be improved with investments in teacher education, training laboratories, libraries and encouraging parents to invest in their children's education. The State Boards of Secondary Education needs to be strengthened.

References

Department of Secondary and Higher Education (2004–2006). *Annual Reports 2004–05 and 2005–06.* New Delhi: Ministry of Human Resource Development.

Gibbons M, Limoges C, Nowotny H, Schwartzman S, Scott P, Trow M., (1994) *The New Production of Knowledge*, Sage Publications, London.

Mahajan Baldev and others (1994), *Education Administration in Madhya Pradesh* (NIEPA), Vikas Publishing House, New Delhi.

Rudolph, S. and Rudolph, L. (1972) *Education and politics in India*. Oxford University Press. Delhi.

Sargent (1968) *Society, Schools and Progress in India.* Pergamon Press. London.

7

Technical Education System

The history of imparting formal technical education in India can be traced back to mid 19th century, although it got momentum in 20th century with the set up of Constitution of Technical Education Committee of the Central University Board of Education (CABE) in 1943; Preparation of Sergeant Report in 1944 and Formation of All India Council of technical Education (AICTE) in 1945. With the country gaining independence in 1947, the development of technical education had become a major concern for the government of India to face the new challenges and move the country forward.

The set up of Indian Institutes of Technology, Indian Institutes of Management and Indian Institutes of Science was a major step in the development of technical education in the country. The quality of education of these institutes have managed to change the outlook of India so much that this ancient country which was earlier known for yoga and mediation is now known for computer engineers. However, it does not mean that the challenge of making technical education accessible to the rural populace and other under developed sections of the society has been overcome.

In order to maintain the standard of technical education, a statutory authority—The All India Council for Technical Education (AICTE)—was set up in 1945. AICTE is responsible for planning, formulation and maintenance of norms and standards, quality assurance through accreditation, funding in priority areas, monitoring and evaluation, maintaining parity of certification and awards and ensuring coordinated and integrated development and management of technical education in the country.

The courses, which are known as 'technical' in India and therefore come under the purview of All India Council of Technical Education are —degree and diploma courses in Engineering, Master degree Courses in Engineering, Master of Computer Application (MCA), Master of Business Administration (MBA), Pharmacy Courses, Courses in Architecture and Applied Arts and Hotel Management and Catering Technology Courses.

As the technical education courses in India are quite diverse, the number of institutes providing technical courses in India is also huge. The number of AICTE approved institutes that offer engineering degree courses in India is —4,39,689. There are around 1244 institutes in India that offer diploma courses in engineering, 415 institutes offer diploma courses in Pharmacy, 63 institutes offer diploma courses in Hotel Management and Catering Technology Courses and 25 AICTE approved institutes that offer diploma courses in Architecture. The number of AICTE approved institutes that offer master of Computer Application courses in India is 1012. Likewise the AICTE also approves institutes from time to time institutes that offer MBA courses, M.E./M.Tech, Architecture and Applied Arts Courses, Hotel Management and Catering Technology Courses.

Given the importance of technical education in the further development of the nation, the Government of India is keen on developing some more institutes in the line of IITs, IIMs and IISCs. The Prime Minister of India has unleashed a plan to establish 8 IITs, 7 IIMs and 5 IISCs to improve the spread and quality of technical education in the country. These institutes along with various private institutes and foreign technical colleges have the potential of making technical education accessible to all sections of society in India without compromising on the quality of education.

Technical Education Programmes

Technical manpower in India is developed through a system of publicly and privately financed training and educational institutions, informal sector apprenticeship-type training arrangements, and the in-plant training programmes conducted by public and private sector enterprises. The formal system of technical education operates at five levels-certificate, diploma, degree, post-graduate and research degree programmes.

Certificate level programmes produce skilled workers and are operated at about 1,900 Industrial Training Institutes (ITIs) run by the Directorate General of Employment and Training (DGET) in the Union Ministry of Labour. Nearly 3,25,000 students are trained annually in about 140 trade areas. The entry requirement to these programmes is 10 years of basic education. Vocational education certificate level courses are offered in agriculture, business, commerce, health and paramedical, home science and humanities areas, in addition to engineering trades. Another 1,500 vocational schools offer these courses, admitting about 72,000 students annually. The National Council for Vocational Training, and the Directorates of Vocational Training in the States look after the planning and operation of these programmes at the national and state levels respectively.

Diploma programmes producing middle-level supervisory staff are offered in about 950 polytechnics. Admission to this programme requires 10 years of basic education. The courses are of three years' duration in the engineering disciplines. About 20% of the polytechnics offer programmes in other fields also. In all, programmes are offered in about 90 engineering and non-engineering disciplines admitting about 1,26,000 students annually. A few institutions conduct post-diploma and advanced-diploma programmes in selected areas.

Degree level programmes in engineering are conducted at the 5 Indian Institutes of Technology (IITs), the IISc and four technical universities, 17 Regional Engineering Colleges (RECs), a few 'deemed university' institutions and University departments and about 350 State-level Engineering Colleges (SECs). The 5 IITs, IISc and technical universities also offer postgraduate and research degree programmes with a bias to technology development and admit about 1,300 students for research and graduate programmes each year. These are national institutions and are fully funded by the Government of India. Of the 17 RECs 14 offer postgraduate and research degree programmes. They have an annual intake of about 5,000 for Bachelor's Degree and 1,400 for postgraduate courses. There are about 350 State-level Engineering Colleges which mainly offer undergraduate programmes with an annual intake of about 68,000 students. About 90 of these institutions also offer post-graduate programmes with an annual intake of about 8,500 students. In addition, there are nearly 50 institutions, including the 4 Indian Institutes of Management providing management education to over 4,000 students annually.

There are considerable imbalances and variations amongst these various types of institutions in the average annual recurring cost per student and in the quality of the graduates they produce. For example, for the degree programmes, the annual recurring cost per student ranges between Rs. 15,000 and Rs. 60,000 in the well established institutions of different types. However, in some institutions with inadequate facilities and faculty the unit cost is much less. The AICTE has worked out the annual recurring cost per student for engineering colleges as Rs. 11,916 at the 1988 price levels. These are based on somewhat liberal norms. If an annual increase of 5 to 10 percent is allowed for, this figure works out to Rs. 15,200 to 19,200 in 1993. These figures are bound to escalate at a much faster rate due to several reasons such as rapid obsolescence of laboratory equipment; emergence of expensive high-tech instrumentation, machinery and equipment; and the phenomenal increase in cost of books, journals and annual maintenance of sophisticated and proprietary equipments and components.

Research and Development

One year after independence, India spent only a meagre Rs. 11 million on R & D activity in the Central Government sector. Four decades later, the figure grew to more than Rs. 30,000 million. In the year 1991-92, Rs. 38,272.3 million were spent on R & D by the Central Government. The approximate corresponding figures for the states sector and the private sector are Rs. 3,719.4 million and Rs. 6,314.7 million bringing the total expenditure on R & D in 1991-92 to Rs. 48,306.4 million.

Another significant factor is the multiplicity of R & D agencies in the country, leading to a particular agency specialising in a particular type of activity. There is a preponderance of Central Government expenditure on R & D in almost all spheres of activity. It is worth examining the growth of R & D in industry. The Government has taken several measures to promote research in industry. By the end of 1990-91, there were 1,164 in-house R & D units, in both the public and private sectors, and it is likely to grow to around 1,500 by the year 1995. The growth of R & D in industry remains, however, unimpressive. In-house R & D activity is bound to receive a set-back at times of severe resource shortages. Advertising expenditure and expenditure required for purchase of plant and machinery etc. compete with R & D expenditure and, in a profit-oriented environment, take precedence for achieving short-term goals.

R & D expenditure by industry, as a percentage of total R & D expenditure, is only 21% in India, compared to 61% in U.K., 63% in Japan and 72% in U.S.A. The time has come for the Indian industry to increase its contribution to R & D through in-house R & D units and/or through supporting research in universities and technical education institutions. This is essential for survival against global competition.

ISSUES AND SOLUTIONS

Technical institutions and university departments offering technical courses are presently faced with the challenge of meeting the steadily escalating cost of salaries, materials and services, maintenance, library books and journals, replacement of instruments and equipment, modernisation of institution and development of laboratories, workshops and other teaching facilities without loss of quality of education. The resource constraints have not affected the private unaided institutions to the same degree as they are able to meet their recurring, non-recurring, and development expenditures mainly through the fees charged from students, the fees being fixed at a fairly high level and revised from time to time. The recent constraints in resource availability for public funding of technical education have compelled the concerned authorities in the Governments and institutions to examine ways and, means of keeping the institution running without loss of quality and slackening of efforts towards modernisation and development.

Planning of Expenditure and Grants

As the Government assistance to meet the requirements of the institutions have until recently been taken for granted, the institutions have not been making any effort towards long term resource planning. A good number of the Government-funded and aided institutions have expanded in size and academic programmes without any consideration of cost effectiveness. As a result, the members of the technical and non-technical supporting staff and infrastructure in these have become large and disproportionate to the strength of students. Several institutions have been established in recent years with uneconomical levels of student intake, both overall and branchwise.

While there is need for long term resource planning by each institution for managing the system in a very cost effective manner, the Governments both at Centre and State levels should have a clearcut policy on consolidation and expansion of technical institutions with emphasis on economy of scale. With the recent Government directives towards freezing of non-plan grants and also reduction in developmental grants despite regular increases in pay and allowances, the institutions have been taken by surprise and are accordingly finding it difficult to bring about the desired economy in expenditure in a short time. It is felt that both the institutions and the Government should undertake realistic planning for the present and the future. Through long term policy guidelines the institutions may be told of their obligations to enable them to prepare plans for running and developing the institutions without loss of quality and without the need for crisis management.

Substantial investments are being made nationally, both in public and private sectors, in engineering industries as well as in service sectors such as energy, petrochemicals, mining, fertilisers, processing, transport, telecommunications, housing, etc., all of which require significant technical manpower support. It is then but natural to expect that a portion of the investments earmarked for these activities is allocated to the development of the required technical manpower and such an approach built into the planning process. With such a philosophy, it is not at all difficult for the governments to mobilise adequate resources for development of technical education.

In a growing economy it is essential to increase the quantum, and quality of technical education. In this context Government support for new programmes in existing institutions and for the establishment of new institutions is unavoidable. Therefore, at a national level there should be a reservoir of funds that guarantees unhindered development of technical education. With such funds earmarked for financing technical education and R & D activities, this sector does not have to compete with other sectors for government support. Such a reservoir of funds can be built up by the Government of India either by collecting educational cess from industries and other user organisations or by setting up an Educational Development Bank of India or both.

A cess on industry is likely to be looked upon as another form of tax; further, other sectors such as health care may also demand similar cess for their development. An educational cess on industry may also be difficult to operate. In contrast, establishment of an Educational Development Bank of India (EDBI) by the Central Government appears to be a simpler and speedier approach. In any case, if and when an educational cess is collected, the proceeds should be fed into the EDBI, augmenting the resource availability.

The EDBI may be set up with shares by each of the State Governments totalling about Rs. 1,000 crores, matching contributions by the Central Government and from International Financing institutions, totalling about Rs. 3,000 crores. Shares may also be given to industrial houses and national and international organisations, augmenting the capital. Funds from the EDBI may be given as soft loans to Government funded, Government-aided and unaided institutions for their establishment and development, including new programmes, replacement and modernisation of equipment and other infrastructure. At the State level every state should also initiate setting up a State Educational Fund (SEF) to give assistance to needy students in the form of loan scholarships.

Enabling Self-reliance of Institutions

The need for self-reliance has been well recognised by the Government-funded and aided institutions though it may not be ever possible to become so self-reliant as to be independent of Government grants like the private unaided institutions. One of the first steps that could be taken in enabling the institutions to become self-reliant is to help them establish a corpus fund by giving initially the seed money and then giving grants periodically to match the fund generated by the institutions for augmenting the corpus fund. To allow the corpus fund to grow at a reasonably fast rate, it is proposed that Government grants to institutions should have three components, viz. Plan, Non plan and Corpus contribution. The corpus contribution should be a significant part-of the total annual grant and in no case less than matching with the contribution raised by the institution in the previous year through donations, savings, etc.

The institutions are expected to be able to attract donations and contributions for a variety of purposes both from individuals and industries in case the giving of donations and contributions is made attractive both through tax exemption and through suitable recognition of the donors by the institutions concerned.

INCREASING COST EFFECTIVENESS OF INSTITUTIONS

Institutions funded and/or aided by Government are not always cost effective. At a policy level, several decisions have to be taken and implemented nationally in order to improve cost effectiveness. Some of the steps that could be taken to increase their cost effectiveness are:

(a) Optimise intake and enrollment strengths. Any new institution to be established should have a minimum intake of 180 with a minimum annual intake of 40 in any discipline. Starting of courses with less than 40 intake should not generally be permitted and starting of institutions with less than 3 disciplines and less than 180 intake should be discouraged. Preference should be given to an annual intake of 60 in each discipline. To take advantage of the economy of scale, institutions should be encouraged to have a total enrollment in the range of 1,500-2,000. Establishment of new institutions should be permitted only after the above criteria have been satisfied by all the existing similar Institutions.

(b) The work load of teaching staff, and the staff/students ratio prescribe by AICTE and presently followed by most degree level institutions in the country are based on the "Madan Committee" norms. These norms are generally considered to be on the higher side in respect of teaching staff requirements. While these norms recommend an overall staff/student ratio of 1:10, a detailed calculation of staff requirements for an undergraduate programme, strictly on the basis of recommended workload norms, will yield only a staff/student ratio of 1:12 including a 10% allowance for leave and training reserve. The staff/student ratio followed even in most of the developed countries is far less than this. AICTE should revise the norms for work load patterns and staff/student ratios in technical institutions, keeping in mind the experience of the developed countries in this matter as well as the special needs of this country. One aspect that should be taken into account is the desirability of using the services of postgraduate students as teaching assistants in return to the scholarship/ assistantship given to them in postgraduate institutions, as is being done in developed countries. In the meantime, it should be possible to reduce the staff-students ratio in degree institutions from 1:10 to 1:15 and in diploma institutions from 1:11 to 1:20.

(c) It is widely acknowledged that the strength of the non-teaching staff in our public sector technical institutions of all types is unnecessarily and abnormally high. There is urgent need to reduce this, both for economy and efficiency. It should also be realised that this is a socioeconomic problem which has its genesis in the climate and attitude favouring employment generation without regard to economy and efficiency that prevailed during the earlier part of our post-independence period.

The AICTE should review the requirements for academic and administrative supporting staff. It is to be noted that except for academic supporting staff, it is not possible to have uniform norms for the non-teaching staff support. Fully residential institutions such as IITs, RECs and some of the universities have to support the municipal services in the campus township. Academically autonomous institutions have to discharge university functions such as those of academic bodies and the examination wing. In contrast, state level government institutions will have many of its administrative functions looked after by the Directorate of Technical Education, the Government Secretariate, the PSC, the PWD, Treasury, Health Service Department, etc. Thus the norms will have to vary between different types of institutions except in the case of teaching staff and academic supporting staff. What is needed is a limit on their numbers as well as their salary component in relation to those of the teaching staff. Detailed norms should be worked out for both academic supporting staff and non-academic supporting staff for different types of institutions. Until this is done there should be a freeze on creating new non-teaching Staff positions and every attempt should be made to reduce the existing positions over all.

(d) The current AICTE norms and standards for the infrastructural requirements of technical institutions are also considered to be on the high side. For example, the norms and standards for degree institutions recommend a dispensary with a plinth area of 700 sq.m and a staff of eight including a doctor, two nurses and a pharmacist. Similarly, a 30 strong staff is recommended for maintenance work. Few engineering colleges of repute and long standing in the country have such facilities nor do they seem to be essential requirements in most cases. Similar is the case with the requirements for journals, particularly international journals, in respect of institutions without postgraduate programmes. Thus there is an urgent need to review and revise the AICTE norms and standards for technical institutions.

In respect of the requirements for certain facilities and amenities, flexibility should be provided in the Norms & Standards so that, where possible, economy may be effected by sharing facilities of neighbouring institutions or the facilities as available elsewhere in the vicinity of the institution. Where possible, sharing of library facilities among institutions and use of INFLIBNET should be resorted to.

(e) The recurring cost per student per year is also to be worked out again by AICTE based on the revisions effected as per the steps at (a) to (d) above for degree and diploma programmes. The figures based on current norms and standards are high for the state level institutions.

(f) The distance mode of education which is less expensive yet effective, if implemented with careful planning, can increase the opportunities available for technical education and in the process, generate substantial revenue to the institutions. In this context, it should be emphasised that, by distance education, what is meant is not the routine correspondence courses offered in certain disciplines. In technical education, the distance mode should include off-campus lecture programmes, video lectures, computer aided instruction, self learning programmes and expert systems, project executed at the place of work with local supervision, supplemented by contact programmes at the institutions, or at selected industrial centres. The emphasis in distance education programmes should be on advancing the skills and knowledge of employed personnel, rather than on awarding basic diplomas and degrees. These must generally be offered in functional and/or interdisciplinary areas, having high employment potential and not in basic conventional disciplines. It should be possible to offer these programmes on a modular, credit based pattern with the provision that on accumulation of adequate credits, a diploma or a degree can be awarded. This kind of programmes can be charged on a "cost-plus" basis, resulting in significant revenue earning to the institutions.

(g) Outdated and stereotyped programmes especially at the postgraduate level should be wound up, and these may be replaced, where possible, with programmes in emerging areas. It should be noted that about 40% of seats created and funded at the post graduate level remain vacant. It may be necessary for the Ministry to monitor continuously the utilisation of seats in every area of specialisation, and persuade the institutions to wind up programmes that do not attract students. Outright winding up of programmes might cause service related problems to the faculty. Therefore, institutions should be permitted to frame new programmes in the place of obsolete ones, without many procedural hurdles. It is necessary to emphasise as a word of caution, that in the name of modernisation, fundamental theoretical subjects of lasting value, should not he sacrificed in favour of glamourous topics of ephemeral value.

(h) Post graduate education is very expensive to the exchequer especially in view of the substantial monthly scholarship being paid to such students. Yet a significant number of these students drop out without completing the programme and there is no effective mechanism nor effort to recover the scholarship amounts already paid to such drop-outs. There is also a feeling in some quarters that too many post-graduates and Ph.D.s are being produced. The high drop out rate and the lack of enthusiasm on the part of most industries to hire post-graduates in engineering appear to indicate that the large investment of the Government in postgraduate education may not be fully justified. In many instances P.G. programmes have become a halfway house between graduation and employment, the post graduate scholarship becoming a handy handout. It is necessary to make available a larger share of post-graduate seats for persons already employed and/or sponsored by industry.

The Government of India should forthwith convert the present grants for payments of scholarships for post graduate education into teaching/research assistantship grant to the institution offering postgraduate programmes. From these grants Post Graduate students may be given TA/RA as remuneration for teaching research work done by them based on the quantum and quality of work done by them. It should be mandatory for all PG students to help in lectures, tutorial, laboratory work, assignment correction and research work. This would help in reducing the requirement of core faculty and technical supporting staff in institutions and thereby improve their cost effectiveness. Furthermore, it enhances the self respect and responsibility of these students and also gives to the benefits of all concerned in all developed countries and even in them training to become teachers. This is a well tested system working excellently some institutions in India.

(i) Educational reforms such as progressive introduction of more and more internal evaluation; change over to a flexible modular credit based system; broadbasing the first degree programme with provision of electives thereby avoiding a multitude of marginally different programmes; centralising laboratory facilities and avoiding duplication of functional areas, equipments and facilities; internalising maintenance and repair services; grant of academic autonomy/deemed university status; etc. can reduce expenses while Improving quality, speed and efficiency. So also can the use of modem equipment and methods such as computers, word-processors and a more decentralised system management. In many institutions, there is also considerable scope for introducing austerity measures by cutting on avoidable activities/facilities without affecting academic quality.

R&D Laboratories

The urgent need for industries, technical institutions and R & D Laboratories to work in a mutually supportive and complementary manner has been much talked about. There are several avenues here which, systematically pursued, will result in additional resources to the technical institutions as well as improvements in both their cost effectiveness and quality of outputs.

P.G. level programmes can be offered in collaboration with specific industries in several functional areas of their interest. Such programmes offered at the industry location can use industry facilities such as class room space, laboratories, computer etc., and experts from the industry for teaching and project guidance. Offered this way, the bulk of the operating expenses can be met from industry sources.

Similarly continuing education/training programmes leading to degrees/diplomas can be offered for employed personnel who are sponsored by the industry. Such programmes can be offered on a net revenue earning basis. Industry problems given to students for their project work can bring in both financial support and personnel support in the form of project guidance and supervision from the industry. Other avenues which will bring in an economic input are consultancy, industrial testing and certification, sponsored research, commercial utilisation of R & D output, etc.. Similarly interaction with R & D Laboratories will enable the institution to share the expertise, equipments and other facilities available with them.

Resource Generation

Though resource generation has been much talked about, the overall achievements have not been noticeable. All the funded and aided institutions should, in the face of diminishing resources, initiate a number of activities for generating resources. The target may be fixed as, a minimum of 15% in the next five years growing progressively to a minimum of 25% of the recurring expenditure in 10 years. It is realised that the achievement of the percentages will vary widely among the institutions.

Increase of Fees and Rationalisation of the Fee Structure

At present the tuition fee contributes only about 1% to 5% of the recurring expenditure per student per year in Government funded and aided institutions. It has been reported that in 1950-5 1, fees contributed to, 37% of the amount spent on higher education. The need to increase the fees to realistic levels has been well accepted. Thus the AICTE had appointed a task force under the chairmanship of Dr. C.S. Jha for framing regulations of fee structure and working out modalities for grant of loans.

The Jha Committee recommended a three tier fee structure for Government institutions, Government aided institutions and unaided institutions. Since then, some of the States have already increased the fees in Government funded/ aided colleges to a level of about Rs. 2,000/-to Rs. 4,000/-per year. While this could be an acceptable level of fees at present for the State level engineering colleges, the fees would need to be prescribed at a much higher level in the Regional Engineering Colleges, IITs, IIMs, technical universities, deemed universities and similar institutions where the unit cost of education is much higher than in State level colleges/institutions. In tune with the recommendations of the task force, it is recommended that the tuition fee for Government funded and aided institutions be revised to at least 20% of the recurring expenditure per student per year. Fees so fixed, may be reviewed, and refixed once in every three years.

There is a general apprehension that such increases would make it difficult for the economically weaker students to undertake professional studies. For protecting the interest of such students, for undergraduate/diploma programmes, full and half freeships as recommended by the Jha Committee should be instituted with the provision that the amount so disbursed be refunded to the institutions by the Central and the State Governments. This includes (i) full freeship to 5% of the students solely on the basis of merit (ii) half freeship to the next 5% of students solely on the basis of merit and (iii) full freeship to 5% of the students on the basis of economic weakness. Such of the needy students as do not qualify for the freeships should be given soft loan at concessional rates of interest. The question of loan scholarships is discussed in detail elsewhere in this report.

The above suggestions have the merits of enhancing recovery of expenditure, removing subsidy from those who are in a position to pay, enabling the financially weaker students to undertake professional studies and also increasing the motivation of the students in studies. Further, it will also change the perception about the value of education. The established Government funded/aided colleges may be allowed to start new specialised programmes for specific target groups on self-financing/net revenue earning basis.

Self-financing Foreign and NRI students are, in a position to pay much higher fees than Indian students.. Such students should be charged fees at international rates. At the present level, a minimum annual fee equivalent to US $ 3,000 appears appropriate. However, the fees would have to be much higher in IITs and IIMs, RECs, technical universities, deemed universities and similar institutions. Selected institutions should be permitted to admit such students charging the higher fees against specially created seats for both the undergraduate and the postgraduate level courses. In respect of foreign students admitted under cultural exchange programmes also, the same higher rate of fees should be paid by the sponsoring agency.

In this context it is worth noting that if we are to attract foreign students at higher fees, we have to remain at the forefront of technical education and maintain high quality. In the early part of the post-independence period, India had been a leader in technical education in the third world. This was possible because of the excellent facilities, infrastructure and faculty we had in our technical institutions.

However, in recent times many of the developing countries have acquired the most modern equipment, facilities and other infrastructure for their institutions, far better than those available in most technical education institutions in India today. If we also do not provide state-of-the-art equipments and other needed facilites in our institutions, India is likely to lose this leadership and fall back in the quality of technical education in comparison with international standards. Hence it is essential to recognise the need for a national commitment to keep technical education at a high level of excellence and to ensure commensurate and continuing inputs to the system.

The fees recovered from the Indian students should not be offset against the Government grants and should be allowed to be retained by the institutions for meeting the recurring expenditures. The fees from the Foreign and NRI students should be deposited in the corpus fund.

All technical institutions, and especially those located in areas of industrial activity, should be able to earn revenue through consultancy and sponsored research. The overall achievement in this regard by technical institutions very encouraging barring a few exceptions.

Whereas Medical professionals, Architects and Management Experts are involved in giving professional services in a big way, this is very much lacking with the technical personnel in educational institutions. Two of the reasons perhaps are the lack of freedom and motivation. Whereas Medical professionals, Architects and

Management personnel are almost always either free or encouraged to offer professional services both for pecuniary and intangible professional benefits, this does not seem to be so in most of the technical education institutions.

So long as professional services can be offered for enhancing professionalism, institutional and individual consultancies could be encouraged on profit-sharing basis between the institution and the faculty, provided the main functions of the institutions do not suffer.

Similarly, teacher-student teams could also render services which are in line with the curricula. This would also give practical experience to both the students and the teachers. This could also be done on cost-sharing basis among the institutions, teachers and students. This would also be monetarily helpful to the needy students. It is understood that a scheme called "Earn While You Learn" is already being implemented in Andhra Pradesh. The services rendered could be in the form of job work, testing, standardisation etc. The income from consultancy should be shared with the teachers and students to keep them properly motivated.

As all institutions have adequate infrastructure, laboratory and workshop facilities, resources could also be generated through such activities as testing and certification, conducting continuing education and part-time courses, production of teaching aids, development of software etc. There are many low technology areas such as computer programming, wordprocessing, DTP, etc. in which short term courses can be offered generating substantial revenue. Similarly, short term programmes in specialised areas like energy management, CAD/CAM, etc. can be offered charging relatively high fees augmenting the revenue.

The higher professional institutions should promote confidence amongst the industries through various means for attracting sponsored research programmes. Such programmes would help finance contract teachers and research staff and will also help in modernisation of research facilities with the added benefit of increasing professionalism amongst the participants in the research programmes. Besides, with such increased industry-institute interaction, the industries will be able to play an effective roll to make the academic programmes more relevant to the needs of the industry; placement of graduates will be quicker; more number of mutually beneficial joint projects will emerge; and thus the function of social audit will be achieved. Institutions should strive to raise dedicated funds for specified purposes such as buildings, library facilities, research facilities, scholarships, fellowships, awards etc.

Loans, Assistantships and Scholarships

The principles of equity and social justice in a democratic set up require that merit is not sacrificed and access to technical education is not denied to the economically weaker sections of the society. This assumes added urgency in the context of increase in tuition fees. Hence the need to provide a system of scholarships, assistantships, loans and such other financial support to the meritorious, motivated but not-so-well-off students.

Today students are assisted in a variety of ways through outright grant scholarships, fellowships and through loans repayable in easy instalments. Further there are a number of schemes of scholarships for weaker sections of the society. These scholarship schemes shall, no doubt, continue. However, the existing loan schemes have several shortcomings which need rectification. These include:

(i) The procedures for securing loans are bureaucratic, time consuming and not user-friendly.

(ii) The present amount and number of loans may be inadequate in a situation where the fees are increased substantially.

(iii) The banks find recovery difficult in many cases.

(iv) There may be genuine difficulty in repayment of the loin for many students in a climate of high unemployment/underemployment.

The loan schemes have to be revised keeping in view the difficulties of the existing set up. Certain guiding principles for such a scheme should be:

(i) Loans may carry only a soft interest rate for a period upto one year after completion of studies or leaving the institution.

(ii) Repayments shall be responsive to earnings.

(iii) Procedures shall be simple and user-friendly.

For the administration of such loans, a National Loan Scholarship Scheme may be set up as a division of the EDBI. The scheme may be operated by EDBI through associate banks in all States/UTs. The disbursement and repayment of loans should be through the associate banks. Loans should always be given on merit-cum-means basis. Depending on the socio-economic background of the student, the loan should preferably cover the cost of tuition and maintenance. The amount of recovery as also the period during which repayments would be made should be flexible, depending upon the paying capacity of the borrower. Where necessary, the terms of repayment may be made renegotiable on the request of the borrower.

The loan should be a 'soft loan' for a period of upto one year after completion of studies or leaving the institution and its repayments should be waived in the case of certain categories of persons such as those who join the armed forces and those who die or become handicapped. It is emphasised that the society has a great stake in the production of highly qualified technical manpower. It has, therefore, to ensure that talent is adequately nurtured and the meritorious students are not denied opportunities of getting technical education for want of the requisite finances. Exclusive reliance on the loan programme, to the exclusion of grant schemes, would not be in the best interests of technical education. We should continue to provide financial assistance to students through a variety of schemes including through loan scholarships. The implementation of a loan scheme should be done with utmost sympathy and consideration rather than in a strictly bureaucratic manner. While encouraging technical institutions to generate internal revenue and become more and more self supporting, it should be emphasised that education and research should not suffer in quality. It is essential that incentives be given for resourse generation by allowing the institutions to retain and utilise such income with no corresponding reduction in government grants. If the grants are correspondingly reduced, it works as a clear disincentive for mobilisation of resources. It is not logical to device a system where the harder one works, the lesser one gets as grants. The institutions shall also be given adequate operational freedom for efficient functioning, especially in matters such as reallocation and redeployment of staff, periodic adjustment of staff positions to suit changes in programmes and in enforcing discipline and accountability.

In a fully developed state it is probably desirable, and even possible, for most educational institutions to be self sustaining, generating the required revenue to meet all expenses including staff salary. However, the conditions prevailing in the country, proximity of the institutions to industries, the ability to mobilise resources, and the general philosophy of establishment of technical institutions hitherto, are not conducive for the implementation of this new concept of substantial self reliance. Thus just at present, it will be unrealistic to expect all institutions to raise adequate funds to meet any significant share of their expenses. Efforts initiated now will start yielding tangible results in about five years' time only. More important, when the resources that can be made available from the entire industrial sector are spread over all technical institutions in the country the result would be either a uniformly insignificant financial contribution or a grossly unequal distribution wherein most institutions get practically nothing. Hence it is essential to guarantee that inevitable expenses like salary, pension, etc. are met by the Government in time.

References

Brodhead, C. W. (1991). "Image 2000: A Vision for Vocational Education." *Vocational Education Journal* 66, no. 1: 22-25.

Kincheloe, Joe L. (1995). *Toil and Trouble: Good Work, Smart Workers, and the Integration of Academic and Vocational Education.* New York: Peter Lang Publishing.

Kincheloe, Joe L. (1999). *How Do We Tell the Workers? The Socio-Economic Foundations of Work and Vocational Education.* Boulder, CO: Westview Press.

Silberman, H.F. (1986). "Improving the Status of High School Vocational Education." *Educational Horizons* 65, no. 1: 5-9.

8

Open Schooling System

The emergence of Open and Distance Learning (ODL) system has been a phenomenal evolution in the history of educational Development towards the later half of the twentieth century. While the conventional system continues to be the mainstream of educational transaction, it has its own limitations with regard to expansion, access, equity and cost effectiveness.

The revolution brought about by the growth in Information and Communication Technology (ICT) has greatly facilitated the expansion of Open and Distance Learning (ODL) system and permitted adopting a flexible, constructivist, learner friendly and multi-perspective approach to teaching learning process.

The Open and Distance Learning (ODL) system is a new paradigm with some elements of shift such as :

— From classroom to anywhere,
— From teacher centric to learner centric,
— From teacher as an instructor to teacher as a facilitator,
— From mainly oral instructions to technology-aided instruction,
— From fixed time to anytime learning instruction,
— From " you learn what we offer " to " we offer what you want to learn".
— From education as one time activity to education as life long activity.

The Open and Distance Learning (ODL) system, during the course of its journey through few decades in India, has seen many stages of

Development in teaching and learning moves/ material and in its delivery mechanisms against the background of unprecedented Development of Communication Technology vis-a-vis shrinking resources of education.

In fact, the ODL system has been gaining wide popularity over the years in India and across the globe since it provides an opportunity to all those who are unable to pursue learning through traditional system.

ORIGIN OF OPEN SCHOOLING IN INDIA

Open schooling in India was first considered in the early seventies. In August 1974, a working group was appointed by the NCERT to examine the feasibility of setting up an Open School. At its meeting held on Nov. 15th 1974 it was agreed in principle that there was great scope for an Open School at the Secondary level. It was recognised that the country is facing a persistent problem of school drop-outs. For every 100 children enrolled in class I, only 40 complete Class VI and only 20 complete Class VII; and only 14 complete Secondary education. It was felt that it is in the interest of both the individuals as well as of the nation that the drop-outs be afforded an opportunity to come back to the main stream and continue their education. It is estimated that there are about 60 million school dropouts in the country and they needed special attention, and this number is growing.

The problem of education of girls and children belonging to rural and economically backward communities also deserved special attention and it was realised that unless an open learning system is provided for, where the children as well as adults can take advantage of the opportunities for education at their own convenience and at their own pace, it will continue to pose a very difficult situation.

In November 1978, the CBSE and NCERT organised an International Seminar on Open School which was attended by experts on Distance Education of international repute and the Open School, the first of its kind in India, was set up by Central Board of Secondary Education, New Delhi, in July 1979.

1980-81 was the year of launching the programme. Wide publicity was given to the scheme through advertisements in the newspapers, radio talks, T.V. discussions, display of slides in theatres, distribution of leaflets and meetings at the grass root level in the villages, in the factories, in the Development Blocks, etc. In this year zero dispatch was also prepared for the learners, which included Study Guide and Entry Behaviour Test.

In 1981-82 the actual registration started and in the 1st session only 1672 candidates were registered. Taking note of this meager figure. the Indian Express. though highlighting and appreciating the scheme gave a Head line in its editorial as "Open School-an Empty School" The annual registration figure, after a decade, was 60,000 students in 1989-90.

In 1983-84 the first examination in the Open School Scheme was conducted by the Central Board of Secondary Education. The results were very encouraging. Hence Open School approached organisations like Shramik Vidyapeeth, Cottage Emporium, Maurya Hotel, C.R.P.F. etc. who sponsored their workers for further education, thus opening avenues for their better future. Open School brought education to their door steps. In 1984-85 the Open School expanded further its network and established a number of Resource Cum Study Centres. These were in Delhi, Madras, Jaipur, Port Blair and Sikkim.

Encouraged by the growing demand for continuing education through the open channel, by the public, the Open School decided to start Senior Secondary Courses in 1986. A scheme of studies was approved by the Advisory Committee and Governing Body of the Board in 1986-87. During 1987-88, the Senior Secondary courses were developed. The work was done on a war-footing and about 300 booklets were prepared and published. In Nov. 1988 the scheme of Senior Secondary was launched and candidates were registered in the first year.

In 1989 the 1st examination in the Sr. Secondary courses of Open School was conducted by the CBSE. In 1987-88, the Deptt. of Education, Ministry of Human Resource Development, initiated the preparation of a Project Report for the establishment of a National Open School, as an autonomous Registered Society. On acceptance of the report, the Govt., on 23rd Nov. 1989, established the NOS and the Open School project of the CBSE was amalgamated with NOS.

The National Open School was established in November 1989 with a mission of providing 'education for all', 'greater equity and justice in the society', and 'the evolution of a Learning Society'. The objectives of the NOS were stated as follows:

— To provide opportunities for continuing and developmental education to interested learners through courses and programmes of general education life enrichment modules and vocational courses up to pre degree level.

— To provide consultancy services and to engage in model building in close collaboration with states and variety of other agencies or institutions,

— To serve as an agency for effective dissemination of information related to distance education and open learning,

— To identify and promote standards of learning in distance education systems and open schools which may be set up in different parts of the country, through research and evaluation and to maintain standards of equivalence with the formal system, while keeping its own distinct character

It is the largest open schooling system in the World. Its client groups include the girls, the women, the Scheduled Castes, the Scheduled Tribes, the rural people, the urban poor, the unemployed, the part-by employed, the under employed, the young and the adult, the partially handicapped etc. The NOS has more than 1000 study centres located in the territory of India and it also has five centres outside the country. The cumulative enrolment of the student exceeds over half a million. The annual enrolment trend shows a steady growth and in the current year the enrolment at secondary and senior secondary level alone is expected over 150 thousand.

MISSION OF NOS

To provide relevant, continuing and developmental education to prioritised client groups, in consonance with the normative national policy documents, and in response to the assessed needs of the people, through an Open Learning System, at the school stage, as an alternative to the formal system and thus make its share of contribution to:

— universalisation of education;
— greater equity and justice in society; and
— the evolution of a Learning Society

NOS aims:

— To provide opportunities for continuing and developmental education to interested learners, through courses and programmes of general education, life enrichment modules and vocational courses, at the school stage, and using a diversity of teaching-learning strategies, including appropriate communication technologies, within the framework of the normative documents and of the mission of NOS;
— To provide consultancy services and to engage in model building, in close collaboration with States and a variety of other agencies or institutions;
— To serve as an agency for effective dissemination of information related to Distance Education and Open Learning
— To identify and promote standards of learning in Distance Education Systems and Open Schools which may be set up in different parts of the country, through Research and Evaluation and to maintain standards of equivalence with the formal system, while keeping its own distinct character;
— To exercise normative and coordinating functions while promoting standards in Distance and Open Learning Systems in the country, and thus to make its own contribution to the evolution of a Learning Society,

Prioritised Client Groups

The prioritised client groups of NOS, selected from the perspective of those who are educationally and socioeconomic most disadvantaged, are as follows:

— Girls, Women, as a category
— Scheduled Castes and Scheduled Tribes
— Rural People and Urban Poor
— Unemployed/Part Employed, seeking jobs/better jobs

— The older than the younger, from 35 years down, in the age bracket of 15-35

FEATURES NOS

Promoting Access and Choices

Research and evolution of theories of Instruction Design and of the processes of cognition, coupled with advances in educational technology and increasing availability and sophistications of the electronic media, as a support to learning, coupled with the rigidities and inflexibility of the Formal System, separately and together ushered in Distance Education and Open Learning, as an alternative to the Formal.

Open Learning System has created opportunities for continuing education for a wide spectrum of students. The precise reasons that prompted them to seek the Open Channel may vary from individual to individual, but some of the reasons are:

— Conditions of educational attainment laid down by the formal

— Economic backwardness Geographical remoteness

— Demands of certificate for employment

— Social, cultural and domestic constraints Age

It is natural to expect that the Open System would attract a growing number of students, who would otherwise find access to continuing education difficult, if not impossible.

Open Entry

Students seeking admission to the Foundation Course (Middle level) or to the Secondary Level are admitted on the basis of a self-certificate by the student, stating that he/she has the necessary educational attainments and is capable of pursuing the course of studies. However, since NOS is a system for education than merely an opportunity for taking an examination, the students must sit for an internal assessment test, 4-5 months after admission and qualify, with at least 25% marks. If not, the student must continue to study till he qualifies and becomes eligible for external examinations.

As such, what looks like making entry very cheap becomes a tougher condition, since it is easier to get a certificate of previous educational attainments than to prove it through an actual test. For the Senior Secondary Course, a certificate of X pass from a recognised Board is required.

Age

The minimum age for admission to the Foundation Course is 14 completed by 31st August of the year of admission. For admission to the Secondary Level Course, a student should have completed 15 years by 31 August. For the Senior Secondary admission, the minimum age is 16 completed by August 31st. There is no upper age limit for any category.

Choice of Subjects

This is an important feature of Open Learning. Students have the freedom to choose the set of subjects that they find useful or necessary. The only compulsion is to choose one of the two languages offered, namely Hindi or English. If a student wishes to choose only ONE subject, for reasons of it being needed to supplement an earlier certificate or because of demand from the employer etc, NOS allows this.

Self-paced Learning

A registered student is given upto five years to complete the course. Part employed or full-employed persons find it difficult to devote much time to study, and this provision is a great help to them to continue their education.

Scheme of Examination

There is provision for two full scale examinations every year, one in May and the other in October. The student has the option to appear in one or more subjects of one's choice or take them altogether. In case of failure, one can appear again, within the five year period. All passes are kept as credit and when the student has acquired the required number for certification, the certificate is issued.

Multi-media Learning Package

The specially prepared printed study materials form the basic source for learning. Prepared specially for the distant learner, incorporating all the features that a good teacher actually does in class, in a face-to-face, situation, the text is a distant teacher in print. Besides, NOS is currently planning the preparation of audio and later video packages to supplement the printed text.

Learning Support Centres

Provision of teachers, who, besides tutoring, may also counsel the students, at the Accredited Institutions would further support the student's efforts to learn on one's own and at one's pace. The system promotes self learning and provides orientation to the students to become independent learners by giving them basic study skills.

Open Education is particularly characterised by the removal of restrictions, exclusions and privileges; by the accreditation of students' exclusions and privileges; by the flexibility of the management of the time variable; hand by substantial changes In the traditional relationship between professors and students. On the other grand, distance education Is a modality which permits the delivery of a group of didactic media without the necessity of regular class participation, where the individual is responsible for his own learning.

STUDENT PROFILES

We could depict the profiles of the NOS students in a variety of ways. One of the most striking is the number profile of those who seek admission to the Open School. The rise in enrolment has been dramatic and is causing some amount of administrative problems because of inadequate provision of student services as well as due to budgetary constraints. Students enroll in NOS from literally every part of the country, from every State and Union Territory, loudly indicating that Open Learning is providing a real second chance for continuing education.

The course profile is another important feature. Of the two course levels offered, though only 7% opted for the Bridge Course (equivalent to the middle stage) in 1982-83, this figure rose sharply to

24% in 1987-88. This is significant, since this group signifies both the most educationally needy group, as a mere primary education of four or five years is barely adequate to cope with life and its demands. Offer of such a Foundation or Bridge course is thus an act of redeeming education and aims directly at the most deprived. Similarly, when the Senior Secondary was introduced and as several jobs and employment avenues are open only to those who pass the Senior Secondary than the Secondary (apart from the opening for tertiary level education in Universities), about 50% of the new student enrolment in the current year (1990-91) were for the Senior Secondary.

The age profile is a clear indication that we are catering, in NOS, to the older than to the younger students. The average age of the NOS students was plus 20, the majority belonging to the age bracket of 17-21. Those in the age group of 14-16 are still appreciable and this is a matter of concern to NOS, as there seems to be an attraction for students in formal schools to take short cuts via the NOS. Hence the entering age specification has been modified as follows:

— 14 completed for the Foundation (Bridge) course;
— 15 completed for the Secondary course;
— 16 completed for the Senior Secondary course

Employment profile is given in the diagram. Though, in the beginning year, the percentage of employed was about 40%, this figure has been coming down, as younger students seek admission to NOS.

The rural-urban student profile is again a difficult one to gauge exactly. For instance, all who come from Delhi UT will be categorised as urban, though they may come from rural parts of the territory of Delhi. The fact that we have students from interior parts of Sikkim, Nagaland, Manipur, Mizoram, Arunachal Pradesh, Andamans and Lakshadweep is proof enough that the rural people in India have also begun to hear and respond to the call for continuing education through open schooling.

Besides, we have other categories of students, such as soldiers and those in the Police, housewives, peons, seeking avenues to move up to the challenge of continuing education. The oldest student who registered with the Open School was 49 years.

Finally, the medium profile. Roughly 80% of the students study through the medium of Hindi while the rest study through the medium of English. These is strong demand for offer of other languages, but NOS is unable to meet this demand from several States, as this will seriously encumber the institution. Besides, it is a task that the States can and must do.

Educational Programmes

Foundation or basic education course

This Course roughly corresponds to the upper primary level of education or Classes VI-VIII. From the beginning, there was provision for a Bridge Course, which would enable one to move on the Secondary, after completing the course. The course offered a real second chance to the many who had dropped out from school and were away for several years. About 20-25% of the new registrations, each year, represented this group. Courses offered were in Languages (Hindi and English) Mathematics, Science and Social Science.

Since the majority of the people of India have not had this level of education, and since a basic minimum of knowledge, skills, and values and attitudes are essential for meaningfully and effectively coping with the many demands of life, in concrete situations, thereby enhancing their quality of life and the life of the community, this is an important area for provision by the NOS. There is an International call and support from several agencies such as UNICEF, UNDP, UNESCO and the WORLD BANK, for provision of such a basic education for ALL. Currently, the existing Bridge Course is under revision as a Foundation or Basic Course. The course is being designed as a functional course, and without the prevalent over-emphasis on mere acquisition of knowledge of facts and data and concepts, without the ability to understand or apply in real life situations. Approaches such as a case study or making a situational statement or posing a problem or presenting an episode as the starting point for introducing a topic or a set of concepts, would bring greater relevance and functionality to the course.

Secondary Level Course

The majority of the students opt for this level of courses, mainly for very practical reasons. A job often calls for a Secondary School

Certificate, as an essential condition or the opportunity to continue education, which had stopped some years earlier. For instance, several thousand teachers in the primary classes in Sikkim availed of the Secondary Certification course and became Matriculates, enhancing their life opportunities, becoming eligible for higher education and getting regular appointments etc.

Currently, the Secondary level courses are also under revision, since these courses were introduced almost a decade ago. Presently, the subjects offered are: Hindi, English, Mathematics, Science, Social Studies, Commerce, Economics, Home Science and Typing (Hindi and English). Like the revision of the Foundation Course, the revision will introduce a qualitatively different course, while maintaining and improving the educational standard. A substantial reduction in content, that does not contribute to quality, is planned, upto 30-40%. In its place, a much larger scale application to real life situations is planned, as part of the curriculum and of assessment, than as an extra. For the Language courses, 25% of the weightage, in terms of curriculum and evaluation, will be for listening comprehension and speaking ability. Projects, as an integral part of the curriculum and hence of evaluation, is another feature.

Senior Secondary Level Course

Introduced in 1989, it has offered opportunities for several thousands to continue their education, after the Secondary Certificate, through the Open Channel. The full range of subjects are offered, in the areas of Science, Commerce and Humanities. The present provision of subjects includes the following:

Hindi	English	Mathematics
Biology	Chemistry	Physics
Home Science	Commerce	Accountancy
Economics	Political Science	History
Geography	Typing Stenography	
Secretarial Practice		

Both as principle and also enabling the students to join higher level courses at the tertiary stage, in formal Universities as well, the standards of the courses are kept the same as those in other Boards of Education, at this stage. While maintaining equivalence, NOS has also introduced certain distinctive features. For example, the language course offers four modules as language for special purposes enabling the student to choose the one best suited. Similar provisions have also been made in Mathematics and Commerce. Such innovations are part of an on-going process. Besides, modularisation is the direction in which NOS would move, which is necessary for purposes of continuous evaluation, including Internal Assessment.

Community Education

Small beginning is being made into provision of community and general education. Currently two projects are being developed by an agency, one on Community Health Education and the other on the Status of Women. Both packages will use the distance education as the basic medium, with supplementary face to face interaction.

Vocational Education

Explorations are also underway for providing practical Vocational Courses, both for the urban and for the rural population. Again, this is being got done by agencies than from within NOS. In fact, as a principle, NOS would get done what others can do as well or better and would only accredit courses thus developed after technically examining them.

Course Development Strategies

The Team Approach

Certain well-established curriculum development strategies, usually in practice, in institutions engaged in distance and open learning, are also practiced in the NOS. The accent is on optimising use of resources, keeping most of the resource persons outside the institution than within, in order to both increase access to greater richness of resources as well as to substantially reduce costs in course development. Hence only a core team is provided in the NOS. This means generally a Tutor is responsible for organising and coordinating the development of a course in one's own subject area. The Director (Academic) is the head of the Department.

A Planning meeting is held, to which academicians, subject and curriculum specialists as well as practitioners are invited to discuss and arrive at a broad consensus on a curriculum framework. Once finalised, it will be normative for all subject-related courses. The conceptual framework will keep in view and incorporate the broad content areas suitable for Open Learning. Subject committees are then set up, who discuss in detail the content areas and approach in the specific subject and decide on inclusion/ exclusion of topics in the course. The depth of treatment of a topic, the weightage to be given to it, the kind of scope for applications or for project or practical work will also be discussed and decided upon. All this will be done within the context of the Curriculum Framework. Audio or video support is also planned at this stage.

Since it is likely that some members of the Subject Committees are unaware of the demands and expectations of the distance and open learning system, orientation is planned to enable the members to examine, understand and accept the Curriculum Framework, its rationale and philosophy. Only those who can arrive at a measure of consensus are associated with the course development work.

Next comes the finalisation of detailed teaching learning syllabus by the members of the Subject committee, which includes teachers, and subject specialists, from special national level Institutions or from Universities as well.

After vetting the detailed syllabus through its exposure for feedback a larger number of teachers and if possible, students, the syllabus is finalised, with weightages to topic or groups of topics, stress on particular areas, approaches in treatment, indication of depth of treatment of a topic etc.

In order to make the detailed syllabus a teaching-learning syllabus, the next step is to organise workshops to define the specific Learning Outcomes, ensuring that all the three, namely the cognitive, affective and psychomotor domains are given their due share of weightage and different levels of difficulty in each area also identified. Thus the cognitive would go well beyond mere memory or recall. Scope is given for experiential learning than only limit to second-hand learning exclusively. This exercise is essential for improving learning effectiveness, for setting clear standards of educational attainments and to facilitate evaluation.

Now the Curriculum Committee or the Academic Committee, which has cross section representation from subject committees would meet to accord its approval. Then the formal approval from the Executive Board obtained and the detailed syllabus becomes normative and prescriptive.

The next step is the writing of the Lessons. A group of lessons are organised into different dispatches. For writing the Lessons, a Subject Team Course Chairman (STCM) and a small team of lesson writers are selected, who either have experience of writing lessons in the specific format required for distance education text (a teacher in print) or are given an orientation through a workshop. The subject Tutor co-ordinates the work. The course is expected to be largely auto-instructional, though additional teaching through face-to-face support is provided.

The orientation takes care of content, format, and pedagogical aspects of the presentation. A few meetings are held by the STCM to review and improve the work of the lesson writers. Graphic inputs are also planned alongside. After final editing by the Subject Tutor, a manuscript is prepared for the press.

The research division engages in getting feed-back from the students about the course, relevance and difficulty level of topics and these are taken into account when the course is revised.

Student assignments are prepared as part of the preparation of lessons. This provides feedback to the students, since answers are provided in the text itself and which the Teachers at the study Centres, use for testing comprehension. In order to provide a meaningful learning package, students are also provided with sample question papers, for practice examinations, along with Marking Schemes. These enable the students to know exactly the criteria that NOS uses for marking and grading the answers.

NOs Operations

Even in advanced countries, where Open Universities operate, and which rely a good deal on the use of electronic media, namely TV and Radio, studies show that the predominant source of learning is still the print medium. NOS has been mainly-relying on the print medium, though it is now actively planning to provide Audio and later, Video support as well.

In the last ten years, print copies of 509 titles totalled about 10,000,000. In 1982-83,150 titles were printed, a total of 4,00,000 copies, using 50 tons of paper. This shot up to 500 titles and 26,00,000 copies, requiring 325 tons of paper in 1988-89. The entire job is got done by a number of presses on assignment basis.

Storage of such a vast quantity of materials, both paper and printed materials would mean renting a very large area and would be quite expensive. The NOS follows the concept of a Dynamic Store than a Static Store. The inflow and out-flow are planned and sequenced, so that, at any time, there is no need for prolonged static storage. Specifically, when the large consignment of paper arrives, it is sent, as required, to the assigned presses directly, and accounted at the press, than at the store, avoiding a lot of storage space and cost. In fact, surely in 1989-90, not a ton of paper was stored in the NOS but all sent directly to the press. Similarly, dispatches are printed and sent sequentially. As the initial dispatches are printed and arrive at the store, they are dispatched to the study centres, so that the store is ready to receive the next batch of dispatches.

NOS has a store space of 6200 sq. feet. If the dynamic store approach were not used, we would require 10 times the storage space. Colour coding is used, for easy identification of different subjects.

The earlier practice of having 10 or more dispatches in each subject was discontinued last year, by putting two dispatches in one cover, thus reducing cost and facilitating better materials handling for dispatch to the study centres.

Similarly, from 1990-91, the earlier practice of sending the dispatches directly to the individual students was discontinued and the materials were sent in bulk, by road transport or by rail to the Accredited Institutions or study centres, for distribution to the students. This has also reduced postage expenses considerably, since we do not have to individually pack literally several hundred thousand dispatches.

The dispatches are printed, using ordinary paper, since the scope of its use is limited and for a short period. However, the cover designs and lay out are made as attractive as possible, within the limitations of remaining cost conscious.

Support Through Accredited Institutions

Even though a basic tenet of the Open Learning System is to promote independent and self-learning and to positively discourage over-dependency on the teacher, it is necessary to have a certain amount of face-to-face contact, for purposes of counselling, tutoring and teaching, Initially, it was envisaged that in selected state capitals, a suitable institution would be identified as a Resource Cum Study Centre (RCSC), which would provide student services, including access to the library, laboratory etc. apart from the personal contact sessions.

Initially, the work of supplying the prospectus, receiving the applications and admitting the students was done directly by the Open School. RCSC's were set up in Sikkim, Delhi, Rajasthan, and Andaman and Nicobar Islands. With the rapid increase in student enrolment, special PCP's were organised in several places, in different parts of the country for the duration of 10 days at a stretch and students were invited to come for the session.

As the enrolment kept increasing geometrically, it became necessary to substantially increase the number of study centres. It also became essential to decentralise the operation, away from the Open School to the Study Centre. Accordingly, on an experimental basis, in 1989, the centres in Delhi were asked to partner with NOS by assuming responsibility for distribution of prospectus, admission of students and for distribution of study materials, apart from the responsibility for conducting the PCP classes. Since the experiment proved largely successful, in 1990, the system was extended to all the study centres throughout the country. No prospectus was sent from the NOS to any, but the students were directed to a study centre.

It worked out seasonally well, but was not entirely satisfactory. Hence for the 1991 registration, a combination of both is being planned, namely allow stud nets to collect prospectus from the NOS as well, but registrations must be done at one of the centres of the student's choice, from among those given in the prospectus.

Currently we have 161 Accredited institutions, spread through the length and breadth of the country, with student enrolment at each centre varying from 40 to 500. Once more study centres become available, we hope to restrict the number to an upper limit of 300.

The administrative responsibilities of the AI's are the following:

1. To distribute prospectus and admit students on behalf of NOS according to norms prescribed by NOS.
2. To distribute study Materials.
3. To maintain accounts of stocks and equipment supplied.
4. To distribute marks sheets and certificates
5. To provide accommodation for conduct of examinations.

EVALUATION OF EDUCATIONAL ATTAINMENTS

Open Learning, especially when offered through distance education mode, can and does pose problems at various stages. At the stage of admission, the compulsion to be open means relaxation of standard admission norms, the production of certificates of achievement etc. NOS does not insist on a formal certificate about previous educational attainments, but is satisfied with a self certificate for admission to both the Foundation and Secondary level courses. Students will cheat? Possibly, Yes. But, NOS insists on all students, regardless of the certificate that they produced, qualifying for appearing at the external examinations, by studying the first two dispatches (about 15-20 lessons) and appearing in an internal test and passing with at least 25% marks. Those who fail are not rejected, but allowed to appear again at the following internal test, till they pass. As a result, the standards have not been reduced, but actually increased. It is much easier to produce a certificate. NOS asks for both evidence of study and of educational attainments.

The internal tests are computer marked, namely through an Optical Mark Reader. In the last Internal Test, there were 1.67 lakh scripts, but thanks to the Optical Mark Reader, the evaluation could be done in about a month and results compiled, centre-wise and despatched. The Infernal Tests do double duty, namely serving as eligibility to qualify for appearing at the external examinations and those who pass at the test have these marks counted for the final Grade, to the tune of 20% of the total.

At the Senior Secondary stage, a formal certificate of pass from a Board or from NOS is insisted on as well as appearing in the Internal

Assessment test. 20% of what the student scores goes towards the final grade in that subject.

As distance education materials are aimed at maximising self-learning, in-text questions are provided at frequent intervals and terminal questions at the end of a unit of lesson. At the end of a series of lessons in a despatch, a set of formal questions are set (similar to the questions that the students will encounter in the public examinations) which the students answer. Earlier these response sheets were sent to the Open School for marking, and returned to the students but now these are taken care of by the teachers at the study centres.

External (public) examinations are held twice each year, in mid May and in mid October. Students have the option to take upto five years to complete the course and they can accumulate credit (passes in subjects) all together or one or two subjects at an examination. Most students take two to three years to complete the acquisition of sufficient credit passes for certification.

The Secondary course remained unbifurcated till the current year but the students of May, 1991 examinations will have the bifurcated course. That is to say, they will have questions at the external examinations only from the portions designated as Certification course. The Foundation course will be for study and as a base for the Certification course. However, for the internal assessment, questions are included from both Foundation and Certification course units. The same applies for the Senior Secondary, where the course is divided into Foundation and Certification units. In the same lesson, parts of it may be foundation, while the rest certification or a whole lesson may be of one or the other category. Such close intertwining of the course units, makes the course equivalent to what obtains in the formal system, though, in the formal also, some Boards test the Class IX/XI course units through a test internally set and examined by the concerned schools.

A small study from a random sample of students of NOS shows that:

a) 07% took the full five years to complete the course

b) 20% completed in four to four and a half years

c) 09% completed in two years

d) 19% took one to one a half years to complete

e) 45% completed in one year.

Though advised to take the number of subjects, depending on one's ability and availability of time to complete the course, 82% of the students in the 1989 examinations had passed 3 subjects earlier, indicating that they take advantage of the flexibility provided.

The NOS does not provide data on the percentage of passes each year, since the students pass in subjects and accumulate pass credits. The diagram as given below shows the average percentage of pass in the different subjects, which indicates a creditable achievement.

The important question of equivalence, recognition and eligibility for jobs, for pursuing higher studies are of relevance. As a matter of principle, the NOS preserves, equivalence of educational standards in the development of courses, something that it invites others to ascertain for themselves. Obviously, the equivalence is different from uniformity or point to point correspondence in the topics prescribed, within a course. Being a newcomer in the field, the NOS will necessarily have to answer questions, experience difficulty in getting equivalence from Boards and Universities. Either it can, while maintaining rigidly standards of attainment, insist on its right and necessity, as a distinct and different system and catering to own clientele, preserve its own identity and flexibility or succumb to the pressure and conform to the demands from the formal. This is a major issue for the very survival and growth of the system. Reforms in curriculum development and evaluation will become teasing illusions, if the Open System surrenders to the formal, for the immediate gains of a pot of porridge.

Staff and Management

When it began as a project of the CBSE in 1979, there was a small staff of 29, which rose to 37 by 1981. With the rapid and dramatic increase in enrolment, the staff strength has also grown, but the tradition of the Open School project was to manage with a lean staff, since over-staffing would have led to drop in efficiency.

Till 1988, most of the student file work (registration of students, and later registration for examination) was manually managed but which have now been fully computerised. The support of the computer was always available for the processing of the results of the public examinations. This year, Internal assessment tests have been introduced. The answer scripts are computer marked, through the Optical Mark Reader, thus ensuring both speed and accuracy. This year, 1,67,000 answer scripts were computer marked, and consolidated reports made ready for despatch to the AIs in about a month. The next evaluation would be speedier from the experience gained from the first exercise.

By the very nature of the work in hand, some work, especially connected with examination, is seasonal, and for this contract staff is employed, who work with the regular staff. This experience has been a happy one and the work quality has been kept at a high level, though, for exacting accurate work, such as for the mailing of dispatches, errors have occurred. Procedures are being standardised and simplified, to reduce the problem areas.

Heavy reliance on the computer, for admission, examination and for various other jobs such as production of identity cards as well as voluminous correspondence, has resulted in the reduction of cost and improvement of the quality of the output. Apart from data entry of students, the editing and updating of data from the checklist received from centres, the computer provides the following:

— subjectwise student data for each centre
— statistics reports on age, course selection, sex, medium of study, economic status, urban/rural etc.
— payroll system for staff salary disbursement
— computerisation of AI's for ready correspondence with individual students through mail-merge Attendance Sheets and other form sheets
— Status reports for various branches

Decentralisation

NOS believes in decentralisation of responsibilities, along with delegation of necessary authority to take decisions. This includes delegation of financial authority as well, upto the level of Assistant Director and Tutors. We have also the system of Impress for easy and ready money availability, while keeping accountability intact.

Levels of Posts

The pyramid is the usual resulting configuration of the levels of posts in many organisations.

Functional Autonomy

Though remaining a grant-in-aid institution, Open School had a good deal of functional autonomy. With the establishment of NOS as an independent registered Society and by reason of its constitution, NOS enjoys a good deal of real autonomy. The earlier Advisory Committee of the Open School, which was the highest body within, has been replaced by an Executive Board, to which all powers of the National Open School Society have been given to manage the affairs of the Society.

The Executive Board does forward planning of policies and programmes of action; takes appropriate decisions, ensures effective implementation and exercises the review function.

The Executive Board has the following representation:

— Chairman of the Society, who will also be Chairman of the Executive Board

— Vice Chairman who will be the Director (Academic)

— Secretary of NOS who will be the Member Secretary

— The Heads of all the Departments of NOS

— Nominee of the Deptt. of Education, MHRD

— Nominee of the Integrated Finance Division of MHRD

— One specialist from each of the following:

—Distance Education

—Development and Education of Women

—Industry

—Media

—Technology

—Vocational/Technical Education

There is also a General Body which shall have, vested with it, the responsibility to assist the Society by providing sound and professional advice and counsel; it well generate a vision and give broad policy directions to the Society; it will receive and critically examine and comment on the Annual Report of the Society; it will receive and approve the annual budget of the Society; in general, the General Body will help ensure that the Society will remain publicly accountable and that it exercises its powers and functions in consonance with the Mission and objectives of the Society and within the framework of normative national documents.

Finances

Open School began with a modest budget of Rs. 40,000 in 1979. Since it was meant to cater to the disadvantaged, the registration fee was kept as low as only Rs. 5 and the course fee was Rs. 25 per subject, which was far from enough to pay even postage charges for dispatch of materials to the students. The course fee was raised to Rs. 40 in 1984. In 1990, the fees were further raised to Rs. 50 for registration (for all) and Rs. 300 (consolidated) for registration and four subjects at the Secondary and Rs. 400 for four subjects, including the registration fee, at the Senior Secondary level.

Due to the rapid increase in student enrolment, the income also increased, even though women, Scheduled Castes and Scheduled Tribes, the handicapped and war veterans were exempted from payment of course fees, upto the Secondary. Except for women, who pay half fees at the Senior Secondary, the other exempted categories do not pay course fees even at the Senior Secondary level. This provision of exemption from course fees was introduced from 1987-88 onwards. The ratio of women candidates, seeking admission to the NOS kept increasing and stood at 37% in 1989-90. The total percentage of all categories exempted from course fees was 58. Clearly indicating that the NOS was actually able to reach to a large measure, the educationally and socio-economically deprived sections of society.

The income for the institution rose from a modest Rs. 1.13 lacs in 1980-81 to Rs. 107.67 lacs in 1989-90. The Central Board of Secondary Education, New Delhi, which initiated the Open School project, also supported the deficit, from its-own funds till March, 1983. Since then, the Department of Education, Ministry of Human Resource Development, meets the net deficit over income, through a grant-in-aid.

CHALLENGES OF NOS

What does an institution for Open Learning at school level hold for the future? What are the futures of the National Open School? It is not an easy question to answer nor can the answers be definitive. But it is eminently worthwhile to dream and envisage some of the future thrust areas of NOS.

While an institution should be happy about its rapid growth, NOS is feeling concerned, because the numbers have grown so quickly that we are unable to cope up with the follow-up student service aspects. As part of the future planning, this aspect of limiting the numbers who will be admitted to NOS and actively exploring with several States to start own state-level Open Schools, with provision of the State language/s, gain urgency. While the pressure of NOS is a problem, its solution through sharing the task with state Open Schools, will offer many new opportunities to the untold millions who seek continuing education.

While an institution System than an appendage to the Formal System, the real test will lie in the ability of NOS and of Open Schools to develop more relevant curricula, with substantial and selective discarding of such content areas that do not contribute to educational standards and appreciably, increasing applications to life situations and conditions. This will help the students to become more competent. Examination, a part of the educational continuum, has for all practical purposes, taken charge and controls and dominates the whole process. A case of the tail wagging the dog and the dog not resenting! Meaningful reforms in the evaluation system, with modularisation of the courses and developing a credit system, and building into it the needed flexibility, to match student needs and interests with corresponding provision in the course units, is another, major challenge for NOS.

Apart from the partnership that we hope to have from States, in setting up own Open School in the State, NOS would actively pursue the identification of partners, already in the field, whether a Government-sponsored institution or a voluntary agency or an organisation, which would collaborate in the evolution of courses and in the administration of such programmes. Since there is still a market demand for recognised courses NOS would assess such courses through technical committees and accredit them. Once accredited, the students offering such courses would get a certificate from the NOS as well. Thus NOS outreach would be extended considerably, not only in geographical terms but in the number and quality of courses offered. Major thrust areas are the accreditation of vocational courses in community education, such as community health, status of women, etc. While some initiatives are already in the pipeline, a search for linkups with courses and programmes to serve the rural people is an important priority area.

Learning to Learn or how to enable the students to become increasingly self-learners or independent learners is a major area of search for practical solutions. This will touch the development and format of the printed texts, the orientation of teachers and tutors at the accredited study centres, which number 160 at present, spread throughout the country and ensuring that the students of NOS are slowly but surely becoming empowered persons (empowered to learn). Since the formal, by practice if not by design, promotes a great deal of unhealthy dependency, thereby making the students more and more incompetent for life, ways for developing this personal power and competence, through built-in features in the curriculum and course designs, teaching-learning approaches and evaluation is among the most important key result areas of NOS.

References

Bates A.W. (1995): *Technology, Open Learning and Distance Education*, London: Routledge.

Ellsworth, J.H. (1994): *Education on the Internet*, Indianapolis: Sams Publishing.

Rumble, G. (2001): The Costs and Costing of Networked Learning, *Journal of Asynchronous Learning Networks,* Vol. 5, Issue 2, September.

South African Institute for Distance Education (1999): *Distance Education and Technology Choices in Southern Africa*, www.saide.org.za, April.

Tait, A. (2000): Planning Student Support in Open and Distance Learning, in *Open Learning*, 15 (3), 287-300.

UNESCO (1985): Final Report: The 4th World Conference on Adult Education, Paris: UNESCO.

9

Development of EFA

Several articles in the Constitution of India bring into focus the general principles governing educational development in the country. These articles are rooted in India's struggle for independence. Basic education was one of the important goals of the freedom struggle and Mahatma Gandhi, even while leading the epic struggle against colonial power, evolved an alternative education system. The Directive Principle contained in Article 45 of the Constitution enjoins that "the State shall endeavour to provide, within a period of ten years from the commencement of this Constitution, for free and compulsory education for all children until they complete the age of fourteen years." The expression "the State" which occurs in this Article is defined in Article 112 to include the government and parliament of India, the government and the legislature of each of the states and all local or other authorities within the territory of India or under the control of the government of India.

Article 29(1) of the Constitution provides that "any section of the citizens residing in the territory of India or any part thereof having a distinct language, script or culture of its own shall have the right to conserve the same." Article 29(2) lays down that "no citizen shall be denied admission into any educational, institution maintained by the State or receiving aid out of State funds on grounds only of religion, race, caste, language or any of them."

Article 30(1) enjoins that "all minorities, whether based on religion or language, shall have the right to establish and administer educational institutions of their choice," while Article 30(2) lays down that "the State shall not, in granting aid to educational institutions, discriminate against any educational institution on the ground that it is under the management of a minority, whether based on religion or language." Article 350-A lays down that "it shall be the endeavour of every State and of every local authority within the State to provide adequate facilities for instruction in the mother-tongue at the primary stage of education to children belonging to linguistic minority groups."

Special care of the economic and educational interests of the under-privileged sections of the population is laid down as ail obligation for the State under Article 46. As per this Article, "the State shall promote with special care the educational and economic interests of the weaker sections of the people, and, in particular, of the Scheduled Castes and the Scheduled Tribes and shall protect them from social injustice and all forms of exploitation."

Till the 42nd amendment of the Constitutional education was in the State List except for certain specified items in the Union List like determination of standards in institutions for higher education or research, establishment and maintenance of central universities as well as specified institutions for scientific or technical education and research. The objective of incorporating education in the Concurrent List was to facilitate evolution of all-India policies in the field of education. Though the parliament was thereby empowered with the authority to legislate on education the Centre has been relying on a consensual process to promote educational development. The concept of concurrency was given an operational meaning by the National Policy on Education (NPE) 1986. This policy envisages concurrency as a "meaningful partnership between the Centre and the States" and placed on the Union Government a larger responsibility in regard to the national and integrative character of education, quality and standards, manpower planning, research and advanced study, and international aspect of education, culture and human resource development.

The Union government has also set up a number of resource institutions at the national level. The National Council of Educational Research and Training (NCERT) has been assisting and advising the Union and state governments in the formulation and implementation of policies and programmes in the fields of school and teacher education. It maintains a national network of field advisors and four Regional Colleges of Education. The National Institute of Educational Planning and Administration (NIEPA) assists and advises the Union and states in the areas of educational planning and administration in the country. Apart from research, it is also engaged in training senior education officials of the Centre and the states.

The Central Institute of Indian Languages (CIIL), Central Institute of English and Foreign Languages (CIEFL), the Rashtriya Sanskrit Sansthan (National Institute of Sanskrit) and the Kendriya Hindi Sansthan (Central Institute of Hindi) are resource institutions for promoting the development of languages in the country.

EFA in India

In the Indian context, Education for All (EFA) would imply:

(i) Expansion of early childhood care and development activities including family and communities, especially for poor, disadvantaged and children.

(ii) Universalisation of Elementary Education (UEE), viewed as a composite programme of access to elementary education for all children up to 14 years of age; universal participation fill they complete the elementary stage through formal or non-formal education programmes; and universal achievement at least of minimum levels of learning.

(iii) Drastic reduction in illiteracy, particularly in the 15-35 age group, bringing the literacy level in this age group at least to 80 per cent in each gender and for every identified disadvantaged group, ensuring that the levels of three R's are relevant to the living and working conditions of the people.

(iv) Provision of opportunities to maintain, use and upgrade their education, and provision of facilities for development of skills, to all persons who are functionally literate and those who have received primary education through formal and non-formal channels.

(v) Creation of necessary structure and setting in motion processes which would empower women and make education an instrument of women's equality.

(vi) Improving the content and process of education to better relate it to the environment, people's culture and with their living and 'working conditions, thereby enhancing their ability to learn and cope with problems of livelihood and environment.

National Policy on Education (NPE), 1986

The NPE, 1986 is a land mark in the Indian education. Based on an in-depth review of the Indian educational system and evolved through a consensual process it provides a comprehensive framework to guide the development of education. The NPE was distinct in that it was followed by a detailed strategy of implementation, accompanied by the assignment of specific responsibilities and financial and organisational support, in the form of a Programme of Action (POA). The Policy and its POA were updated in 1992 through a similar consensual process involving all state governments, resource organisations and educationists.

The extant policy and its POA give unqualified priority to UEE, adult literacy and education for women's equality; this priority is reflected in the budget allocations during the current five year plan (1992-97). What the policy posits is a 'dual track' approach, desired to promote simultaneously adult literacy and primary education, with focus on girls, and disadvantaged groups. In the extant policy, there are several points of departure in the pursuit of EFA:

(i) The emphasis has shifted from enrolment per se to enrolment as well as retention and achievement. As the POA, 1986 put a crisply "enrolment by itself is of little importance if children do not continue beyond one year, many of them not seeing the school for more than a few days."

(ii) Taking a realistic view of the enormous task of achieving UEE in its entirety (access, retention as well as achievement), the NPE envisages that free and compulsory education of satisfactory quality should be provided to all children up to 14 years of age before the commencement of the twenty-first century.

(iii) The policy seeks to address the more difficult aspects of access. It was for the first time, in 1986, that an educational policy had admitted that the school would not reach all children, particularly millions of girls and working children whose participation in school system is thwarted by socioeconomic parameters. The policy called for a large and systematic programme of Non-

Formal Education (NFE) as an integral component of the strategy to achieve UEE. NFE should have enough flexibility to enable the learners to learn at their own pace and at the same time would have quality comparable with formal education.

(iv) The policy postulates integration of the gender perspective in all aspects of the planning. There is a pronounced policy shift from an equalisation of educational opportunity to education for women's equality. The policy enjoins that the national education system should play a positive, interventionist role in the empowerment of women, foster the development of new values through redesigned curricula, textbooks, the training and orientation of teachers, decision-makers and administrators, and the active involvement of educational institutions. The removal of women's illiteracy and obstacles inhibiting their access to, and retention in, elementary education are given an overriding priority.

(v) UEE is contextual; contextuality entails local area planning with disaggregated target-setting and decentralised participative planning. The focus has shifted from educationally backward states to educationally backward districts.

(vi) While financial resources are important and necessary they are not sufficient for achieving EFA. A host of measures, both on the supply side and the demand side, mobilisation of community support and enlisting NGOs need to supplement higher financial outlay.

(vii) The policy recognises that unattractive school environment, unsatisfactory condition of buildings and insufficiency of instructional material function as demotivating factors for children and their parents. The policy, therefore, called for a drive for a substantial improvement of primary schools and provision of support services.

(viii) The NPE, 1986 commended the adoption at the primary stage of a child-centred and activity-based process of learning.

(ix) The NPE, 1986 and its POA postulate a large programme of restructuring of teacher education, pre-service as well as in-service.

(x) The total literacy campaigns (TLCs) with their unique social mobilisation, forging of a broad based alliance between the district administration, NGOs and social activists, and the innovative use of the confluence of culture and communication and the new pedagogy of improved pace and content of learning (PCL) with its inbuilt mechanism for evaluation of learning outcomes, are to be the main vehicle for promoting adult literacy.

(xi) The policy shifts from sectoral to a multisectoral approach with convergence of all developmental inputs; the resultant synergy is expected to improve the delivery of services and enhance the efficiency of resource utilisation. Thus in primary education convergence is sought between schooling, child services, nutrition and primary health care and other basic services. In non-formal education and adult literacy, convergence is sought between education and development, themes like population education, immunisation, nutrition and afforestation.

STATE POLICIES

State policies closely follow the national policies as the states have been closely associated with the formulation of the NPE and its POA significant development of the 1992 review NPE and POA has been that states have undertaken to formulate state POAs harmonising the situational imperatives with the national policy framework.

Several states have already come up with their own POAs. In the spirit of concurrency, states have been associated in tilt, formulation and implementation of national programmes like total literacy campaigns, operation blackboard, teacher education and the new district primary education programme. All the five year and annual plans of states have minimum needs component which includes adult literacy and elementary education. The release of central assistance to state plans is linked with the performance in the minimum needs component.

Incentive schemes of different kinds are already a well established feature of elementary school system. These are almost entirely in the state sector. The coverage as revealed by the Fifth All India Educational Survey (1986) indicated that of about 0.53 million primary schools, no less than about 0.15 million schools were providing mid-day meals of some sort to about 13.6 million children. About 0.25 million schools were providing free uniforms to 11 million children and about 20.2 million children were getting free textbooks in 0.35 million schools. At the upper primary level, as many as about 10.3 million children were getting free books, 4.3 million were getting free uniforms and 7.1 million some sort of mid-day meal. Education is free for girls up to class XII. Other incentives, including scholarships, also exist in different places.

STATUS OF EFA

At the time of Independence, India inherited a system of education which was not only quantitatively small but also characterised by the persistence of large intra and inter-regional as well as structural imbalances. Only 14 per cent of the population was literate and only one child out of three had been enrolled in primary school. The low levels of participation and literacy were aggravated by acute regional and gender disparities.

As education is vitally linked with the totality of the development process education being "the basic tool for the development of consciousness and reconstitution of society," in the words of Mahatma Gandhi-the reform and restructuring of educational system was recognised as an important area of state intervention.

The need for a literate population and universal education for all children in the age group of 6-14 was recognised as a crucial input for nation building and was given due consideration in the Constitution as well as in successive five year plans. This has resulted in a manifold increase of spatial spread, infrastructural facilities, increased coverage of various social groups; but the goal of providing basic education to all continues to be elusive.

India home to 16 per cent of world's population, is spread over 3,287,590 sq. km with a population of 1,028,610,328 (Census 2001), among them 532,156,772 being males and 496,453,556 females. The Census of India 2001 records an increase 12.6 percentage points over the literacy rate of 1991, the highest in any decade. For the first time the absolute number of illiterates has fallen from 328 million in 1991 to 296 million in 2001, despite the continuing rise in population. The nation is posed on the doorstep of total literacy with three-fourth of the male population and more than half of the female population and more than half of the female population now being literate. The female literacy rate has increased by 14.4 per cent from 39.3 per cent in 1991 to 53.7 percent in 2001. The corresponding increase in male literacy is about 12 per cent.

There have been several major interventions in India over the years to speed up pace of education for all. Such interventions are new national and state policy frameworks, planning mechanisms, new schemes, programmes and projects.

India's commitment to education for all was pronounced right at the dawn of her Independence as indicated by Article 45 of the Constitution. The commitment was reaffirmed subsequently. The major landmark in policy was the National Policy on Education 1986, inspired by the vision of then Prime Minister Late Shri Rajiv Gandhi, that laid the foundation of several schemes and projects for education for all. This resolve was strengthened by the international movement on education for all beginning with the Jomtien Conference in 1990.

The new Government that came to power in 2004, has made several important pronouncements indicating the new policy thrust on education for all, and has adopted a National common Minimum Programme (NCMP), which makes an unequivocal commitment of providing at least 6 per cent of GDP for education. The Government has also decided to levy a cess of two per cent on all Central taxes thereby generating an additional revenue of about Rs. 50 billion or $ 1 billion a year, for providing universal education to all children in the age group of 6 to 14 years. The new Government has also decided to create a non-lapsable Primary Education Fund so that the revenue generated for elementary education may not be diverted to other expenditure.

Both on the literacy and the primary education fronts, India has been implementing a number of specially designed programmes to move towards the goals of ensuring universal primary education and of eradicating adult illiteracy. As a follow up to the Dakar Framework of Action for EFA, an attempt has been made to link national goals and targets with the global targets on EFA, as stated earlier. The Central Advisory Board of Education (CABE) recognised that the World Declaration on EFA was, from the national point of view, a reaffirmation of the policy orientation given to elementary education in the NPE 1986. The CABE endorsed the Declaration and called for further strengthening of the processes initiated through the NPE 1986.

Other important developments have included the following:

— A separate Department of Elementary Education & Literacy, headed by an independent Secretary, was created in November 1999 within the Ministry of Human Resource Development to specifically focus on EFA goals.

— Constitutional Amendment Act was passed by the Parliament making elementary education Fundamental Right.

— Public expenditure on education as percentage of GDP increased from 3.82 in 2001-02 to 3.97 in 2002-03.

— Gender Parity Index has significantly improved from 0.38 in 1950-51 to 0.85 in 2002-03 in Elementary Education.

— Early Childhood care and Education provided coverage to a large majority of the 5652 blocks.

The introduction of New Education Policy in 1986 heralded an era of gradual expansion of education with a rise in the number of Centrally Sponsored Schemes (CSS) with targeted assistance to primary education. Gross enrollment ratios (GERs) in primary education increased from 81.9 percent in 1993-94 to 96 percent in 2001-02, and that in upper primary education, from 54.2 percent to 60.2 percent. The most remarkable improvement was in the education of girls, rural and poor children. During this period not only did GERs rise overall, but also the gap between rural and urban enrolment narrowed, as did the gender gap and the expenditure gap.

Early Childhood Care and Education (ECCE)

Early Childhood Care and Education (ECCE) was designed with dual objectives to provide necessary maturational and experiential readiness to the child for meeting the demands of the primary curriculum, and simultaneously providing substitute care facility for younger siblings. The integrated concept of ECCE, clearly represents the spirit of holistic development. The programme of ECCE has been under implementation on a large scale in rural areas through Integrated Child Development Services (ICDS) Scheme. Pre-school education in urban areas, which is fairly wide spread and is continuously expanding, is largely in the hands of the private sector.

Elementary Education

Universalisation of Elementary Education (UEE) is a national goal. NPE 1986 redefined UEE, shifting emphasis from enrolment to retention and achievement. This has been captured in the comprehensive scheme -Campaign for Education for All (Sarva Shiksha Abhiyan).

The Sarva Shiksha Abhiyan (SSA) is a nation-wide programme with an unprecedented outreach and comprehensiveness to universalise elementary education through community-ownership of the school system. The programme has subsumed the erstwhile District Primary Education Programme (DPEP), which covered about 270 districts in the country. The magnitude of the thrust under SSA can be estimated from the fact that from 01.04.2001 to 30.09.2004, about 160,000 new schools, 748,000 additional teachers, 127,000 new school buildings and 241,000 additional classrooms were sanctioned under the programme. Total enrolment at the elementary stage increased from 157 million in 2000 to 169 million in 2002. At the primary stage dropout rate for boys fell from 62 per cent in 1961 to 40 per cent in 2002-03, while the rate for girls came down even more sharply from 71 per cent to 34 per cent in the same period. Number of out-of-school children is estimated to have decreased from 35 million in 2000 to about 8 million by September 2004.

SSA provides special components for girls, children from SC/ST and other backward, and minority communities. Its focus is on educationally backward blocks, and it includes special programmes like Education Guarantee Scheme, Alternative & Innovative Educational Scheme (EGS & AIES); it has also converged with several of the schemes already initiated for UEE.

Empowering Women and Girls

The Mahila Samakhya programme, especially designed for empowering women, has / been implemented in 9,000 villages in 57 districts in 10 States. The programme views education as the critical factor for the empowerment of women, with adult education, non-formal education, and vocational training introduced in a phased manner, responding to the needs and priorities expressed by women. Under SSA, National Programme for Education of Girls at Elementary Level (NPEGEL) and Residential Schools for Girls (Kasturba Gandhi Balika Vidyalaya) have been introduced. The NPEGEL is targeting girls' education in the 2656 educationally backward blocks with a predominantly SC and ST population. In the residential schools scheme, nearly 750 residential schools, catering mainly to girls belonging to SC, ST, other backward classes (OBC) and minority groups are being set.

Out-of-school Youth and Adolescents

The development of adolescents falls under the purview of several ministries of the Government of India with the Ministry of Youth Affairs and Sports designated as the nodal ministry for the development of adolescents. The draft National Youth Policy 2001 provides a comprehensive overview of youth issues and concerns. The policy highlights several areas of concern for adolescents and youth in the country and emphasises an inter-sectoral approach, stressing empowerment and gender equity and underlines the importance of youth participation in all programmes. It gives a special focus to the educational needs of adolescents, including non-formal education and vocational skills requirements. Special mention has been made about developing a health package for adolescents and enforcing the legal age of marriage. The National Policy for Empowerment of Women 2001 recognises the girl child as a separate category and within this category, adolescent girls. The policy covers their nutrition, education, health, violence and sexual abuse against them, and the rights of the girl child.

Adult Education and Literacy

Adult literacy was taken up in a mission mode and the National Literacy Mission (NLM) aimed at full literacy (i.e., a sustainable threshold level of 75 per cent by 2007), focusing on functional literacy in the age group 15-35. Consequently, despite the population growth rate of more than 2 per cent per year, the absolute number of illiterates has steadily declined; the 12.6 percentage points increase in literacy between 1991 and 2001 is an all time high.

Adult literacy programme has been provided support through Continuing Education (CE) Programme and Jan Shikshan Sansthans (JSS). The CE programme has been made operational in 235 districts. Another 7500 CEs would be established in the districts covered by the literacy programmes, and full time facilitators appointed. Under JSS at present, more than 250 types of courses and activities are offered and 200,000 persons have been imparted vocational training so far. To accelerate the outreach, 30 JSSs have been selected for expanding activities to one additional neighbourhood district and funds are being sanctioned by NLM.

To provide a fillip to the literacy programme the National Literacy Mission has identified 45 districts in the country where the level of female literacy was below 30 per cent as per the 2001 Census. Most of these districts are in the States of Uttar Pradesh, Orissa, Bihar, and Jharkhand. The NLM is implementing local-specific interventions in these States with the participation of NGOs and local communities and is accelerating the implementation process over a period of 6-12 months.

Quality Concerns

The elementary school system in India has grown in size consistently, achieving an enrolment of more than 169 million. This obviously poses a major challenge not only for efficient management but also for mobilising resources needed to maintain even a reasonable level of quality. Quality improvement is a complex question and there is no single-factor solution for the problem. The Government has pursued a four-fold strategy consisting of (a) improving the provision of infrastructure and qualified teachers for primary education; (b) providing improved curriculum and teaching-learning material; (c) improving the quality of teaching-learning process through the introduction of child-centred pedagogy; and (d) increasing attention on measuring learner achievement levels.

Partnership with Development Agencies

To effectively achieve the targets of Universalisation of Elementary education external funding has been tied up for various programme like District Primary Education Programme, Shiksha Karmi

Programme, the Sarva Shiksha Abhiyan (SSA) Programme largely with World Bank, Swedish International Development Agency (SIDA), UNICEF, European Commission (EC) and UK Department for International Development (DFID). The 3 External Agencies (WB, EC and DFID) have agreed to fund SSA as an ongoing programme, accepting the existing framework, guidelines and implementation mechanism of the programme. The total amount of funding committed is around 1 billion dollars (Rs.4700 crores) of which 500 million dollars (around Rs.2250 crores) is from the World Bank, 190 million pounds (around Rs.1550 crores) from DFID and 160 million Euros (around Rs.900 crores) from EC. This amount is over and above the funds being provided by Government of India from domestic resources. The Department of Women and Child Development is also receiving approximately 20% funding for its ICDS programme from IDA. Beside that various international agencies such as ILO, UNESCO, UNAIDS, UNICEF are extending technical assistance to achieve targets of EFA.

A critical element in India's march towards education for all is the partnership between the Centre, the States and the civil society (including NGOS) within the federal structure. With broad policy, planning and financial parameters designed at the central level, Central Government also acts as a mentor encouraging States to innovate and generate local specific approaches to planning and implementing of education for all, which is essential because of the enormous diversity of India.

The SSA programme provides opportunities for NGOs and private sector to contribute towards the achievement of these goals and lead towards a community owned initiative for universalising elementary education. Over 4000 NGOs are currently participating in the programme for enhancing educational level for girls, urban children, children with special needs and flexible/alternate learning system.

The campaign for education for all is meticulously planned with the involvement of the community, primarily through decentralised district based planning. Implementation is continuously reviewed and is an ongoing process that provides meaningful feedback for midcourse corrections.

Financing and Expenditure Framework

Two key aspects of the Indian fiscal system that impinge on resource availability for the education sector are the division of taxation powers and the arrangements for fiscal transfers between the two levels of government.

Two types of transfers from Central to state governments exist – general purpose and specific purpose. The former include Finance Commissions awards, which devolve fixed shares in specified central taxes to states to support states' recurrent expenditure and Planning Commission Awards to support States' development expenditure for specific purposes. These CSSs may involve matching grants from the state in ratios specified in the scheme.

For the education sector in a state, thus there are multiple sources of finance:

— The state's own receipts (tax revenues and non-tax revenues)
— The statutory transfers of the Central governments
— The block assistance for the state plan
— The CSS of the Central Ministry of Human Resource Development.

The expenditure by education departments as a percentage of GNP at current prices has increased from 0.68 per cent in 1951-52 to 3.97 percent in 2002-03. It is hoped that the outlay on education would uniformly exceed 6 per cent of the national income by the end of Tenth Five Year Plan i.e., by 2007.

Elementary education has received a more favourable treatment since the Eighth Plan. In the Ninth Plan, the government allocated Rs. 249,080.38 million for education against an expenditure of Rs. 85,218.9 million in the Eighth Plan. The Ninth Five Year Plan (1997-2002) allocation for elementary education was 163695.9 million, which was 65.72 per cent of the total allocation for education. In the Tenth Five Year Plan (2002-07), the outlay for basic education has been fixed at Rs. 300,000 million in the total outlay of Rs. 438250 million for all education programme's indicating 68.5 per cent share of basic education. This highlights the proactive role that the central government is playing towards achieving the goal of EFA.

Resource Projection for EFA

India has consciously decided to align the planning process of EFA with the planning process of the country, which is reflected in the five-year plans. While formulating the goals of the Tenth Five Year Plan (2002-07), it has been attempted that requirements of the EFA goals set in Dakar are fulfilled in the Plan period itself. The sectors covered in the Tenth five Year Plan (2002-07) are: (i) Early Childhood Care and Education (ECCE), (ii) elementary Education, (iii) Mid-day Meal in Schools, (iv) Education of Girls and Women Empowerment, (v) Teacher Education, (vi) Education of Out-of school Youth and Adolescents, and (vii) adult Education Programme. As is apparent, the above sectors target all the six EFA goals.

Total fund requirement for implementing the National Plan of Action for EFA is Rs. 941,190 million as indicated in Table below:

Table 1. Total Funds required for EFA Rs. in Million

Sl.No.	*Sector*	*Centre*	*State*	*Total*
1	ECCE	122470	0	122470
2	Elementary	397600	125200	522800
3	Mid-day meal	66000	110000	176000
4	Girls' education	25750	3750	29500
5	Teacher Education	9500	0	9500
6	Youth & adolescent	11020	6500	17250
7	Adult education	63400	0	63400
	Total	695740	245450	941190

Additional resource required for elementary education and mid-day meal are being generated through an Education Cess @ 2 per cent on income tax, excise and customs duties and service tax levied from 2004-05. This new Cess will yield about Rs. 50, billion in a year, which will be earmarked for financing Elementary Education including the Mid-day Meal Scheme. This Education Cess would flow into a separate, dedicated fund called National Elementary Education Fund, and the amount accrued as Cess would neither lapse at the end of the financial year nor would be diverted to any purpose other than elementary education.

More education need not and should not mean diluted education. A democratically oriented mass education system is necessarily more resource intensive. As aptly put by Philip Coombs, while not all problems of education can be solved by throwing money at them, without money to procure the essential physical inputs (buildings, equipments, other material supplies) and human resources (teachers and administrators) educational systems would collapse to empty structures. In the ultimate, resources and management would define implementation of the strategies outlined for achieving the goals and objectives of EFA.

INTERNATIONAL COOPERATION

Assistance from UNESCO

India actively promotes international cooperation in the area of basic education mainly at the regional anti sub-regional levels through various programmes of UNESCO and the SAARC Technical Committee on Education and Culture. India, as one of the promoters of UNESCO's Regional Programme of Educational Innovations for Development of Asia and the Pacific (APEID), participates in APEID programmes and activities at a significant scale. A National Development Group (NDG) for APEID in India was set up which functions as an identifier, stimulator and coordinator of activities of educational innovations for development within the country. The NDG, comprises representatives of concerned Ministries and departments and pioneering institutions engaged in educational research. On the lines of NDG, State Development Groups (SDGs) were established in States and Union Territories which function in close collaboration with the NDG. The NCERT, one of the principal associate centres of APEID, acts as the secretariat of NDG and facilitates dissemination of information about APEID activities, innovative experiences in the country.

Another important regional programme of UNESCO in which India has contributed significantly is the Asia-Pacific Programme on Education for All (APPEAL) which was launched from New Delhi by UNESCO in 1987. A high level National Coordination Committee has been set up to coordinate activities under APPEAL and the follow up of the Jomtien Conference.

UNESCO has also sponsored, through Japanese Funds-in-Trust, an innovative Pilot Project on Promotion of Primary Education of Girls and Disadvantaged Group in the State of Haryana. This project is being implemented by the NCERT. India has the distinction of being awarded UNESCO Literacy prizes for three successive years; The King Sejong Literacy Prize awarded to the Kerala Sastra Sahitya Parishad, Thiruvananthapuram in 1990 and Puduvai Arivoli Iyakkam of Pondicherry in 1992 and the Noma Literacy Prize to the Government of West Bengal in 1991.

Assistance from UNICEF

UNICEF's cooperation with Government of India in the field of education is intended to support the national goals of improving opportunities for basic education for all children and women, improving social and economic opportunities for women and reducing disparities in education among different groups and between genders.

Working closely with both the Department of Education at Union level and national institutions such as NCERT and NIEPA as well as departments in focus states, UNICEF has provided financial as well as technical support to the implementation of experimental projects for introduction of Minimum Levels of Learning (MLLs), projects for evaluation and documentation of Total Literacy Campaigns, the development of literacy and post-literacy materials, innovative media activities such as Project Radio Education in Adult Literacy (PREAL) and production of weekly broadsheets for neo-literates, etc. During 1992, UNICEF provided support for developing and implementing district specific projects in a number of states. The most significant of these was in Madhya Pradesh where teacher education project in five districts is being experimented. The project is establishing teacher resource centres at cluster level and aims at institutionalising continuous in-service teacher support and training. In Andhra Pradesh, UNICEF has focused on the issue of education for girls and is supporting demonstration activities in Mehboobnagar and Anantpur districts. In Bombay, a project implemented by the Bombay Municipal Corporation seeks to improve the quality of primary education in deprived urban areas and reduce the high drop-out and repetition rates.

Support has also continued for two innovative projects-Project on Integrated Education for the Disabled (PIED), and the Area Intensive Education Project (AIEP). PIED, which is being coordinated by NCERT, seeks to develop appropriate strategies for integrating disabled children into mainstream primary education and strengthen the central government's Integrated Education for Disabled Children Programme at primary levels. AIEP is an attempt to operationalise the concept of micro-planning and is being undertaken in six states and union territories. This is being coordinated by the respective SCERTs/ SIEs.

UNICEF has collaborated in the areas of promotion and planning of "Education for All" at national and state levels and in developing demonstration projects in support of key elements of the national programme of action, focusing on activities at district level. In addition UNICEF is also supporting a comprehensive basic education project in Bihar, viz. Bihar Education Project.

Andhra Pradesh Primary Education Project (APPEP)

This project is being implemented in Andhra Pradesh, since April 1983 with the assistance of Overseas Development Administration (ODA) of U.K. The objective of the project is to improve the quality of primary education in the project area by (i) enhancing the professional competence of teachers and supervisors of primary schools through HRD programme which emphasises child-centred learning and (ii) assisting construction of primary school buildings. The project covers all the primary schools in the state and envisages an outlay of Rs.31.2 million over the period 1990-92. AJs a pre-omtien project, its scope is partial and does not cover important components of basic education such as demand generation, non-formal education and the focus on girls. An important institutional innovation is the organisation of in-service teaching training at sub-districts levels.

The Bihar Education Project

The Bihar Education Project (BEP) represents the first major attempt in India to include the broad range of national EFA concerns, issues, approaches and strategies in one, large-scale operational programme. It is regarded as the UNICEF's "flagship" EFA project. The BEP covers all components of elementary education and will be expanded in a phased manner in 20 districts. Project activities have begun in seven districts. An outlay of Rs.3600 million is envisaged during 1990-95; UNICEF has pledged US $8 million from general resources and $100 millions from supplementary resources.

An important institutional innovation has been the constitution of an autonomous state level body, registered as a society, for the implementation of the project. The creation of this structure is rooted in the wide-spread realisation that the existing administrative structures are inadequate to implement special time-bound educational programmes which call for intense participative process and which require a mission mode of implementation with a spirit of despatch and resolve. There are two main organs of the society—the general Council under the chairmanship of the Chief Minister and the Executive Committee under the chairmanship of the State Education Secretary. The Government of India, the Government of Bihar, NGOs, teacher representatives and distinguished women and educationists are represented in these bodies so that planning and monitoring are done in a participatory manner. Similar participatory structures have been set up at district level. Village Education Committees play an important role in the implementation of the project at the village level. This insitutional innovation has come to be a key feature of all subsequent projects like the U.P. Basic Education Project and the District Primary Education Programme (DPEP).

The UNICEF-GOI mid-term review of the project in May 1993 had noted :

1. Despite a slow start, implementation picked up considerably in the second half of 1992. The 1993-94 financial year represents the first year for which systematic planning has taken place for each of seven districts. District planning has emerged as an important project strategy.
2. Project management structures established at state level and in seven districts though to a varying degree of effectiveness.
3. In line with the open-ended approach of the Project, some components have been given higher priority than others for the time being in accordance with local/district priorities and implementation capacity. Overall, the initial emphasis on

mobilisation and literacy activities in 1991 has shifted to a strong focus on primary education. Activities related to women's empowerment are also emerging as key interventions.

4. Though coverage within districts is still uneven and varied in terms of components, a 'standard' package of service delivery inputs and quality interventions for primary education is beginning to emerge (community mobilisation, provision of facilities, basic materials, teacher training, etc.) in the seven districts taken up so far. Provision of facilities with extensive community mobilisation and involvement has emerged as a strong entry point.

5. Important policy interventions are being developed and applied (e.g., teacher rationalisation). Major strategies for key components with state-wide implications are being developed: BEP has provided impetus for a complete overhaul of the teacher education system in the state; alternative approaches for in-service training developed and tested including establishment of a model District Institute of Education and Training.

6. Project has had major impact on attitudes in Bihar towards education at political, administrative and community levels. Project has also played a major role in mobilising greater national and international interest in basic education. It is regarded as the pioneering effort for other large-scale projects which are now being taken up in several states. Lessons learnt have also been applied in the national District Primary Education Programme."

The project 'Lok Jumbish : People's Movement for Basic Education for All : Rajasthan' Is being implemented in Rajasthan with assistance from Swedish International Development Authority. The project relies heavily on people's mobilisation and seeks to bring about maximum possible decentralisation of management, accountability and relevance to the educational system. The overall goal of the project is to achieve education for all in Rajasthan by the year 2000. As of now, it is in the pilot phase (1992-94) with a coverage of 25 blocks.

Uttar Pradesh Basic Education Project

This is the first major primary education project funded by the World Bank in India. Covering ten districts the project envisages an outlay of

Rs.7280 millions approximately over a period of years spanning 1993-2000. The World Bank has approved a credit of US $ 163.1 million for the project. As with BEP the management would be through a participative state level autonomous society and VECs would play an active role in the implementation of the project at the grass-roots level. A key institutional innovation is the State Institute of Management and Training, UP which, in collaboration with NCERT and NIEPA, is expected to play a major role in the training of educational functionaries and communi ty leaders.The project also attempts to operationalise the concept of school complexes, suggested as early as 1964-65 by the Education Commission, to provide resource support to schools.

CHALLENGE FOR EFA ACHIEVEMENT

The new millennium begins with new expectations. The revised framework of the National Literacy Mission proposes to reach a literacy rate of 75 per cent by the year 2007. The Sarva Shiksha Abhiyan (SSA), which is the flagship programme of the national government, expects to achieve the goal of EFA by 2010 (five years ahead of the International commitment made at Dakar). This would mean that all children (in all states) would complete at least five years of schooling (or its equivalent through non-formal means) by the year 2007; all of them would transit to upper primary schools and complete at least another three years of schooling by 2010.

There is no doubt that the SSA targets are ambitious, surpassing the international expectations articulated in the Dakar Summit, which sets the target of 2015 for achieving the goal of EFA. While one can debate on the relevance of setting such ambitious targets, ignoring the practicability of mobilising necessary physical, financial and human resources, an important point needs to be borne in mind. For the poor and the marginalised, basic education continues to be the only hope and means of redemption. But across socio-economic considerations, a deep sense of desperation is setting in the minds of the people with respect to the capability of the state to meet their educational needs. An urgent requirement is to dispel this sense of despair and re-establish public faith in the state-sponsored delivery mechanisms, be it primary schools or adult literacy programmes. This can be done only through actual demonstration of effectively functioning institutions that produce desired results and meet the aspirations of the society. It is this resolve and determination of all those concerned with EFA in the country to persist with accelerated efforts that holds the key for achieving the goal of Education for All.

Considering the strong political will, assistance from civil society / NGOs, institutional arrangement at State and lower level and sustainable financial arrangement such as imposing Cess on Central taxes for education, the country is hopeful to achieve target of EFA.

Educational administration has long tended to be too pre-occupied with provision of facilities-schools, school buildings and appointments of teachers to the neglect of the processes required to make the system work. There is enough empirical evidence on the mismatch between access and enrolment which cast doubts on the propriety of this institutional pre-occupation. It is this exclusive concern with the facilities of schooling that was impugned by Mahatma Gandhi in his Chatham House address: "I say without fear of my figures being challenged successfully, that today India is more illiterate than it was fifty or a hundred years ago, and so is Burma, because the British taking hold of things as they were, began to root them out. They scratched the soil and began to look at the root, and left the root like that, and the beautiful enough for the British administrator, so he came out paraphernalia, building, and so forth... I defy anybody to fulfil a programme of compulsory primary education of these masses inside of a century. This very poor country of mine is ill able to sustain such an expensive method of education."

This is said not to belittle the importance of such facilities to schools but to emphasise that the construction of school buildings and lower pupil-teacher ratios are not the be all and end all of UEE. The education system, the state and the civil society at large should internalise a broader functional view of education, a view which conceives education as a dynamic, cumulative lifelong process, encompassing a wide diversity of learning opportunities, applying to all people, but laying stress on girls, children and youth, particularly those belonging to the disadvantaged groups. But here again rhetoric is not enough. -Strategies are needed to bring about the perceptional change. Innovation and dissemination are important components of any such strategy. Nothing can bring about the perceptional changes faster than the development and dissemination of viable and scalable models of non-formal education. Regional and international co-operation can facilitate innovation and dissemination.

The importance of financial resources cannot be exaggerated. It is reasonable to hope that, as the economy is reformed, as state intervention gets re-focused and as public expenditure is restructured more budgetary resources would flow to education, articularly to EFA. To this end educational reform needs to be fitted into the "architecture that our (economic) reforms seek to create".

The 73rd and 74th amendments to the Constitution provide yet another opportunity to decentralise educational administration and render the system accountable to the community. This opportunity should be grasped through legislative and administrative changes in consonance with the spirit underlying these costitutional amendments. If the past experience is any guide devolution of functions Should be complemented by simultaneous devolution of commensurate powers and resources; peoples' representatives as well as the educational functionaries need to be prepared to cope with the transition and to discharge the responsibilities that the pursuit of EFA would entail, such as microplanning and monitoring. The role of training for this purpose cannot be emphasised enough; training should encompass motivation, content and process. Designs for reform should not overlook routine business of education. "If schools do not open their doors, if teachers are not paid, the best policies, plans, or reforms will serve very little... the improvement of administrative machinery must always begin with everyday functions of delivery. This is already a challenging and difficult undertaking, requiring 'time, political commitment, and the enlistment of social support".

The task ahead is daunting but one need not despair. To despair is not only to sin but to miss the silent revolution that has been transforming India. The democratisation process has transformed India into a "land of million mutinies". Social groups which have been hitherto quiescent are yearning for social and economic advancement. It is the collective psyche of unrest that offers the greatest hope for EFA.

References

Brossard, Mathieu, and Luc-Charles Gacougnolle. 2001. "Financing Primary Education for All: Yesterday, Today and Tomorrow." United Nations Educational, Scientific, and Cultural Organization, Paris.

Colclough, Christopher, and Keith Lewin. 1993. *Educating All the Children: Strategies for Primary Schooling in the South.* New York: Oxford University Press.

Devarajan, Shantayanan, Margaret J. Miller, and Eric V. Swanson. 2002. "Goals for Development: History, Prospects and Costs." *Policy Research Working Paper* 2819. World Bank, Washington, D.C.

De, Anuradha, and Jean Dreze. 1999. *Public Report on Basic Education in India (PROBE).* New Delhi: Oxford University Press.

Delamonica, Enrique, Santosh Mehrotra, and Jan Vandemoortele. 2001. "Is EFA Affordable? Estimating the Global Minimum Cost of Education for All." Innocenti Working Paper 87. United Nations Children's Fund, New York.

10

Teacher Education System

Education has always been linked with society. It has both a personal and a social dimension, and like the two sides of the same coin, they are Inseparable. Accordingly, the goals and priorities of the nation must necessarily be reflected in the objectives of the teaching profession and of the teacher, since these are intrinsically and casually linked. For the same reason, as the priorities and thrusts of a nation undergo a certain amount of change from time to time, so must educational priorities and objectives, to enable education to retain its currency and relevance. Hence we have given the report the title The Teacher and Society.

For the proper fulfilment of the national educational goals, the teacher's role assumes great significance. The teacher must actively and feelingly associate himself, as an essential and responsible partner, in the great tasks which face the nation. If the four national goals were to become the actual motive force and the ideals that every man, woman and child in our land would live by the teacher must intervene in a big way. The formation of character, a character evolved in response to the national goals, would constitute his primary task. He will indeed prepare students for examinations and open to them the world of knowledge. But these will count for little unless he has helped them become persons of character. There is the personal aspect of character-building to develop qualities like honesty and integrity and there is the social aspect which defines national character. Such a character identification must not be based on cultural and religious traditions of any one group but must find acceptance by all sections of the people. The teacher must provide suitable challenges to children and guide them through personal contact to strive continuously to raise performance to their highest level ability.

An aspect of modernisation of particularly relevance to our national needs today is productivity. How we produce more, produce better, improve designs and processes and update standards if attitudes continue to be traditional ? This is where the teacher has a critical role to play to develop in the child proper modern attitudes. Science today is compulsory at the secondary stage. But if science is taught merely as a body of information and facts to be passed on to the students for later retrieval during the examination, if the teaching and learning of science does not bring about a real change in the students' attitudes, then science teaching will remain largely a wasted effort. What is important in learning science is that the student must be able to question, to hypothesise, to search for evidence, insist on objectivity all the time in search for solutions to simple and everyday problems. He must demand and insist on accuracy, exactness and order in his work. Science must enable the student to see reality differently, to perceive self, others and nature, in a new light. Teaching science today, we feel, is largely teaching something about science and achieves little by way of modernising the child's thinking and approaches. The highest priority must belong, therefore, to the systematic orientation of science teachers so that they can help the students understand and appreciate science and the true value of the scientific method.

Today's classrooms, for the large part, exhibit stark medievalism. The absence of even the most essential physical facilities and even more, the absence of any kind of aids and equipment to facilitate teaching and promote learning makes the task of teaching science difficult and, in many instances, virtually impossible.

If the teacher does not care, he cannot expect his students to care either. If he does not know what tenderness or kindness is, he has the impossible task of fostering compassion in others. In a brief report like this, we can only provide certain directions and clues to path-finding rather than provide complete answers. This would be the responsibility of teachers, teachers organisations and educational agencies. Caring, must begin in the classroom and in the school campus. The child should be taught to develop an effortless sense of equality with others, even though he sees differences of colour, caste, religion, abilities, etc. This will naturally result in considerateness and the desire for mutual help.

If brighter children could help the weaker ones, would so many children fail? Outside the classroom same considerateness can extend to the younger ones at school, to the handicapped, and to strangers? When such feelings and relationships are fostered individually and collectively, the school climate becomes humane and caring.

While taking up programmes of community service, children come into live contact with people, and when these experiences are backed up by group discussion and reflection, they gain insight into the inter-relatedness of man with man, and begin to see a close link with other members of the community, no matter by what name or label the other is identified. Similarly the teacher must take a lead role in promoting kinship with environment. Good environment, whether human or physical, has a humanising element. Without having to incur any major expenditure, simple initiatives on the part of the teacher and the head will enable each school to present a much cleaner and more beautiful look as a place of learning. Trees and flowers could become a part of every school. A collective effort by teachers and pupils would transform our present drab classrooms into attractive places of which both the students and the teacher could legitimately feel proud and happy. It will also enable pupils to work together cooperatively and in a team spirit. Starting with developing an eye for beauty and order in their immediate environment, teachers can help pupils observe the environment outside the school, in their neighbourhood or beyond, the dirt and the squalor, poverty and degradation as well as the beauty and loveliness of nature and of man. Concern for environment grows with such observation.

Status of the Teacher

There has been a feeling of grievance on the part of the teachers that they net receive the status and respect from society that their profession And role demand. True. The fault, however, does not shop lie at the door of the community alone. Teachers, teacher attitudes and teacher performance have contributed to the sad status quo. Their new sense of commitment and effective linkage between their work and the attainment of national goals and purposes, will restore in full measure the reverence that traditionally was given to the teacher. Status, by reason of a title or position will become increasingly difficult to come by, we feel. Status, in other words, will have to be earned, by the teacher, as by any other professional worker. It may be recalled that the Guru never demanded reverence but the Shisya, his parents and the adult community gladly and gratefully proffered it to the teacher. So must the new teacher earn status through achievement. The closer the teacher is able to link himself and his vocation with the mission of the nation, the more relevant he will become and the more revered by students, parents and society. We underscore that the primary task of the teacher is concerned with man-making, namely the making of the Indian of tomorrow.

The role of the teacher has been well recognised in the traditional Indian thought through the centuries. The 'Guru' (teacher) was to be revered as an imparter of knowledge and a guide. In the present context, the role of the teacher remains as critical as ever.

The teacher plays a major role in implementing the policies and schemes formulated to achieve a breakthrough in the quantitative expansion and qualitative improvement of education. Reflecting the crucial role of teachers in national development, the NPE 1986 called for a substantial improvement in the conditions of work and quality of teacher education.

System of Teacher Education

The NPE 1986, called for an over-haul of the Teacher Education System in the country. It emphasised the need for continuing education for teachers to meet the thrust envisaged in the policy. A new Centrally Sponsored Scheme of Restructuring and Reorganisation of Teacher Education was launched in 1987-88 which primarily envisages establishment of DIETs to provide pre-service and in-service training to elementary school teachers and to AE and NFE personnel. In addition, upgradation of Secondary Teacher Education Institutions into Colleges of Teacher Education (CTEs), establishment of Institutes of Advanced Studies in Education (IASE), strengthening of SCERTs and University Departments of Education through the University Grants Commission are components of this restructuring which has the basic objective of providing training and resource support to elementary and secondary education at the grassroots level.

Central assistance is meant for the construction of buildings, procurement of books and equipments, additional expenditure on staff salaries and training programmes. In view of the high priority accorded to the achievement of the target of UEE, emphasis under the Teacher Education Scheme has so for been on setting up of DIETs. It was proposed to establish DIETs in 425 districts in the country (as per 1987-88 configuration when there were 451 districts in total) by the end of the VIII Five Year Plan. Against this target, 424 DIETs have been sanctioned as on 1st March, 96. Seventy three CTEs and 34 IASEs have also been sanctioned. Eighteen SCERTs have been assisted under strengthening of SCERT component of the scheme.

A Special Orientation Programme for Primary Teachers (SOPT) has also been taken up during the VIII Plan period. Started in late 1993, this programme is aimed at orienting an estimated 1.8 million primary teachers in the country in the use of Operation Blackboard material and MILLs strategy. The NCERT is the apex body implementing this programme through state nodal agencies which are mostly SCERTs. Ministry of Human Resource Development releases grants to the NCERT based on the needs. Within the provision of the Centrally Sponsored Scheme of Restructuring and Reorganisation of Teacher Education, so far about Rs. 450 million has been released to the NCERT for the purpose. According to the NCERT, State Governments have reported training of about 0.3 million primary teachers under the SOPT. Details on the implementation of Teacher Education Scheme have been presented earlier.

Qualifications and Training

The minimum general qualification prescribed by some states for the recruitment of primary school teachers (teaching grades I-V) is 10 years of formal education (matriculation/ secondary), whereas, it is senior secondary or 12 years of education prescribed in certain states (e.g., Haryana, Maharashtra, Tamil Nadu, Uttar Pradesh and Delhi). The minimum qualification prescribed by most states for the appointment of upper primary school teachers (teaching grades VI-VIII) is graduation (second level diploma) whereas in some states it is matriculation/senior secondary (first level diploma). The educational qualifications of teachers have been gradually increasing. According to the Fifth All India Educational Survey in 1986 (NCERT, 1990), as many as 2.1 million (77 per cent) primary and upper primary school teachers had been trained through first level diploma (under-graduation), 0.5 million (18 per cent) through second level diploma (graduation) and 0.1 million (5 per cent) through third level diploma (post graduation and above).

All states in India require at least a graduation degree (second level diploma) for secondary school teachers (grades VI-X and post-graduation degree (third level diploma) for higher/ senior secondary school teachers (grades XIXII). As many as 58 per cent teachers teaching at the secondary and higher secondary levels had second level diploma, 33 per cent had third level diploma and only about 9 per cent had first level diploma (under-graduation).

Pre-service Teacher Training

The Fifth All India Educational Survey (NCERT, 1990) indicates that about 87 per cent primary and upper primary teachers are trained, that is, they have acquired a primary or elementary teacher training certificate of one or two years' duration or bachelors degree in education. There are, however, significant regional variations. The percentage of trained teachers at primary and upper primary level is more than 99 per cent in the states of Haryana, Tamil Nadu, Chandigarh and Delhi. It is less than 50 per cent in Arunachal Pradesh, Meghalaya, Sikkim, Nagaland and Tripura.

The Centrally Sponsored Scheme of Restructuring and Reorganisation of Teacher Education taken up in 1987-88 in pursuance of NPE 1986 envisages, on the one hand, strengthening of institutional base of teacher training and on the other, takes up special programmes for training of teachers in specified areas and other non-institutional programmes of orientation for teachers. The Scheme provides for the setting up of DIETs to provide training and resource support to elementary education (both formal and non-formal) and AE systems at the grassroots level.

The scheme for establishing the DIETs envisaged raising the general education of primary teachers to 12 years of schooling. With the establishment of DIETs, almost all states are now moving towards a two-year diploma in education for those teaching at the elementary level following 12 years of schooling.

Of the total number of teachers working in high or higher secondary schools, approximately, 90 per cent are trained, i.e., they have acquired a bachelor's degree in education (B. Ed.)/, The percentage of trained teachers at both the levels is the highest in Chandigarh and lowest in Assam. A comparison between male and female teachers indicates that the number of male untrained teachers is more than that of female teachers at all school levels in the country.

The National Council for Teacher Education

The NCTE was established in May, 1973 by a Government resolution to advise Central and State Governments on all matters pertaining to teacher education, with its Secretariat located in the NCERT. The NCTE's status and role till 1993 have been purely advisory and it did not have statutory powers to enforce its guidelines. As per the provisions laid down in the NPE 1986 and the Programme of Action for its implementation, the NCTE has been conferred statutory status as per the NCTE Act No. 73 of 1993 passed by the Parliament and assented to by the President. It has come into existence with effect from 17th May, 95. The Act provides for establishment of the NCTE with a view to achieving planned and coordinated development of teacher education system throughout the country, regulation and proper maintenance of norms and standards in the teacher education system and for matters connected therewith. Programmes and activities taken up by the NCTE so for include:

— Preparation of a framework for competency-based curriculum for elementary teacher training institutions.

— Restructuring of pre-service teacher education curriculum for all stages.

— Human Rights and National Values-preparation of materials and orientation of teacher educators.

— Preparation of a video film on teacher training in physical education.

— Preparation of a project proposal on Teacher Education in States/UTs-current status, issues and future projections.

— Development of material for teacher educators on specific subjects.

Instructors in NFE

In the NFE system, the instructor is the key person. The instructor is a nominally paid volunteer who is usually employed on a part-time basis. He/she could be an educated housewife, a girl from the village, an educated unemployed youth, a retired teacher, a qualified social worker, an Anganwadi worker or even a professional semi-skilled person. Among the qualities expected of an instructor are dedication to work, and volunteerism. Girls' NFE centres have only lady instructors. The minimum qualification of the instructor is class 10 pass. But studies show that the qualifications of instructors vary from class 8 to Master's degree with a professional degree in education. In fact, there are many remote areas-rural and tribals-where individuals who have studied beyond class 8 are not available. In such cases, the VEC is empowered to relax the minimum qualification of the instructor. In the case of lady instructors, this problem is even more acute.

The basic skill which an NFE instructor is expected to have or develop is multi-class teaching as the group of learners he/she has to deal with is a heterogeneous one. The methodology of teaching at the NFE centre has to be different from the one used in formal schools. Therefore, to orient the instructor in the teaching methodology and also to acquaint him with the content of the learning materials, a four-tier system of training has been developed. A group of mastertrainers from each state is trained by the NCERT, who in turn train Project Officers of NFE at the state level. The Project Officers thus trained, are responsible for training supervisors and instructors at the block level.

During the first year, the minimum training period for the instructor is 30 days and in the subsequent year it is 20 days. The first phase is usually divided into three phases and focused on training in pedagogy, content, evaluation and monitoring. The second phase of training is devoted to discussion focused at finding solutions to the problems faced by the instructors while teaching at the centre.

Various packages of training materials have been developed to cope with the needs of training. The training of instructors at the district level is done through DIETs. The overall responsibility of training NFE functionaries at the state level rests with the SCERTs.

In the NFE centres, the instructor is the link between the centre and the community and is expected to perform a more dynamic role. He is also expected to take care of the individual needs of the learner and help him/her in solving day-to-day problems. The responsibilities of instructors include the organisation of the daily activities of the centre, identification of out-of-school and non-school going children, the selection of the site for the centre in consultation with the VEC, organising teaching-learning activities by drawing on supervisors, primary school teachers, TLC volunteers, ECCE Centres, the community, nearby voluntary agencies, mobile village library, Block Development Office, Primary Health Centres, etc.

The monitoring of the NFE programme is done on a continuous basis at all levels viz. village, district and state through the VEC, DIETs, SCERTs and Directorate of Education.

The teachers working under TLCs are volunteers and are not paid any salary for their services. Since the qualification of these volunteers is not fixed, any educated person capable of working as a volunteer is appointed and trained. The responsibility of training volunteers of TLCs is that of the State Resource Centres (SRCs).

Conditions of Work

Good conditions of work play a significant role in attracting and retaining the right type of persons in the teaching profession and enabling them to function efficiently. The working conditions include teacher's salary and benefits, availability of a suitable school building and essential facilities in the school, teacher's workload, method of recruitment, availability of teaching and non-teaching materials and opportunities for promotion.

Today, teacher's pay is probably the most important element affecting the quality of education. The salaries of different levels of teachers are established separately by each state and are determined on the basis of academic qualifications, training and experience.

In addition to salary, price-index linked 'dearness allowance' is given to all teachers. Various other allowances are also granted to all categories of teachers to compensate them for the special stress under which they work. These allowances are: city compensatory allowance, house rent allowance, hill allowance and other special allowances such as winter allowance, backward, remote and tribal area allowance, island allowance, etc. These allowances differ from state to state and within the state from stage to stage of education. Entry level salaries for trained primary teachers are only slightly higher than those for untrained teachers. The maximum salary for a trained teacher is 3 to 4 times his/ her entry salary, and is achieved only after 1620 years of service in most states.

In the majority of states, the salary scales of trained and untrained graduate teachers in upper primary/middle schools are at par with those in secondary and higher/senior secondary schools. Teachers with a Master's degree working in higher/senior secondary schools have separate salary scales and are designated as post-graduate teachers (PGTs) or 'Lecturers' (School Cadre).

There is a provision of selection grades for all categories of teachers. Twenty per cent of senior teachers of different categories get selection grades after, 10 to 15 years of service. In addition, most states provide fixed medical allowance or reimbursement of medical expenses, advances for house building and purchase of conveyance, and free education for the children of teachers, as well as retirement benefits of pension, gratuity and group insurance. In the majority of states, there is also a provision of incentives for some special categories of teachers. For instance, in Assam, Bihar, Gujarat, Maharashtra and Tamil Nadu, a certain percentage of elementary (primary and upper primary) women teachers working in rural and remote areas are given residential accommodation. In some states, physically handicapped teachers are offered conveyance allowance.

Teaching Material

Recent studies at primary level in selected educationally backward districts have revealed, that charts, maps and globes were available in the blocks covered by the Operation Blackboard (OB) Scheme introduced by the Central Government to provide some minimum infrastructure to primary schools e.g., two classrooms, a kit consisting of some teaching-learning materials and provision of an additional teacher. Teachers in remote areas now handle 2-3 classes, whereas, earlier they used to handle 4-5 classes. Thus, it is evident that the minimum essential facilities needed for a smooth school functioning and a teaching-learning process need to be upscaled at all school levels, particularly, at primary level.

Promotional Prospects for Teachers

In most states, the promotion of teachers in government primary and secondary schools is either on the basis of seniority or seniority-cum-merit. Acquiring higher qualifications also helps in promotion provided a departmental vacancy exists which suits the qualification of the candidate.

In the case of teachers working in private and aided schools, the chances of promotion are rare because in privately managed schools there is a shortage of senior positions and so only one or two persons have the opportunity to reach the level of headmaster/head teacher. In secondary and higher secondary schools, a Trained Graduate Teacher (TGT) may become a Post-Graduate Teacher'(PGT) provided he gets some higher qualifications i.e. a Master's degree in any school subject and depending upon the availability of a vacancy in the school. It may well be that teachers in private aided schools or privately managed recognised schools or public schools remain in the some post from the beginning to the end of their service of 30 to 35 years.

Teachers in government schools can aspire for higher administrative posts in the Education Department of the Government of India. Though a certain percentage of posts in the higher categories of education are reserved for teachers, yet, avenues of promotion in the teaching profession are comparatively more limited than in other sectors such as industry, commerce and business.

Teacher Support Material

A number of agencies such as the NCERT, NIEPA, SCERTs and Departments of Education in universities have developed documentation services for teachers. A number of educational journals addressed to school teachers are published by national and state institutions such as NCERT, SCERTs, Boards of School Education, Teachers' Associations, NGOs and private publishers to disseminate research findings and information regarding innovations attempted by teachers, teachers' educators or researchers in different settings.

Materials (multi-media packages, self-learning materials, etc.) for training and upgrading the knowledge and skills of teachers/ functionaries of minority institutions through Distance Education are prepared by the NCERT, IGNOU, NIEPA and NOS, etc.

Some leading newspapers also sometimes bring out supplements or special editions on education. In addition, several institutions and NGOs bring out educational material in audio and video format. Professional associations have also made their contribution in this field. The UGC supports these efforts at the higher education level through a chain of EMRCs (Educational Media Research Centres) and AVRCs (Audio Visual Resource Centres). These efforts are coordinated through a Consortium of Educational Communications (CEC). The IGNOU also has a media programme service. These programmes are telecast throughout the country under the programme 'Country-wide Classroom'. Even though the programmes are targetted at students, teachers are also able to upgrade content and methodology-related delivery and evaluation techniques. Computer software has also been developed to upgrade the knowledge content in various school subjects.

At the school level, the CIET in the NCERT and the SIETs which have been set up in six states are responsible for producing these programmes. Besides these, broadcasts and telecasts cater to regular and out-of-school children and teachers at the primary and secondary level. Several other technological aids and other audio-visual aids have been developed to help teachers in their instructional tasks. A large number of films have also been produced on teacher training, including the teaching of difficult concepts and content areas to children. The films produced include films on the methodology of teaching science, and the needs of children with special problems. Science kits, too, have been developed to enable children to perform experiments related to the prescribed syllabi.

Influenced by the advent of new technologies of communication, the teacher's role has been changing rapidly and teacher education curricula have been revised periodically reflecting this. Interpersonal skills for making instruction interactive and the two-way communication effective have become an integral part of the changes. These curricular reforms have provided teachers an opportunity to participate in the designing of instructional material using locally available resources.

A number of newspapers and magazines extend support to teachers in their work. Many teachers, through their writings in newspapers and magazines, provide additional material to students.

School broadcast and school telecast programmes addressed to students of different levels are organised with the help and cooperation of practising teachers. Teachers participate in the planning, organisation and evaluation of these programmes. Since, these programmes are meant to provide syllabus-based enrichment material to children, they supplement the work of teachers. The government provides a satellite channel to educational and development programmes, the telecast of which is available to students in all parts of the country, This would also give a boost to the development of educational software.

Efforts for Teacher Development

Private educational establishments-government-aided and government recognised but unaided-make special efforts to maintain their teachers' motivation. Both incentives and disincentives are used. Good work in these institutions is rewarded by giving additional responsibility which is often linked with monetary incentives. In government schools, this is not possible as the head of the institution is not empowered to extend monetary incentives to teachers. Teachers in private education establishments have relatively less security of service. It is relatively easier to dispense with their services if their performance is not found satisfactory. In government schools, though teachers are accountable, teachers' unions make it difficult to enforce accountability, and it is extremely difficult to dispense with their services.

Teachers are involved in the formulation of education policies, development of curricula, syllabi and instructional material. They are also represented on decision-making bodies of universities, boards of school education, SCERTs and DIETs. This is in keeping with the UNESCO-ILO Recommendation Concerning the Status of Teachers that:

> Teachers' organisations should be recognised as a force which can contribute greatly to educational advancement and which, therefore, should be associated with the determination of educational policy

Moreover, teachers are autonomous in the management of their own classes. They are encouraged to undertake experimentation and action research and are provided incentives both at the state and national level. Every year, the NCERT conducts an All India Competition of Innovations and Experiments undertaken by school teachers and Teacher Educators. Teachers are invited to submit papers on the basis of the work done by them in their schools and as many as 50 primary school teachers and 20 secondary teachers are given national level awards. Similar-awards are also available for elementary and secondary teacher educators.

In the management of educational institutions, teachers at some places enjoy partnership in decision-making. The School Education Acts in vogue in some states have a provision for the membership of teacher representatives on the managing committee of the institution. For example, in the Delhi School Education Act and Rules, 1973, teacher representatives have to be on the managing committee of every recognised school. In the last few years there has been a move that even government schools should have an advisory or managing committee with representatives of the teachers working in the school as members.

To ensure parental support, many schools have either Parent Teacher Associations or Mother Teacher Associations. Parents are invited periodically to the school to discuss the performance of their children with the teachers. In some schools, particularly private schools, parents support the teachers in the organisation of co-curricular activities, art education activities and work experience activities by providing the materials required for these activities. In the DPEP, large scale efforts are underway to facilitate a constructive involvement of parents and the community with the school through the formation of grassroot structures such as VECs, Mother Teacher Associations and Parent Teacher Associations.

Another aspect of enhancing motivation is through the instititution of an annual Teachers' Day, on September 5 "This day is observed in all the schools throughout the country, according a special place to the teacher. Under the aegis of the Ministry of Human Resource Development, a National Foundation for Teachers' Welfare has been set up. This Foundation provides facilities for teachers' welfare.

Similarly, with the objective of raising the prestige of teachers and giving public recognition to teachers, the Scheme of National

Award for Teachers was launched in the year 1958-59. Primary, middle and higher secondary school teachers are eligible under the scheme.

The enrolment in universities has been on the rise over the post years, with approximately a teaching staff of 0.301 million, catering to a student population of 6.1 1 million students. The pay scales of university teachers have been revised periodically and are considered to be on par with the highest pay scales of civil servants. Benefits include provident fund, residential accommodation, retirement benefits, etc.

Various incentives exists for teachers to improve their qualifications during their service by way of training and research. They are sent abroad under bilateral programmes of research, area studies, conferences, etc. There are fellowships and scholarships offered by various countries besides travel grants to go abroad. Approximately, 250 scholars visit various countries under these programmes.

Involvement of teachers in decision making is also a vital component of teachers' service conditions. University and college teachers, are involved in the formulation of curricula and the management of university/college affairs. They are autonomous in planning their research. In Autonomous Colleges, teachers have been given the freedom to formulate and teach their courses of general curricula and evaluate their students. A scheme of Academic Staff Colleges provides training programmes in various subjects as a support for professional development of University and College teachers.

With a large network of technical institutions established and developed since independence, and the programmes and initiatives launched in India during the successive plan periods, the technical education system has made significant contributions in producing one of the largest reservoirs of technically trained manpower which has been a source of strength for scientific and industrial development. The role of teachers in technical education is quite central and crucial. To be effective in their task, the technical teachers have to maintain fine balance between their professional competence and teaching potential.

Schemes and Programmes

The Government of India, over years has taken a series of steps for developing the overall performance of the technical teachers. Significant among them are mentioned below:

Quality Improvement Programme (QIP)

The programme was launched in 1970 with an objective of upgrading the expertise and capabilities of the teachers of engineering colleges and polytechnics in the country, The aspect of upgradation of academic qualifications is achieved with the help of seven major centres located in the IITs, University of Roorkee, IISc., Bangalore and 18 other centre through which the engineering college teacher can acquire their masters and doctoral degree with full salary and allowance. They are also paid a monthly stipend. Over the years, about 2,000 engineering college teachers have acquired Ph.Ds and about 1,700 teachers have acquired masters degrees in engineering/technology.

The ISTE, a national professional body in technical education conducts summer/winter schools for improving the knowledge, skills and capabilities of engineering college teachers as well as polytechnic teachers. The ISTE conducts a large number of short term courses and programmes at various institutions and industries in the country. The teachers are provided travelling and other allowances as per the rules. So for over 25,000 college level teachers have participated in such programmes and over 4,500 polytechnic teachers have been benefited under such programmes.

In addition, QIP centres in the IITs, IISc., Bangalore and University of Roorkee also have established curriculum development centres for upgrading curricula of engineering colleges with the help of teachers and experts.

The statutory AICTE has also launched some innovative schemes for teachers of technical institutions which include:

- — Travel Grants Scheme
- — Seminar/Conference grant
- — Career award for young teachers
- — Emeritus fellowship

— Professor of Eminence.

Under the scheme of continuing education programmes, presently handled by AICTE, the working professionals in the industry are provided knowledge-based skills and training with the help of teachers of various technical institutions, both at the degree and diploma level. Continuing education has been a very significant aspect of the World Bank assisted project for polytechnics as also the CIDA funded Canada India Institutional Cooperation Project for 12 polytechnics in Southern India.

Despite several measures taken so far, the overall position of filling up the sanctioned posts and attracting competent engineers/ technologists to the teaching profession has been a matter of concern and debate. Efforts are, therefore, afoot to launch some new schemes and programmes for attracting brilliant young teachers by taking them up at a young age and sponsoring them for acquiring higher qualifications. At the same time, designing some new scientific methods of selection and providing adequate research facilities and challenges so as to keep the teachers motivated, professionally satisfied and result-oriented. Several new measures are also required in order to fill up the existing vacancies and the vacancies likely to be created because of mass scale retirement in the near future, especially, in the old reputed technical institutions. The aspects of providing need-based training and also to engage eminent experts as visiting faculty and contract faculty are also being encouraged.

UNESCO-ILO recommendations

The recommendations concerning the Status of Teachers adopted on 5th October, 1966 by the Special Inter-governmental Conference on the Status of Teachers convened by UNESCO, Paris in cooperation with ILO in 1966 recognised that the document was a unique instrument which recognised that education is fundamental to development and that teachers are the key to educational process. In the Indian context, the major aspects of the recommendations viz. the guiding principles recognises the importance of education and the fact that the status of teachers should be given its due regard in society. This is already incorporated in the NPE.

As far as the educational objectives and policies are concerned the items concerning the interface between the world of learning and the world of work in the field of education is well recognised and has been implemented in India. In fact, the EFA commitment speaks of a financial commitment to the extent of 6 per cent of the GDP by the turn of the century for the education sector.

In the recommendations concerning Preparation for programmes, Educational objectives and policies and Preparation for the profession, there is evidence that there is widespread availability of teacher training facilities as well as comprehensive selection and recruitment facilities for each in the country. The various incentives that are given to employment and career opportunities to teachers have also been well documented. The security of tenure is particularly well established in government run schools.

In the domain of the Rights and Responsibilities of teachers, the Indian context enjoins a fair degree of freedom and flexibility based on a framework outlined by the respective state governments on the issue of freedom of association. In every state, teaching and non-teaching personnel have their unions/associations. These organisations have powers of collective bargaining to secure better service conditions for their members. State level organisations have joined together to form federations of educational organisations for primary, secondary and college stage of education. These federations negotiate with the central government to secure better pay scales and other service conditions. The central question under Indian laws is whether a 'teacher' can be equated to a 'workman', the latter being defined in the Industrial Disputes Act 1947. Various suggestions in this respect are being considered by the Ministry of Labour to amend the Industrial Disputes Act and initiate reforms to grant teachers the same protection as other workers. On the question of the rights of teachers, (in particular, salaries), these are structured as per government norms as laid down by the government from time to time.

On the Conditions for Effective Teaching and Learning, due consideration has been given in the context of the Indian teachers incorporating the recommendations of ILO. According to NPE 1986, development of Teachers' Code of Professional Ethics has been the responsibility of National level Teachers' organisations and they have themselves evolved such a code. On the issue of Teacher Shortage and

Social Security, there are provisions for various benefits and salary revisions commensurate with inflationary trends that protect the pay of teachers.

Training and Recruitment

The professional skills of teachers in all categories of institutions except the unrecognised ones are determined by the regulations of the state education departments and examining bodies. The level of professional skill required is fixed in terms of academic and professional qualifications which are taken into consideration for granting recognition and affiliation. Therefore, institutions of various types set up in the public and private sectors adhere to the norms prescribed by the state. Initial training of teachers (pre-service teacher training) is organised at the following three levels, i.e., pre-school teacher education, elementary teacher education, and secondary teacher education

Pre-school Teacher Education

Pre-school teacher education is organised to prepare teachers for teaching pre-school classes, i.e., nursery and kindergarten. The minimum qualification for admission into the pre-school teacher education programme is secondary or senior secondary examination, i.e., 10 years or 12 years schooling. The duration of the course is one to two years. Preschool teacher training institutions are mostly unaided private institutions. In the case of nursery teacher education and primary teacher education courses, State Education Departments prescribe a minimum percentage of marks in the qualifying examination as a requirement for admission. Some universities have also fixed a minimum percentage of marks in the B.A./B.Sc. examinations for admission to the Bachelor of Education (B.Ed.) course.

Elementary Teacher Education

Elementary teacher education is organised to train teachers mainly to teach primary classes from I to 5. The minimum qualification for admission into the elementary teacher education programme is either

10 or 12 years of schooling. Recently, most states have prescribed 12 years schooling as the minimum requirement though some states still have the entry qualification as secondary school examination pass. The programme duration in the majority of states is two years, while in others it is one year. Elementary teacher training institutions are of three types-government, private aided and private unaided. Recently, DIETs have been set up in all the states. An important feature of these is that besides ; providing pre-service teacher education, they also provide in-service education to teachers. Thus, both pre-service and in-service education are provided under one roof. The number of such institutes is 424. These institutes are government institutions and are fully financed by the Central Government. The total number of elementary teacher training institutions is 1,179.

Secondary Teacher Education

Secondary teacher education institutes prepare teachers to teach classes 6 to 12. The minimum education required for admission to a secondary teacher education programme is graduation in science, social sciences, humanities, commerce, agriculture, etc. A large number of postgraduates also seek admission to these training institutions.

Secondary teacher education is offered by secondary colleges of education which are affiliated to different universities. Some university departments also offer a secondary teacher education programme. The minimum qualification for admission to this programme is graduation. These institutes are of three types: government, private aided and private unaided. At present, there are around 586 secondary colleges of education.

Four Regional Institutes of Education (RIEs), constituent units of the NCERT offer a 4-year integrated course in secondary teacher education. The minimum qualification for admission into this programme is senior secondary, i.e., 12 years of schooling. Recently, the University of Delhi has also started a four year programme in elementary education leading to the degree 'Bachelor of Elementary Education'.

Teacher education institutions follow the reservation policy of the Government of India with regard to the disadvantaged sections of society like SCs and STs and Other Backward Classes (OBCs). At present, 15 per cent posts in the Education Departments and seats in teacher education institutions are reserved for candidates belonging to the SCs. Likewise, 7.5 per cent posts are reserved for candidates belonging to STs. Recently, 27 per cent posts in all services including teaching have been reserved for candidates belonging to OBCs.

Curriculum for Teacher Education

The primary teacher, specially, in the first three grades is expected to teach mainly literacy, numeracy and life skills. Besides these, the teacher is required to have knowledge of the process of a child's growth, development and learning. At the secondary stage, a teacher is expected to be familiar with adolescent psychology and social processes, in addition to knowledge of school subjects.

The curriculum for primary teacher education is developed by state governments/State Boards of Teacher Education and is reviewed from time to time. The curriculum for secondary teacher education developed by universities is also reviewed and updated periodically in the light of changes in the school curriculum, advances in pedagogical science, societal demands, technological advancements and changes in the socioeconomic structures in the country.

The NCERT has developed model curricula for elementary and secondary teacher education. State governments and universities may adopt/ adapt this in their teacher education programmes. The NCERT revises these curricula from time to time.

The pedagogical component has received a weightage of 80 per cent in the curriculum. The curriculum lays a great deal of emphasis on teaching through child-centred, activity-based and cooperative learning approaches. Enriching the trainee's knowledge of the content of school subjects is also an important objective of the curriculum. The components of the secondary teacher education curriculum are the some as that of the elementary teacher education. There are, however, variations in courses depending on the stage for which the teachers are prepared.

Teacher Training for Special Needs

To look after children with special needs, the NPE 1986,

recommended integrating children with locomotor and mild disabilities in general schools. The implementation of the UNICEF assisted 'Project Integrated Education of the Disabled' (PIED) in ten demonstration sites in different contexts further encouraged policy makers to integrate children with moderate disabilities in general schools, The Multi Site Action Research Project also promoted the need to develop 'effective' schools for all. All these experiences focus on the preparation of the general school system to meet the special needs of not only those with physical impairment but also of those with mental impairments and learning disabilities. A provision has thus been made by the NCERT to orient all teachers and education officers by incorporating a component on special needs in all major in-service training programmes. The emphasis is on preparing general teachers and also moving towards the organisation of primary schools as inclusive schools focussing on meeting individual needs in the classroom. Teachers receiving this training are supported by multi-category trained teachers who were, provided training by 4 RIEs of the NCERT. Teachers absorbed into special schools, mostly single disability schools or those with multiple disabilities such as spastics, cerebral palsy, etc., are trained under the guidance of the National Institutes for the Handicapped as well as some non-governmental organisations with courses accredited by the Rehabilitation Council of India. A number of universities have also started offering B.Ed., and M.Ed., courses in special education.

Recruitment of Teachers

Different states follow different recruitment procedures. In some states, the recruitment is made on the basis of the candidates performance in a competitive examination, whereas, in some other states, recruitment is made on the basis of the academic and professional background of the candidate. The merit of each candidate is determined on the basis of his/her score in the examinations he/she has passed in addition to previous teaching experience, if any. In some other states, a combination of the two procedures, i.e., performance in a competitive examination and merit determined on the basis of academic credentials is adopted, Some weightage is given to the performance of candidates in an oral examination held through interviewing the candidates.

The qualifications required for the recruitment of * Lecturer in a university/college are:

— Qualifying in the National Test conducted by the UGC or any agency approved by it.

— A Master's degree with of least 55 per cent marks or its equivalent grade and a good academic record.

At the higher education level, 45 Academic Staff Colleges are involved in teacher training and university departments also organise orientation programmes and refresher courses.

Institutional Infrastructure for Training

The infrastructure for in-service training of teachers exists at the central, state, regional, district and sub-district levels. At the national level, there are the NCERT, the NIEPA, the Central Institute of English and Foreign Languages (CIEFL), Hyderabad, and the Central Institute of Indian Languages (CIIL), Mysore.

At the regional level, there are Regional Institutes of Education located in the four regions of the country-Northern, Western, Eastern and Southern. One Regional Institute has been set up recently at Shillong for the states in the northeastern part of India.

At the state level, there are the SCERTs, State Institute of Education (SIE), State Institute of Science Education, IASE, CTEs, SIETs.

Districts have DIETs and In-service Training Institutes. DIETs cater to the in-service education of teachers working at primary and upper primary level. In-service education of secondary teachers is being looked after by CTEs. It is proposed to strengthen 200 CTEs, of which 73 have already been established. The IASEs are looking after the in-service education of senior secondary school teachers, including principals of these schools and the faculty of DIETs.

Recently, in-service training centres have been set up at sub-district level, i.e., block and cluster level. To begin with, these centres are being established in the districts covered under the DPEP.

In-service Training

In the context of the NPE 1986, the Government of India formulated a national scheme of in-service training of teachers to reach out to primary and secondary school teachers. The objectives of the scheme known as the Programme of Mass Orientation of School Teachers (PMOST) was to sensitise teachers to the emerging concerns in education, UEE, use of learner-centred approach, action research, the emerging role and responsibilities of teachers, enrichment of their knowledge in curricular areas, and other thrust areas enlisted in the NPE. The duration of training was 10 days. The programme was in operation from 1986-90 and about 1.8 million teachers were covered by it. The training programme was strengthened by media support. Films relating to various modules constituting the training print package were telecast on the national network for the benefit of teachers in different parts of the country. Each viewing session was preceded and followed by discussion. A participatory, interactive approach was followed in the training. The programme was implemented by the NCERT in collaboration with the SCERTs in different states.

After the PMOST, another programme/scheme known as the Special Orientation Programme for Primary School Teachers (SOPT) was launched from the year 1993-94 to improve the quality of primary/ elementary education as part of the strategy to achieve UEE. The main focus of this programme is implementing the MLLs identified for the primary stage, training in the use of Operation Blackboard materials provided to primary-school teachers, and encouraging teachers to adopt a child-centred approach to teaching. It envisages covering 0.45 million teachers every year. During the past few years, these two schemes of moss orientation have covered more than 2 million teachers. Like PMOST, this programme too, is strengthened by media support. Films on various themes covering the course design are shown to teachers during training programmes.

In most of the states, pre-service teacher education is essential for appointment as a teacher. Therefore, most states do not organise induction programmes for new entrants. However, some organisations like Kendriya Vidyalaya Sangathan and Navodaya Vidyalaya Samiti do organise a short induction, programme for newly appointed teachers.

In-service programmes are organised to realise three objectives—awareness, content upgradation and fine-tuning of teaching skills. The duration of a course differs from the others depending upon their nature, objectives and content. At present, the in-service education of teachers through distance mode is organised on a very limited scale. In-service education is mostly provided through face to face modality. However, recently a programme has been developed to provide in-service education to primary school teachers through distance education mode in the districts covered under the DPEP in which a multi-media approach would be used. The programme will be implemented by the IGNOU in collaboration with the NCERT. Recently, NCERT has successfully experimented with using interactive teleconferencing for training of Primary teachers of Karnataka and Madhya Pradesh, This intervention will be upscaled as an important strategy for in-service education.

Besides sensitisation to general problems and priorities of education, the in-service training of teachers is also focused on specific areas requiring different kinds of competencies. These specific competencies include educating groups with special needs like SC and ST children, disabled children and those belonging to minority communities. Since, these groups have different social, linguistic and physical problems, training and orientation programmes for key persons and teachers working with them have been formulated keeping these in view.

From time to time, the NCERT provides orientation at the national level to key persons working for the education of SCs. This orientation is used by them during the training and also during the orientation programmes they organise for teachers of their states associated with the education of the SCs. The Welfare Department/ Tribal Development Departments in the states, and the UGC through the state colleges also organise remedial programmes to enrich and facilitate teachers working in the areas predominantly inhabited by the SCs and STs.

Training programmes addressed to teachers working in educational institutions of minority groups are in the formulation stage and will be implemented in the coming years. However, as a start, NCERT has designed some orientation and training programmes to help educationally backward minorities. Steps have also been initiated to update the list of minority concentration districts and these shall be made available to voluntary agencies and SCERTs requesting them to include teachers/functionaries of minority schools from these areas in their training programmes.

References

Ashby, P., Hobson, A., Tracey, L., Malderez, A., Tomlinson, P., Roper, T., Chambers, G. and Healy, J. (2008). *Beginner teachers' experiences of initial teacher preparation, induction and early professional development: a review of literature*. London: DCSF

Frederick, R., et.al. (2009). Teacher candidates' transformative thinking on issues of social justice. *Teaching and Teacher Education* .doi:10.1016/jtate.2009.05.004

Garet, Porter, Desmoine, Birman, Kwang, (2001) What makes professional development effective? *American Education Research Journal* 38(4) 915-946.

Huling-Austin, J. (1988) A systhesis of research on teacher induction programs and practices; papre presented to the Annual Meeting of the American Educational Research Association, New Orleans LA, April 5-9.

Snow-Renner and Lauer, (2005) 'Professional Development Analysis (synthesis of 54 studies), McREL.

Wong H; (2004) Induction programs that keep new teachers teaching and improving; *NASSP Bulletin* Vol. 88 No. 638 .

11

Non-formal Education System

Development in the education in India was seen mostly after independence. The educational system in the country was modified to a great level and it was structured. Different forms of education were introduced in the society. The 86th Constitutional Amendment Act was passed by the parliament to make education a fundamental right. Formal and non formal educational systems were popularised in India. Non-formal education in India achieved world wide recognition.

Non-formal education in India is the concept of recurrent and lifelong learning. In addition to that non-formal education is about 'acknowledging the importance of education, learning and training which takes place outside recognised educational institutions'. According to Fordham four characteristics can be associated with non-formal education that includes: Relevance to the needs of disadvantaged groups, Concern with specific categories of person, a focus on clearly defined purposes and Flexibility in organisation and methods.

The notion of Non-formal education in India refers to education that mainly takes place outside of the schools that are formally organised. Moreover, non-formal is term which is used to refer to adult literacy and continuing education for adults. This educational policy is preferred by the rural as well as urban communities as it is not compulsory and does not lead to a formal certification. The non formal education is likely to be state-supported.

The programme Non-formal education in India was launched by the Government of India during 1979-80. According to the Non-formal Education or NFE is designed to provide education to the children of 6-14 years age group and to those who have constrains in attending regular schools. The non formal education policy also helps those students who are school drop-outs, working children and children from areas without easy access to schools. This policy of education is extended to all parts of the country including urban slums as well as hilly, tribal and desert areas. The programme is functional in all the states and Union territories of India with voluntary assistance to centres offering non formal education.

Conceptualisation of NFE

At the outset, it would be relevant to mention that although life-long learning has entered the academic discourse, the NFE sector in India still tends to equate education with basic literacy and numeracy while other skills are relegated to acquisition of technical skills as in a vocational education programme.

The basic conceptualisation of NFE is substantially influenced by the UN definitions. Formal education in India refers to the hierarchically structured education system running from the kindergarten through the university, including institutions of technical and professional education and training. 'Informal education', also often termed as 'incidental education', is seen as the unorganised education acquired during the entire life span of an individual through interaction with other members of the society. Hence, informal education is in fact accepted as a life long process through which every individual acquires attitudes, values, skills, and knowledge, to a large extent conditioned by his/her environment.

NFE is conceptualised as an organised educational activity, occurring in the traditional framework of formal education system. Formal education is highly structured and rigid. It is characterised by uniformity to a large extent. The major characteristic feature of NFE in India is its flexibility in terms of organisation, timing and duration of teaching and learning, clientele groups, age group of learners, contents, methodology of instruction and evaluation procedure. It is this characteristic feature of NFE, which has made it a critical mode for reaching out to the hardest-to-reach group of children and youth, both in rural and urban India, in order to achieve the much desired goal of education for all.

National Literacy Mission (NLM)

The National Literacy Mission (NLM), the most important state mechanism for imparting NFE, defines literacy as acquiring the skills of reading, writing and arithmetic and *the ability to apply them to one's day-to-day life*. Thus the goal of the NLM goes beyond the simple achievement of self-reliance in literacy and numeracy of functional literacy. The achievement of functional literacy implies:

— Self-reliance in the 3 Rs.

— Becoming aware of the causes of deprivation and moving towards amelioration of their condition by participating in the process of development

— Acquiring skills to improve their economics status and general well-being

— Imbibing values of national integration, conservation of environment, women's equality, and observance of small family norms.

— The acquisition of functional literacy results in empowerment and a definite improvement in the quality of life.

Poverty and equity comprise major distinctive elements of the conceptualisation. The 3 Rs have been characterised in the NLM thus:

Reading

— Reading aloud, with normal accent, and at a speed of 30 words a minute, a simple passage on a topic of interest to the learner.

— Silent reading at 35 words a minute, of small paragraphs in simple language.

— Reading with understanding the road signs, posters, simple instructions and newspapers/broadsheets designed for neo-literates.

— Ability to follow simple written passages relating to one's working and living environment

Writing

— Copying, with understanding, 7 words a minute.

— Taking dictation at 5 words a minute.
— Writing with proper spacing and alignment.
— Writing independently, short letters and applications, and filling in forms of day-today use to the learner

Numeracy

— Reading and writing numerals 1-100.
— Doing simple calculations (without fraction) involving addition and subtraction up to 3 digits, and multiplication and division by 2 digits.
— Working knowledge of metric units weights, measures currency, distance, area and unit of time.
— Broad idea of proportion and interests (not involving fractions) and their use in practical situations.

Life Skills Education

The concept of life skills education as the focus of all educational programmes and processes has been adopted by the Ministry of Human Resource Development (MHRD), Government of India.

The Government seeks to follow an integrated approach to literacy. "This means, the Total literacy Campaign and the Post Literacy Programme will operate under one literacy Project. This approach would enable the enormous illiteracy problem to be tackled in a holistic manner. By treating the imparting of functional literacy as a continuum rather than as a one of benefit for the illiterate person, progress of literacy efforts would be made goal-directed. Literacy campaigns would continue to run in those areas where there are large pools of residual illiteracy. At the same time, for those who have crossed the basic learning phase, programmes of consolidation, remediation, vocational skills, integration with life skills and such other aspects would be considered the basic unit".

The characterisation of life skills is not available; but speaking to MHRD officials; it appears that they follow the standard international definitions in relation to NFE. Some NGO NFE providers ordered the life skills differently for the Indian context in a 2001 UNESCO-supported study conducted by an Indian NGO, REMEDIA Trust, on life skills education within the NFE sector; with a view to address issues related to drug abuse and HIV/AIDS prevention.

According to the NGOs participating in the study, 'self awareness is the first necessary life skill. By using the Socratic Method, the students can be helped to debate the issue of an individual's place in a family, a social group, a community, and a country. The young people can be made aware of their rights and duties and their responsibilities to themselves and society. The need to preserve their physical and mental health has to be realised. The twin essence of self awareness is the life skill of empathy. Awareness of self should be counterbalanced by awareness of others, their different thinking, feelings, desires and wishes. This requires some imagination and fellow feeling. It is part of a process of socialisation and self control. Indian culture emphasises empathy with human beings, animals and the nature around us. This skill has to be cultivated carefully, especially among street and slum children as they often exhibit an aggressive stance in self protection.

Critical thinking and creative thinking is the next pair of life skills. Training in thinking is very rare in formal as well as non-formal classrooms in India; and today as the media sends out a constant stream of messages, it is important to begin critical listening and asking the right questions. Training young people to ask for cause-effect relationship and then for rational thinking is essential, if they are going to withstand pressure.

Decision making and problem solving comes somewhat easier to children who are on the streets rather than to children who are protected by the family. Since, in India, the group rather the individual are given importance, these skills may be fostered by debates where individual differences can emerge and can be defended by logical arguments.

Coping with emotions and stress first requires admitting emotions and stress. In the Indian society, emotions and stress are regarded as shameful and stoicism is encouraged. Therefore, the discipline of standing aloof from one's emotions, recognising them and coping with them is an exercise that has to be carefully taught so that the extreme positions of either denying emotions or totally giving in to emotions are avoided.

Effective communication and interpersonal relations skills are important to young people in order to maintain both their independence and their friendships. In India, friendship between young people of the same sex has been more highly regarded than elsewhere. Even in India, family bonds, though strong, need careful nurture. Drugs do not tempt whose family bonds are strong. Families offer the young protection from drugs and stress.

Two major life skills necessary are spatial orientation and orientation in time. The nonverbal spatial skill is needed to practice arts and crafts, which are part of the Indian way of life. Most vocational programmes depend on spatial skills. Orientation to time helps the young to plan for their future. It has been discovered that the disadvantaged do not have this orientation, so they tend to live in the present and do not save or invest money they earn for their morrow.

If the young who come to the NFE centres begin to understand the time-line and the cause and effect relationship, they will begin to appreciate how their effort of today will bear fruit tomorrow. Many young people do not have a clear notion of how yesterday, today and tomorrow are linked. They have a vague notion of weekdays and months but if they are going to participate in the modern world of technology, they must have orientation to both space and time.

Considering the large number of out-of-school children, an important human resource in India, it is necessary to device ways of giving them these life skills that will help them handle adult responsibilities without failure and stress; making them the strengths of their communities'. It is, however, not known or reported how this set of characterisations are actualised in the Indian setting.

Lifelong Learning

Lifelong learning is emphasised, at least in theoretical terms, in the Indian NFE context. One of the most interesting set of proposals with respect to lifelong learning in India was advocated by Gandhi as Indian independence approached. He saw that Indian education was bookish and European in outlook—and totally inappropriate to the majority of people who were villagers. At the same time Gandhi was completely against the idea that there should be two types of education—urban and rural. He felt that there was a great need for city dwellers to have more contact with the land.

The programme that Gandhi proposed was that manual work should be the basis for three or four hours per day and that training of the mind should stem from this. The central craft that he recommended was that of spinning—firstly, because spinning wheels or *charka* were cheap, traditional and simple to use. Secondly, because it was a good example of 'bread labour' (it had a useful social function). Thirdly, because spinning then led to other activities, that could be performed with skill. He argued that mental powers of inquiry and research must find scope for development through craft. He also said that craft must be collective, with teacher and students joining in service to the community. Vinoba Bhave, one of Gandhi's followers, gave the following list of the essential areas of knowledge that all children should have: facility in speech, knowledge of great poems by heart, discussion of the ideas of Gandhian philosophy; the basic concepts of science and the laws of health, nutrition, hygiene, and cookery. All this formed part of Gandhi's work around combating untouchability and cultivating common reconciliation and village rehabilitation.

The Gandhian approach had more of a philosophical mooring than a practical one. In the later decades, on a more pragmatic level, the NLM was launched to impart functional literacy to non-literates in the country in the age group of 15-35 years in a time bound manner. The NLM eventually aims at ensuring that the Total Literacy Campaigns (TLC) and their sequel, the Post-Literacy Programme (PLP), successfully move on to Continuing Education (CE), which provides a life-long learning and is responsible for the creation of a learning society.

Moreover, through the Open Universities and distance learning initiatives, mechanisms are in place to upgrade skills at regular intervals and develop new competencies. People's needs of lifelong learning are constantly expanding. The Open University System was initiated in the country to augment opportunities for higher education as an instrument of democratising education and also to make it a lifelong process. The first Open University in the country was established by the state government of Andhra Pradesh in 1982. In 1985, the central government established the Indira Gandhi National Open University (IGNOU).

NON-FORMAL EDUCATION SYSTEM

Non-formal education in the Indian context has developed a restricted meaning of an alternative delivery system of education for children who are not able to participate in the formal elementary school. Non-formal Education has therefore, been limited to providing a second chance to those children who are out-of-school. Broadly speaking, such children are often described as drop-outs. However, a very large number of such children are, in fact, pull-outs from school because of economic and cultural compulsions. Many children may be called stay-outs because the reach of the primary school system in India is not universal. Besides pull-outs and stay-outs, a very large number of children are what may be termed as push-outs. These children do not find the primary school attractive or meaningful. In order to fulfill the constitutional goal of providing free and compulsory education to all children upto the age of 14, we have to provide education which is both relevant and interesting. For a variety of reasons the formal school system has tended to leave out millions of rural and urban poor children who are not able to attend a full time day-school. Consequently, there is a need for developing a viable alternative system of education which would provide Basic Education for All children in the country. Non-formal Education has evolved as one such alternative.

Non-formal Education as an alternative to formal Elementary Education was experimented with as early as 1976 at which time nine educationally backward states in the country were pursuaded to initiate experimental NFE centres. In 1988, following the introduction of the National Policy on Education (1986), a full-fledged scheme of Non-formal Education supported by the Central Government was introduced primarily in ten educationally backward states, as well as all over the country in urban slums, remote areas, desert and hilly regions.

Since 1986 there has been a growing National concern for achieving Basic Education for All in the shortest possible time. Several programmes of support to primary and elementary education in the country have been initiated in order to achieve this goal. The experience gathered since 1976 and particularly since 1988 in the area of Non-formal Education clearly demonstrates that Universal Elementary Education can only be achieved if Non-formal Education is made available as a viable alternative to formal school education.

Despite Limited success, Non-formal Education has become acceptable to a large section of the rural poor parents who are keen and willing to send their children to school but find the formal full-day school not suitable in their economic condition. The feasibility of Non-formal Education has become enhanced in the last eight years. Participation in the Non-formal Education programme by nearly 650 voluntary Agencies has added to its credibility and acceptability.

Department of Non-formal Education

In 1988 when the Centrally Sponsored Scheme of the Non-formal Education was formulated by the MHRD, a full-fledged Department of Non-formal Education was established in the NCERT Prior to 1988, Non-formal Education functioned as part of other departments. With the establishment of a Department, Non-formal Education became recognised as an alternative to elementary education. From 1988-1995 the department was also given the responsibility of overseeing Education to Scheduled Castes and Scheduled Tribes since Non-formal Education emphasised reaching these communities where large number of children were out-of-school. In 1995, the department was re-organised and renamed Department of Education in Non-formal and Alternative Schooling. This reorganisation has vindicated the significance of Non-formal Education as an essential alternative to Formal Elementary Education. The department is now poised to play a significant role in the achievement of Universal Elementary Education which has been a goal for the country.

Functions of the Department

Following the 1988 Central Scheme of Non-formal Education the department was designated as a National Resource Centre for Non-formal Education. The functions and roles of the department included the following :

— providing academic and technical support to State agencies as well as Voluntary Agencies implementing the scheme of Non-formal Education;

— evolving training models and providing training for functionaries in Non-formal Education at all levels;-

— developing materials and methodologies for the implementation of Non-formal Education;
— conducting fundamental and action research in all aspects of Non-formal Education;
— providing extension services to all agencies (State as well as Voluntary) concerned with Non-formal
— carrying out programme in pupil evaluation in Non-formal Education; and
— creating and maintaining capacities at the State level for successful implementation of the scheme of Non-formal Education.

Programmes and Activities

The department has attempted to fulfill all its roles and functions enumerated above in the eight years of its existence. The department has carried out numerous activities and has attempted to create academic and technical capacities in the States and amongst the Voluntary Agencies implementing Non-formal Education.

Scenario of NFE

A large number of children in then age group 6-14 continue to remain outside the formal system due to socio-economic constraints. These include working children who assist in domestic, chores, like fetching fuel, fodder, water, attend to siblings, graze cattle, etc., children from scattered habitations with population below the permissible school norms drop outs and over-age children. Any strategy for UEE must, therefore, take into account alternative strategies to reach this important but marginalised group of children. The National Policy on Education (NPE), 1986 and the Programme of Action, 1992, call for a large systematic programme of Nonformal Education (NFE) as an integral component of the strategy to achieve universalisation of elementary education.

The term Non-formal Education (NFE) has been used in a specific context in India to denote education of out-of-school children. Although planned and concerted efforts in Non-formal Education is barely two and half decades old in India, it has, travelled a long way from the early beginnings in 1970s to a full-fledged scheme of the Government of India reaching out to nearly seven million children in the age group 6-14.

NFE was experimented bit the NCERT in early seventies and was later initiated as a centrally sponsored scheme in 1978. It was originally available in nine educationally backward states. viz. Andhra Pradesh, Assam, Bihar, Jammu and Kashmir, M.P., Orissa, Rajasthan, U.P., and West Bengal. Later it was extended to Arunachal Pradesh and the educationally backward pockets of the remaining States.

The NFE programme seeks to provide out-of-school children with opportunities for primary education which are decentralised, flexible and permit them to study at a convenient place, pace and time. The programme is operationalised by setting Lip NFE centres in rural areas and urban slum with average enrolment of 20 learners under the charge, of a local instructor with modest academic qualifications who is paid an honorarium of Rs. 200/p.m. The village community is expected to provide for space and make other arrangement for running these centres. NFE centres are expected to run for 1 1/2 to 2 hours for 6 days a week. As a majority of the centres are being run at night, lighting arrangements are generally made by kerosene lanterns.

The NFE course is condensed into 4 semesters of 6 months each for which specially developed teaching-learning materials and stationery is provided to children free of cost. There is a provision for testing and certification of children of NFE centres to facilitate their entry into formal schools. Instructors are provided with training by District Resource Units (DRU) in District Institute of Education and Training (DIETs). For supervision, monitoring and evaluation of the NFE programme a supervisory structure has been put in place which includes a part time supervisor for every 1 0 NFE centre; a Project Officer for 100 NFE centres, district and state level functionaries.

States are being given 60% of central assistance for co-educational centres and 90% for girls centres. Voluntary Agencies are given 100% assistance. The scheme covers around 70 lakh children (majority of whom are girls) in 21 States/UTs in about 2.79 lakhs centres. While 1.18 lakh centres are exclusively for girls, 38,000 centres are run by over 500 voluntary agencies. There has been a steady increase in the number of girls centres and also in the participation of NGOs in NFE in last few years.

While the NFE programme saw a major expansion during the Seventh Plan, it has been extended and consolidated during the 8th Plan. At present, there are 2.79 lakh NFE centres covering about 70 lakh children in 21 States/UTs. Of these, 2,40,787 are being run by State Governments and 37,808 by 544 Voluntary Agencies. Five States viz. U.P., Bihar, Andhra Pradesh, Madhya Pradesh and Orissa account for 81% of NFE centres. The scale of NFE programme is moderate in Rajasthan, and Assam. Coverage is very limited in Jammu and Kashmir and North-Eastern States. Arunachal Pradesh has started the programme recently.

Non-formal Education Projects

Lok Jumbish Project

Lok Jumbish Project (LJP) in Rajasthan seeks to achieve Universalisation of Elementary Education through a community based and decentralised approach. The project which commenced in 1992 with support of SIDA, GOI & GOR in the proportion of 3:2:1 has taken up non-formal education as one of the strategies for achieving UEE in rural areas of the State. Currently the programme covers about 20,000 children through approximately 1000 NFE centres. A detailed evaluation of the programme conducted by Operations Research Group (ORG), New Delhi commends it as a feasible design for providing primary education to out-of-school children who are working or have crossed the school admission age. The ORG study recommends that the NFE model of UP deserves to be studied with care for improvement of the State NFE programme in Rajasthan and other parts of the country. The following features of the programme have been highlighted in this context:-

— Efficient and decentralised system of management.

— Effective community mobilisation.

— Adoption of successful strategies for motivation and training of instructors.

— Clear focus on girls' enrolment (girls constitute more than 2/3rd of children enrolled).

— Stress on equivalence with the formal system.

Some of the other steps taken by UP to improve efficiency of the NFE programme are as follows:-

— Appointment of local instructor in consultation with the community.

— Substantial increase in honorarium of instructors and supervisors from Rs.200 to Rs.550 per month and from Rs,500 to Rs,1000 per annum respectively.

— The per centre expenditure has been enhanced to about Rs. 19,000/-per annum.

— It has been decided that number of women instructors should be increased to about 1/3rd and special reorientation courses are organised for women instructors.

— Opening of NFE centres on the basis of community-based school mapping and micro-planning exercise,

— Experienced and innovative voluntary agencies have been entrusted with important responsibilities in implementation of NFE.

— A system of intensive, recurrent and rigorous residential training of NFE functionaries has been designed and developed in partnership with NGOs.

— Modifications in curriculum and text-books to Incorporate MLLs and, contextually relevant materials.

— Flexible duration of study for different age groups within the eligible group 6-14 years.

— Development of a comprehensive MIS for NFE.

— System of monthly review of NFE programme at the cluster and block levels and quarterly review at State level.

Shiksha Karmi Project

The largest experiment in Non-formal and alternative education outside the Centrally Sponsored NFE scheme has been undertaken under the Shiksha Karmi Project (SKP) in Rajasthan which was launched in the year 1987 with the assistance of SIDA to revitalise and expand primary education in the remote, inaccessible and backward villages of Rajasthan. The Shiksha Karmi Project (SKID) has utilised the services of local youth who are specially selected and are trained rigorously and regularly, to revitalise primary schools in the most difficult areas of the State. Currently the project is being implemented in 1590 villages and covers approximately 1.32 lakh children in day schools, Prehar Pathshalas (Schools of covnenient timing) and Aangan Pathashalas (Courtyard Schools).

Prehar Pathshalas (PPs) in SKID provide Non-formal Education to out of school children in the age group 6-14 years who are unable to attend day school due to socioeconomic and cultural constraints. It is obligatory for every shiksha karmi to run a PP in his/her village outside school hours, in addition to running a day school during regular school hours. The number of PPs is 3534 indicating that there are 2 PPs in every SKP village. In few villages no PP has been running as all school age children have been enrolled in and attend primary schools during the day regularly. One of the significant features of PPs is that out of 32570 children enrolled, as many as two-thirds are girls.

The other noteworthy features of this scheme are:

— use of condensed version of school textbooks;

— development of curriculum of each semester, on the basis of minimum levels of learning;

— availability of teachers guides to enable Shiksha Karmis to handle multi-grade classes;

— special inputs on running of PPs during initial and recurrent training of shiksha karmis;

— provision of 2,000 solar lanterns for righting in PPs;

— continuous efforts to encourage children of PPs to enrol in day schools;

In addition, SKP has experimented with the concept of Aangan pathshalas (APs) i.e. Courtyard schools for young girls who cannot travel long distances to attend either day schools or PPs. A local person, preferably a woman, is selected to run a Aangan Pathshala in her own home after necessary training and provision of other inputs. At present 58 APs have 2,415 students of which more than half are girls.

Achievements of NFE

During the last 17 years the concept of NFE as an instrument for providing primary education to out of school children in educationally backward areas has been by and large accepted and validated, However, NFE is subject to criticism in certain quarters as a low cost inferior and ineffective alternative for full time school. A few critics have gone to the extent of saying that NFE seeks to legitimise child labour as it is based on the assumption that poor and deprived children must work and, therefore, cannot attend regular schools. Nevertheless it cannot be denied that despite numerous shortcomings, NFE has provided access to primary education for millions of children in remote and inaccessible rural areas and urban slums, specially girls, and disadvantaged sections of society.

In this context, NFE may be seen as an evolving model emerging from existing socioeconomic realities. Where it has been effectively and properly implemented, NFE has been useful as a stepping stone for formal schooling, in addition to improving the self esteem, confidence and social skills of children. A few voluntary organisations have been able to provide vocational inputs to NFE thereby improving the employment prospects of children. More importantly, NFE is recognised as an alternative by parents and the community. Currently, the NFE programme has the potential of enrolling nearly half the number of children enrolled in the formal school system. Together, the formal primary school and NFE can fulfil the demand for primary education for all children in the country in the age group 6-11.

LEGAL FOUNDATIONS OF NFE POLICIES

The Indian Constitution in its 86th Amendment Act, 2002 stipulates: Right to Education, "The State shall provide free and compulsory education to all children of the age of six to fourteen years in such manner as the State may, by law, determine." However, the most important official confirmation of the need for expanding adult education services in India came in the form of the National Policy Resolution of 1968. The first important initiative in adult education—the National Adult Education Program (NAEP) –was not established until 1978. It defined education as literacy, functionality, and conscientisation, and although its structures were eventually established, they did not always function effectively. In 1980, the program was renamed (it was now simply called the AEP—Adult Education Programme) and expanded from a 10-month to a 3-year program with emphasis on health, family planning, and functional programmes. Unfortunately, the AEP was not extremely successful either. The main thrust of the new National Program of Adult Education is like its predecessors in that its main thrust is efficiency rather than equity and its general mode is technocratic.

The 1986 education policy envisages a national system which will take determined action to bring about universal primary education and promote the spread of adult literacy, thereby helping to reduce inequalities. The education system will be based on a national curricular framework which contains a common core as well as components specific to each region. The core will cut across subject areas and will be designed to promote such values as India's common cultural heritage, egalitarianism, democracy and secularism, equality of the sexes, protection of the environment, observance of the small family norm, and the scientific approach.

Pace-setting schools called Navodaya Vidyalayas will provide quality education to particularly gifted children, irrespective of their families' means, and will promote excellence as well as equity and social justice. The 1986 policy also emphasises the need to raise the level of investment in education from about 4 per cent of national income in 1986 to 6 per cent by 1990 and even higher thereafter. It has to be noted that education in India is on the concurrent list, that is, it is the joint responsibility of both the Centre and the States. This leads to a considerable amount of confusion and indeed passing the buck in the actualisation of responsibilities in imparting education.

While India is a signatory to the EFA processes, in terms of legislations, the education processes are governed by Government Orders (GOs) passed from time to time. The framework does not seem to be justifiable in the sense that the state cannot be taken to court for non-implementation of the education policies.

Governance and Finance

The major implementing bodies of the NFE come under the Ministry of

Human Resource Development (MHRD). The MoLE (Ministry of Labour and Employment) is accountable for some modular vocational training courses. Moreover, according to various officials, there are some 17 Ministries and Departments, which claim to provide NFE vocational training through various schemes and programmes. Information on this is not readily available.

Supervision

In terms of supervision of NFE, the National Policy on Education, 1986, instructs the need for a substantial strengthening of the supervisory and administrative apparatus of NFE. Rather than depending on the urban-oriented bureaucratic model, emphasis is laid on taking up well designed projects of approximately 100 NFE centres, in a compact and contiguous area. Supervisors should be selected from the local community and if possible, an experienced and committed NFE Instructor. These persons should be intensively trained and wherever possible, there should be the involvement of an organisation of continuing education programme. Village Education Committees should be set up as envisaged in NPE/POA (National Policy on Education / Programme of Action) to involve the local community in the programme and also to make the NFE centre in-charge accountable to it. The broad aim of this scheme is to effectively involve voluntary agencies, public trusts, non-profit making companies, social activist groups and the rest, in the implementation of NFE programme.

Monitoring

Monitoring of literacy campaigns is one of the important activities of the Directorate of Adult Education. In order to ensure reliability as well as steady flow of information in literacy campaigns, the State Directorate of Adult Education (SDAEs) have been asked to monitor literacy campaigns. The Directorate has taken steps to strengthen the monitoring system by involving State Directorates in regular monitoring of the progress of literacy campaigns in each of the districts. Detailed guidelines were evolved and issued by the Directorate for strengthening of monitoring system under these guidelines. SDAEs are required to hold monthly meeting in which the presence of Secretary, Zilla Saksharata Samitis, Director, SRC and other resources persons has been made mandatory. The State Directorates are now required to consolidate the district reports at the state level and forward the same to the Central Directorate of Adult Education, which is to examine critically these reports and submit feedback to the State Directorate. The Status Reports of Literacy and Post Literacy Campaigns are brought out at the end of each quarter.

Evaluation

With a view to ensuring effective implementation of the literacy campaigns the NLM has now introduced more meaningful and rigorous evaluation system. Each literacy campaign is now required to take up concurrent evaluation of the ongoing programme through an outside agency nominated by the State Directorates of Adult Education. The State Directorates have been asked to empanel agencies for undertaking concurrent evaluation. Concurrent evaluation aims at quick mid-term appraisal of a project to assess the strengths and weaknesses of an ongoing programme and to identify correctives for improvement of the programme.

Guidelines on Concurrent Evaluation are evolved and circulated to all literacy campaign districts and State Directorates. The NLM had planned for a comprehensive and systematic M&E, anticipating data flows from learners groups on the ground on to the district headquarters, to the states and then to the Centre. Internal monthly monitoring was also expected to be complemented with formal internal evaluations when required. External spot checks were also part of the monitoring plans. The hope was to collect policy oriented feedback that could be collated for use at 6-month intervals. Concurrent Monitoring as well as Quick Appraisals were to be conducted at all the various levels and locations of the overall system. Data in the Monitoring system was to be used to develop program evaluations in all the aspects of formative evaluation, evaluation of instruction, and outcome evaluation.

In addition to in-house monitoring and evaluations, large-scope evaluations of TLC's were mandated that were to be paid for by the central government. At least three evaluations had to be conducted in each TLC: (1) a quick appraisals at the beginning; (2) a mid-term evaluation; and (3) an end-term evaluation. The list of questions that evaluations should find answers to were also established. The state governments had to contract these evaluations with outside experts—in university departments, specialised institutes, or NGO's who have acquired a reputation for doing good evaluation work, and were on the approved list. Normative frames for methodology, for testing achievement, for definition of success are also provided. In addition, an official of the Ministry of Human Resource Development of the rank of a Deputy Secretary has been assigned to oversee all the matters pertaining to the scheme of Teacher Education and of monitoring the TE scheme in the country as a whole. By 2002, some 14 years after its launch, the NLM, using goal-oriented, area-specific and time-bound strategies, had covered 574 of the nation's 598 districts. As many as 302 districts were already offering continuing education programs. Total enrolment had touched 125 million adults, with some 12 million volunteers leading learners groups. As many as 71.45 million had become literate.

Research and Training

The National Institute of Education Planning and Administration (NIEPA), under the MHRD is the government body conducting research and training in the NFE sector. The Institute comprises of the Department of school and Non-formal Education, whose prime focus is on the critical issues of school education, non-formal and adult literacy providing strong empirical base in order to contribute more meaningful inputs for developing and improving education. The Department maintains close linkages with government, non-government and international agencies with the objective of restructuring educational system at subnational, national and international levels. Apart from NIEPA, civil society organisations like ASPBAE and Nirantar are actively involved in training and research in the NFE sector.

Departments of NFE at the National Universities

The University Grants Commission (UGC) has played a key role in shaping the character of University Adult Education in India since the launching of the National Adult Education Programme in 1978. During the last two decades, the UGC has not only formulated a number of guidelines on adult continuing education programmes, but has also provided one hundred per cent funding support to universities to implement the programmes. Today as many as 93 universities have set up Adult Education Departments and they have implemented a variety of programmes.

Training of NFE Educators and Trainers

The history of adult education in India shows that due emphasis and importance has been given to training strategies, programmes and policies. With the launching of the NLM, Project Formulation Guidelines were issued. These guidelines were supposed to be implemented in operationalising the Literacy and Adult Education Programme throughout the country At the *National Level* Training Programmes are designed by the NLM, Directorate of AE, and Management institutions. At the *State Level* the Programmes are designed and organised by the State Resource Centres (SRCs), State Literacy Mission Authorities (SLMA) and other educational institutions. At the *District Le*vel the training programmes are designed and organised by SRCs, the District Institutions for Educational Training (DIET), The Zilla Saksharata Samities (ZSS), Jan Shikshan Sansthans (JSS) and the NGOS, while at the Community Level the training programme is run by the ZSS, the JSS, NGOs, the Block Resource Centres (BRC) and the Literacy Resource Centres (LRC). To conduct training programmes at different levels a pyramidal approach is adapted, with the Core Group, the Resource Persons, Master Trainers and lastly the Implementers. The training of core group and key resource persons is conducted by SRC. The Resource persons train the master trainers and the master trainers train the Implementers. The funds are provided to district agencies by National Literacy Mission (NLM) through the State Literacy Mission Authority (SLMA).

The training Programme available for NFE facilitators have facility for Pre Service (basic role and responsibilities), In service (when new issues are introduce to programme) and Short Course which is need based. The programmes are organised in the following methods: the SRC training group travels to the districts for training, the Core group Conducts District Resource Persons (RP) training, the RPs go to Block for Master Trainers (MT) training, and the MTs go to the Panchayats for Volunteers (VTs) training. For occasional courses, they go up to the district / block or to the State level also.

The main contents of the training programme are to explain the participants the Concept of Continuing Education programme and its importance; the establishment of CE Centres (CEC) and Nodal CECs; the management of CEC and Nodal CEC; the programmes organised at these CECs; the roles and duties of a facilitator and the strengthening of the CEC and launching innovative programmes and skill development programmes.

The participants of the training programmes are selected at District/Block/Panchayat level by the ZSS (District Literacy Committees) while for the Core group and the other special training; SRC gives the criteria for selection of trainees. The SRC assesses the usefulness and impact of the training programmes through its Research and Development Cell. The State also assesses by monitoring and external evaluation.

NFE Initiatives

There are many, many providers of NFE programmes in India. Apart from the NGO initiatives, including the famous ones like the BGVS and Nirantar, there are Central Government and State Government Initiatives too. It really would not be an exaggeration to say that almost every ministry except the Defence, Home and External Affairs runs some kind of programme or the other. This is apart from the TLC initiative under the NLM. The medium of instruction is the State vernacular that is in the dominant language of the state. Thus in Uttar Pradesh, Bihar or Jharkhand, it is Hindi and field observations show that this creates problems for, say, the ethnic indigenous groups like the tribals. Also, the official language of the state is the standard colloquial one and often not followed by the speakers of particular dialects.

The teaching-learning methods of the programmes are generally hard to come by. For most programmes, (the exception being the TLCs of the 1990s) there are hardly any comprehensive evaluation reports available in the public domain on these aspects. Sometimes it is even difficult to pin-point who runs a particular programme. The NIOS and the NCVT (National Council of Vocational Training) schemes are run by the government approved centres (ITIs) as well as NGOs like Don Bosco.

The picture gets more complicated as one tries to compile an indicative list of programmes that are supposed to provide basic literacy plus, that is try to impart life skills and/or economic development (income-augmenting) skills. The bigger picture that has to be kept in mind is that of the low literacy rates (65.4 percent overall, 75.4 percent male and 54.1 percent female in 2001) as well as the elementary school (class 1-5) dropout rate (31.4 percent in 2003-4) in India. Also, insofar as skill training (that is imparting literacies apart from basic literacy and numeracy) is concerned, it has to be kept in mind that "the actual number of persons expected to enter the labour force is about 12.3 million persons per annum…the number of those entering with some degree of formal training is about 1.5 millions". The numbers of those who are possibly provided for, the government and NGO initiatives put together just don't match the high demand. Against this background, the rest of this section gives a glimpse of some of the major NFE initiatives in the country.

One of the major government initiatives, the Total Literacy Campaign (TLC) run by the National Literacy Mission (NLM), was started in 1988-89, initially as an experiment. It was area specific, time bound, volunteer based, outcome oriented and had a mass programme character. The core activities of the programme were literacy and numeracy. The targeted age group was illiterates in the age of 15 to 35. After the campaign was over, the neo-literates moved on to Post-literacy Programmes (PLP) and Continuing Education (CE). The minimum duration of the TLC was 6 months with PLP and CE was 3 months. The programme was imparted in the vernacular and the trainers were local volunteers. In the initial phases, literacy was the only competency focused on.

However, In the light of EFA goals and targets set up in the Dakar Framework for Action and clearly aligned to social and gender equity thrusts, the NLM, under the aegis of MHRD in 2003, felt the necessity to effect a certain re-focusing of its strategies pursued since 1999. The EFA-NPA's (National Plan of Action) new "thrust areas" in literacy include achievement of 75 percent literacy level by 2007, a multipronged strategy to address regional, social and gender disparities in literacy, refocusing literacy, post-literacy and CE programmes to increase and strengthen women's participation, to bridge gender gap in literacy, encouraging PL and CE districts to pay special attention on mobilisation and organisation of women into neo-literate and self-help groups (SHGs), special attention to socially disadvantaged groups like Schedule Castes / Scheduled Tribes and women.

Another government-run programme for UEE, with a view to Alternative Schooling and alternative education to a section of drop-outs, is the Sarva Siksha Abhiyan (SSA), started in 2001. The important features of SSA are Education Guarantee Scheme (EGS) and Alternative and Innovative Education (AIE) that seeks to base itself on strong community involvement and micro planning exercises. The EGS & AIE generally cover children in the age group of 6-14 years; however, for children with disabilities, it covers children up to the age of 18 years, complying with the provisions of Persons with Disabilities (Equal Opportunities, Protection or Rights and full Participation) Act, 1995.

The SSA has laid down various strategies for adolescent girls too. They are similar to interventions adopted under the Mahila Samakhya programme and several other NGO run programmes in different states. These include Jagjagi centres, short duration motivational and literacy centres which are residential in nature, from where the girls could go on to attend longer duration residential camps. The focus of these motivational/preparatory centres, apart from inducting the girls into the formal system is also impart to life oriented and gender sensitive education. The learners apart from reading and writing get information regarding legal aid, health care, environment and women issues. The SSA also offers bridge Courses, remedial courses, Back-to-School Camps with a focus on mainstreaming out of school children into regular schools.

Jan Shikshan Sansthan (JSS), originally known as the Shramik Vidyapeeth, was first established in the country in Worli, Mumbai in 1967. JSS or the Institute of People's Education was initially launched as a polyvalent or multi-faceted adult education programme aimed at improving the vocational skill and quality of life of workers and their family members. The programme was evolved to respond to the educational and vocational training needs of numerous groups of adult and young people living in urban and industrial areas and for persons who had been migrating from rural to urban settings. Now with the emergence of millions of neo-literates through the total literacy campaigns and the transformation that has taken place in the economic and social set up over the years, the role and scope of these polyvalent educational institutes have widened manifold.

In the changed scenario, the focus of JSS is now shifting from industrial workers in urban areas to the numerous neo-literates and un-skilled and unemployed youth throughout the country. The Sansthans act as district level resource support agencies especially in regard to organisation of vocational training and skill development programmes for the neo-literates and other target groups of the continuing education scheme. Originally the JSS scheme was restricted to urban, semi-urban and industrial areas. Now, the area of operation has been extended to the entire districts including rural areas. As per the revised guidelines issued by the Government of India, at least 25 percent of the beneficiaries of the Jan Shikshan Sansthan should be neo-literates.

The JSSs offer around 255 different types of vocational courses—from candle and agarbatti making, sewing and embroidery to computer courses. Earlier, the JSSs were set up under the aegis of non-government organisations, State Governments and Universities. On the other hand, JSS Delhi is directly under the Government of India. However, as per the revised guidelines issued by the Government of India, the Jan Shikshan Sansthans will function only under the NGOs. Efforts are on way to transfer all the Jan Shikshan Sansthans to run under the aegis of the State Governments to the NGO sector. In the year 2004-5, there were 157 institutions with the training capacity of 0.35 million, with 0.15 million trained so far.

Established in 1989 as National Open School (NOS) by MHRD, Government of India, the National Institute of Open Schooling (NIOS) was renamed in July 2002 and is the largest Open Schooling System in the World Providing Alternative Schooling System. The NIOS has 1805 academic study centres and 917 Vocational study centres throughout the country with 249 Centres for Open Basic Education. The enrolment for the last 5 years has been 1.4 million students.

The NIOS offers open vocational education, package courses, six months and one year vocational courses, life enrichment courses, stand-alone vocational subjects, as well as vocational subjects in combination with academic subjects. The broad vocational areas comprise subjects ranging from agriculture, Computer Science and IT, Engineering and Technology, Teacher Training to Business and Commerce as well as Health and Para-Medical courses. The NIOS curriculum can be largely placed in the categories of equivalency or alternative schooling, life skill training, as well as training in income generation programmes.

Skill Development based on Modular Employable Skills (MES). Very few opportunities for skill development are available for the out of school youth and existing workers, especially in the informal sector. Most of the existing skill development programmes are long term in nature. Considering their educational, social and economical background, it was concluded that the poor and less educated persons can not afford long term training programmes due to higher entry qualifications and opportunity cost.

Consequently, a new framework for Skill Development for the informal sector has been evolved by the DGET (Directorate General of Employment and Training –Ministry of Labour and Employment) to address the above mentioned problems. MES would benefit different target groups like workers seeking certification of their skills acquired informally; workers and ITI graduates seeking skill upgradation, early school drop-outs and the unemployed. The curricula has been developed ranging from agriculture to food processing and banking and accounting. The curriculum is approved by the NCVT (National Council of Vocational Training) and the time taken to gain the qualification will vary according to the pathway taken and will be kept very flexible for persons with different backgrounds and experience.

The government of India runs various NFE schemes for adults in the realm of income generation. There are about 17 governmental departments and ministries offering training in various areas. Some of the schemes are:

— *DWCRA:* Introduced in 1982-83, as a sub-scheme of the Integrated Rural Development programme, DWCRA aims at developing income-generating skills and promoting activities among poor women in rural areas, subsequently improving their social and economic status. The basic unit under this scheme is a group of 10-15 poor women (though the size may be smaller in different areas). The programme is implemented by the District Rural Development Agencies. Any economic activity suited to groups of women in line with their skills, aptitudes and local conditions can be taken up under the scheme. NGOs are also involved in the implementation of the programme and are supported by the Council for Advancement of People's Action and Rural Technology (CAPART), an organisation set up under the Ministry of Rural Areas and Employment to coordinate the development work of voluntary agencies in India.

— *TRYSEM:* Established in 1979, the Training of Rural Youth for Self-Employment is aimed at developing technical and entrepreneurial skills among rural youth from families below the poverty line aged from 18 to 35 years, to enable them to take up income-generating activities. Training given under this scheme is based on the needs of the area, and is provided at such training centres as the ITIs, community polytechnics, extension training centres, Krishi Vigyan Kendras, khadi and village industry boards, state institutes of rural development or institutions run by voluntary agencies. Training under this scheme is normally for six months, during which the trainees receive a stipend. Besides, financial assistance is also provided to the training institutions and master craftsmen.

— *Prime Minister's Rozgar Yojana:* Launched in October 1993, the Prime Minister's Rozgar Yojana (PMRY) aims at providing wage employment and self-employment to educated unemployed youths aged between 18 and 35. The scheme envisages compulsory training for entrepreneurs for a period of 15 to 20 working days for the industrial sector after a loan is approved. The scheme is targeted to provide assistance to 220,000 educated youths during the year 1999-2000. An evaluation of this programme revealed that it generates employment for about 2.4 persons per unit. The employment generation potential is found to be more in the case of industrial units (3.5 persons) than in the service (2.2 persons) and trade (1.9 persons) sectors. Training has been useful for an overwhelming majority of the beneficiaries (81 per cent). Many more youth seek assistance under the PMRY.

Apart from the schemes mentioned above, there are various other schemes which offer informal apprenticeship as well as on-the-job training by various ministries. They are:

— Vocational Training in Krishi Vigyan Kendras—Farm Science Centre.
— Vocational Training in Khadi and Village Industries
— Swarn Jayanti Gram Swarojgar Yojna
— Stree Shakti
— Swarn Jayanti Sahari Rojgar Yojna
— Testing and certification of skills of workers engaged in the Informal sector (DGET) and many more.

Information on these schemes and programmes are hard to come by as there is no comprehensive/systematic documentation centrally available. Apart from the purely government set up and run NFE schemes, there are some initiatives run by the NGOs. Foremost among them is the BGVS. The impetus to initiate a mass action for renewal was propelled from such an understanding. A voluntary agency, Bharat Gyan Vigyan Samiti (BGVS) was formed to initiate a mass action for renewal, out of many voluntary groups working under the loose umbrella of the 'People's Science Network' (PSN). BGVS considers literacy as a possible starting point for social transformation, and a means for a crusade against conditions that maintain illiteracy, a crusade against communalism, a crusade against dependence and oppression.

Looking at how a broad democratic movement, with the participation of the state machinery, can reach out to millions of people and overcome traditional hurdles, BGVS, in collaboration with various PSN groups, has been exploring further areas of development and possibilities for intervention. It is intervening in areas such as universalisation of elementary education, science popularisation, participatory watershed development programmes, rural enterprise programmes, library and cultural movements, health, environment protection and sustainable models of development.

References

Coombs, P. (1985) *The World Crisis in Education,* New York: Oxford University Press.

Graham-Brown, S. (1991) *Education in the Developing World*, Harlow: Longman.

Jeffs, T. and Smith, M. K. (eds.) *Using Informal Education. An alternative to casework, teaching and control?*, Milton Keynes: Open University Press.

McGivney, V. and Murray, F. (1991) *Adult Education in Development. Methods and approaches from changing societies*, Leicester: NIACE.

Rubenson, K.(1982) *Interaction Between Formal and Non-Formal Education* Paris, Paper for Conference of the International Council for Adult Education.

Tight, M. (1996) *Key Concepts in Adult Education and Training*, London: Routledge.

UNESCO (1972) *Learning to Be*. Paris: UNESCO.

Bibliography

Ashby, P., Hobson, A., Tracey, L., Malderez, A., Tomlinson, P., Roper, T., Chambers, G. and Healy, J. (2008). *Beginner teachers' experiences of initial teacher preparation, induction and early professional development: a review of literature*. London: DCSF

Basu, AN (1947), *Education in Modern India, Orient Book Co.*, Calcutta.

Bates A.W. (1995): *Technology, Open Learning and Distance Education*, London: Routledge.

Brennan J., Kogan M. and Teichler U., (eds.), (1996). *Higher Education and Work*, Jessica Kingsley, London.

Brodhead, C. W. (1991). "Image 2000: A Vision for Vocational Education." *Vocational Education Journal* 66, no. 1: 22-25.

Brossard, Mathieu, and Luc-Charles Gacougnolle. 2001. "Financing Primary Education for All: Yesterday, Today and Tomorrow." United Nations Educational, Scientific, and Cultural Organization, Paris.

Chen, D. (2001). "Restructuring through Amalgamation in China." *International Higher Education* Fall.

Clarke, B. R. (1998). *Creating Entrepreneurial Universities: Organizational Pathways of Transformation*. Oxford, UK: IAU Press, Pergamon.

Colclough, Christopher, and Keith Lewin. 1993. *Educating All the Children: Strategies for Primary Schooling in the South.* New York: Oxford University Press.

Coombs, P. (1985) *The World Crisis in Education,* New York: Oxford University Press.

Dayal, Bhagwan (1955), *The Development of Modern Indian Education,* Orient Longman, Bombay.

De, Anuradha, and Jean Dreze. 1999. *Public Report on Basic Education in India (PROBE).* New Delhi: Oxford University Press.

Delamonica, Enrique, Santosh Mehrotra, and Jan Vandemoortele. 2001. "Is EFA Affordable? Estimating the Global Minimum Cost of Education for All." Innocenti Working Paper 87. United Nations Children's Fund, New York.

Department of School Education, Government of Madhya Pradesh, Bhopal, *Annual Administrative Report* (1996-97).

Department of Secondary and Higher Education (2004–2006). *Annual Reports 2004–05 and 2005–06.* New Delhi: Ministry of Human Resource Development.

Devarajan, Shantayanan, Margaret J. Miller, and Eric V. Swanson. 2002. "Goals for Development: History, Prospects and Costs." *Policy Research Working Paper* 2819. World Bank, Washington, D.C.

Directorate of Public Instruction Madhya Pradesh, Bhopal, *Basic Educational Statistics* (1997).

Ellsworth, J.H. (1994): *Education on the Internet*, Indianapolis: Sams Publishing.

Elzkowitz, H., and L. Leydesdorff, eds. (1997). *Universities and the Global Knowledge Economy: A Triple Helix of University-Industry-Government Relations*. London: Cassell Academic.

Frederick, R., et.al. (2009). Teacher candidates' transformative thinking on issues of social justice. *Teaching and Teacher Education* .doi:10.1016/jtate.2009.05.004

Garet, Porter, Desmoine, Birman, Kwang, (2001) What makes professional development effective? *American Education Research Journal* 38(4) 915-946.

Gibbons M, Limoges C, Nowotny H, Schwartzman S, Scott P, Trow M., (1994) *The New Production of Knowledge*, Sage Publications, London.

Gore, MS (1995), *Indian Education : Structure and Process,* Rawat Publication, Jaipur.

Graham-Brown, S. (1991) *Education in the Developing World*, Harlow: Longman.

Haq, Ehsanul (1997), *Education, Polity and Society,* Shipra Publications, Delhi.

Huling-Austin, J. (1988) A systhesis of research on teacher induction programs and practices; papre presented to the Annual Meeting of the American Educational Research Association, New Orleans LA, April 5-9.

International Finance Corporation. 2005). "India's Issues and Challenges for Future Private Investment in Higher Education." Unpublished presentation, IFC, Washington, DC.

Jeffs, T. and Smith, M. K. (eds.) *Using Informal Education. An alternative to casework, teaching and control?*, Milton Keynes: Open University Press.

Jolly, KG (1992), *Literacy for All by 2001 : Strategies at District Level*, D.K. Publishers, New Delhi.

Kincheloe, Joe L. (1995). *Toil and Trouble: Good Work, Smart Workers, and the Integration of Academic and Vocational Education.* New York: Peter Lang Publishing.

Limaye, PM (1945), *Education in India Today*, Deccan Education Society, Poona.

McGivney, V. and Murray, F. (1991) *Adult Education in Development. Methods and approaches from changing societies*, Leicester: NIACE.

Mehta, PL and Poonga, Rakhi (1997), *Free and Compulsory Education*, Deep and Deep Publications, New Delhi.

Naik, JP (1975), *Elementary Education in India : A Promise to keep*, Allied Publishers, Bombay.

Premi, MK (1972), *Educational Planning in India*, Sterling Publishers, New Delhi.

Rudolph, S. and Rudolph, L. (1972) *Education and politics in India*. Oxford University Press. Delhi.

Rumble, G. (2001): The Costs and Costing of Networked Learning, *Journal of Asynchronous Learning Networks*, Vol. 5, Issue 2, September.

Sargent (1968) *Society, Schools and Progress in India.* Pergamon Press. London.

Sinha, Amarjeet (1998), *Primary Schooling in India*, Vikas Publishing House, New Delhi.

Snow-Renner and Lauer, (2005) 'Professional Development Analysis (synthesis of 54 studies), McREL.

South African Institute for Distance Education (1999): *Distance Education and Technology Choices in Southern Africa*, www.saide.org.za, April.

Tait, A. (2000): Planning Student Support in Open and Distance Learning, in *Open Learning*, 15 (3), 287-300.

Tight, M. (1996) *Key Concepts in Adult Education and Training*, London: Routledge.

Tilak, JBG (1992), *Educational Planning at Grassroots*, Ashish Publishing House, New Delhi.

UNESCO (1972) *Learning to Be*. Paris: UNESCO.

Zellener, A. A. (1951), *Education in India*, Bookman Associates, New York.

Index

ISBN 978-93-5919-641-1

Published by : **Daya Publishing House®**
A Division of
Astral International Pvt. Ltd.
– ISO 9001:2015 Certified Company –
4736/23, Ground Floor, Ansari Road
Darya Ganj, New Delhi-110 002
Ph. 011-43549197, 8130496929
e-mail: info@astralint.com
Website: www.astralint.com

Printed at : **Replika Press Pvt Ltd**

Chromatography

Javid Ahmad Sofi

2026

Daya Publishing House®

A Division of

Astral International Pvt. Ltd.

New Delhi – 110 002